Twentieth-Century Popular Culture in Museums and Libraries

Twentieth-Century
Popular Culture
in
Museums
and
Libraries

Edited by Fred E.H. Schroeder

Bowling Green University Popular Press
Bowling Green, Ohio 43403

Copyright © 1981 by Bowling Green University Popular Press

Library of Congress Catalog Card No.: 80-85197

ISBN: 0-87972-162-6

Contents

To
Ray B. Browne and Russel B. Nye
who have done so much for
popular culture studies in
museums and libraries

The world is so full of a number of
things, I'm sure we should all be
as happy as kings.

Robert Louis Stevenson, A Child's
Garden of Verses XXIV

'The degree to which both
museums and libraries have
ignored our popular culture is
appalling even when one thinks of
documents and artifacts whose
value for the future is
unquestionable."

Fred E.H. Schroeder,
"Introduction: A Little History and
Some Prevues of Coming
Attractions"

I

The introductory essay by the editor provides a brief historical background of the popular culture movement in American colleges and universities, the antecedents of popular culture collections and exhibitions in museums in the eighteenth and nineteenth centuries, and the development of popular culture collections and services in three kinds of libraries—academic, research and public. The rationale for this volume is explained and the common topics and themes among the contributed articles are mentioned, with reference to certain of the contributions. It will be noted that no definition of "popular culture" is provided in the introduction, but that it is left to the reader to infer the specific aspect of popular phenomena that is being considered in each article. These variously include mass-produced and commercial artifacts and publications, electronic media, vernacular and folk architecture, furnishings and costumes; popular and populist entertainments and political activities, and the everyday lifestyles of common people. In short, popular culture can be viewed as a wide range of concerns about any non-elite and non-establishment aspects of human activities and environments.

Fred E.H. Schroeder is Director of the Program in Humanities at the University of Minnesota, Duluth. In addition to several dozen articles on art, architecture, literature, history, biography and teaching, Dr. Schroeder is the author of *Outlaw Aesthetics; Arts and the Public Mind* and editor of *5000 Years of Popular Culture; Popular Culture Before Printing,* both published by Bowling Green University Popular Press. He has written a Technical Leaflet for AASLH entitled *Designing your Exhibit: Seven Ways to Look at an Artifact* and is a frequent consultant to schools, museums and historical societies. A member of the Board of Trustees of the St. Louis County Heritage and Arts Center, he has served on planning committees for the Depot Square "old town" reconstruction and for the interpretive programs for the Immigration Room of the Union Depot in Duluth.

2

Fred E.H. Schroeder

Introduction:
A Little History and Some Prevues
of Coming Attractions

POPULAR CULTURE is a relatively new term, gaining currency only since about 1965, but most particularly after the founding of the *Journal of Popular Culture* in 1967 by Ray B. Browne at Bowling Green State University and the establishment of the Popular Culture Association at the 1969 national meeting of the American Studies Association in Toledo, Ohio, under the leadership of Professors Browne, Marshall Fishwick and Russel B. Nye. The term has been a locus for controversy since the beginning, and, as many of the essays in this collection indicate, controversy continues on many fronts. Opponents of popular culture speak of "cheapened standards," "triviality" and "pandering to the masses," while proponents respond with attacks of "elitism," "irrelevance" and a "reactionary establishment." The controversies seem to have more to do with the word than the reality, however, because both the study of popular culture in the academy and the collection, preservation and dissemination of popular culture in the museums and libraries is almost as old as these institutions themselves.

In the world of academic scholarship, the origins for the study of popular culture are early in the nineteenth century in the *volkeskund* studies of peasant culture by the brothers Grimm, out of which have evolved the studies of folklore, cultural anthropology and linguistics, while at about the same time in France, Auguste Comte initiated the science of sociology, with its characteristic concern with the *people* as a whole rather than with leaders alone. Later in the century, literature in translation and popular forms such as vernacular modern short stories and the novel crept into the traditional curriculum, and, by the early decades of the twentieth century, such popular subjects as "American literature" and "modern history" (both terms being self-contradictory, the conservatives argued) had begun to replace classics in the cultural curriculum. In addition, a number of critics and scholars began to pay serious attention to the documents of popular entertainment. Possibly the first of these was Gilbert Seldes' *The Seven Lively Arts* (1924) which gave critical attention to movies, comics and the popular stage. Constance Rourke's *American Humor: A Study of the*

National Character (1931) selected a non-elite road into American culture, using such materials as jokebooks, ballads and minstrel shows. Frank Luther Mott published the first part of his monumental *History of American Magazines* in 1930, and later chronicled "the story of best sellers in the United States" in *Golden Multitudes* (1947). In 1950 two more major milestones appeared with James D. Hart's *The Popular Book* and Henry Nash Smith's *Virgin Land: The American West as Myth and Symbol*, which in its use of Dime Novels as historical sourcebooks set the "American Studies" movement firmly on a course that inevitably led to the creation of the Popular Culture Association. It should be noted also that two magazines that incorporated popular history to a large extent were founded at the same time: the scholarly *American Quarterly* (1949) and the more popular but no less authoritative *American Heritage* (1947). However, these, and other works of the first half of this century were sheltered by more acceptable categories: social history, literary history, social criticism and American studies. The culmination of this period is unquestionably Russel Nye's *The Unembarrassed Muse: The Popular Arts in America* (1970). This book, with its bibliography, should be the starting point for museum personnel and librarians who are new to popular culture. Most of the rest of the history can be found in the pages of the *Journal of Popular Culture,* while those who are interested in research methodologies are referred to the bibliographic afterword in my *5000 Years of Popular Culture* (Bowling Green Popular Press, 1980).

Two articles in the present collection are recommended as well to newcomers: Barbara Moran provides a succinct account of the recent popular culture movement as it relates to the academic library, while Thomas Schlereth is encyclopedic regarding newer approaches in many non-academic settings relevant to museum work, including above-ground archaeology, vernacular architecture, industrial archaeology, urban studies, landscape geography and historic preservation.

The early history of "popular culture" in museums is in part an outgrowth of the *Volkeskund* movement, as C. Kurt Dewhurst and Marsha MacDowell explain in their article on the European folk museum, and it is probably true that for the *research* aspects of museums, there is a development parallel to that of the academic institutions as explained above, with the additional influences of classical and near-eastern archaeological collections and the exotic culture collections of natural history museums which influenced the discipline of ethnology. Both archaeology and ethnology tended to reflect the *whole culture*, not so much because of a dedication to studying the "life of the people" as because of a curiosity about the strange, remote and primal—after all, as Edward Green points out in his essay, many museum collections such as the British Museum began as cabinets of *curios*. The *exhibit* aspects of museums are in a large part outgrowths of popular phenomena, as Dewhurst and MacDowell indicate. Wax museums, such as Mme. Tussaud's (in

Paris until 1800 and since in London) are one influence, as are the equally sensational popular "museums" of P.T. Barnum in the 1840s, while the great "world fairs" are another. One direct result of the 1851 Crystal Palace exposition, for example, was the Victoria and Albert Museum, which continues to be particularly strong in such popular material culture as home furnishings, ceramics, tools, musical instruments, costumes, stagecraft and industrial and architectural design. The Chicago World's Columbian exposition of 1893 was among those that included several village reconstructions and craft demonstrations, precursors of both serious and entertainment museums such as Colonial Williamsburg and Disneyland.

Many state and local museums, like America's national museum, the Smithsonian Institution, have been collecting and exhibiting popular artifacts under other rubrics, especially in such areas as "period furnishings" and business, transportation and manufactures. In the first article of this volume, Edith Mayo shows how established areas of collection in the Political History Division of the Smithsonian provided a consistent rationale for developing a popular culture program, and undoubtedly many museums could do likewise. On the other end of the scale, the new museum of the city of Oakland dedicated an entire room to the expression of local and regional life, history and values through popular culture, and we cannot help but wonder what substance there could be to American life if we were to remove mass-produced commercial cultural artifacts. Both transportation and manufactures have a considerable museum history, dating back in America to the 1876 Centennial Exposition in Philadelphia, and with a number of truly major later collections such as the Museum of Science and Industry in Chicago and the Henry Ford Museum in Dearborn. In our volume, Maurice Duke sets forth to identify in a descriptive index the motor vehicle museums in the United States, including private and commercial collections. Finally, in the popular culture field of electronic media, the History and Technology Museum of the Smithsonian is one of the most comprehensive: for example, expansion of communications technology to include the popular arts carried by the media (films, snapshots, recordings, radio and television) was a fortuitous extension of the narrower definition of "technology."

The history of popular culture in libraries should be divided into public libraries and research-academic libraries. Although the original impetus of public libraries was "cultural uplift" (for better, the *mission* persists; for worse, the *image* clings), with the advent of Carnegie libraries at the turn of the century, the die was cast for "populist" libraries, free to all and excluding no one. By 1900 most public libraries had also suffered the little children to come unto them, and while they forbade the children their Horatio Alger *Tom Swift,*and *Oz* books, the Rover Boys, the Nancy Drew mysteries and comics until more than half the century was past, adults were accustomed by the thirties to find special shelves for current best-sellers and for detective, western and science fiction.

Although Leslie Fiedler, one of the greatest advocates of popular literature as *literature*, has referred to this as "ghettoizing" popular arts, professional librarians know that this is a service to popular tastes, not a value commentary. No, the public library, despite its lingering images of genteel "Silence!" scolding old maids, locked cases for sex manuals, explicit and implicit censorship and exclusiveness can provide patterns for popularization that have only in recent years been emulated by other "cultural" institutions such as museums, orchestras, theater and ballet troupes. Such early innovations as branch libraries and bookmobiles, free meeting rooms and cooperative programs with schools have continued in "mail-a-book," circulating collections of recordings, films and framed art works and similar expanded services.

Not everything has been positive. Censorship is a reality, and deliberate or *de facto* denial of services to minorities continues. Moreover, for every library that has popular film programs, collections of popular gothic novels, pop and country-western music, or circulating radio and video cassettes, there are a score that haven't. Some resistance is from the community: fundamentalists, activists of all kinds and stuffy cultural conservatives among them. But as Wayne Wiegand and Bruce Shuman indicate here, library schools, library associations and librarians themselves are hampered by attitudes and traditions of print-orientation, restrictive cultural definitions and intellectual and social elitism.

The academic library is not a public service institution like the public library, although insofar as American higher education is a popular phenomenon, one might strain to define it so. But as Wiegand and Barbara Moran point out, the college library must serve the curriculum, and they document a significant number of popular culture courses that have no library back-up (for all of the reasons given in the prior paragraph), while B. Lee Cooper has prepared an "opening day" collection in recent popular music as a direct remedy.

Research libraries and archives, whether academic or not, are different from museums and public and college libraries in that they are rarely popular institutions themselves, except for limited exhibition functions as in the Presidential Libraries, the National Archives or "rare book room" lobby display cases. Only during the past decade have a few libraries developed popular collections *per se*, and Barbara Moran notes these. Two different kinds of popular audio collections are described in detail by Maurice Crane and William Schurk. But by and large it can be said that, historically, popular culture collections in research libraries are accidental and unwanted bequests of antiquarian scholars and monomaniac nostalgics. Love me, love my dog: take my million for a new building, but make a home for my penny dreadfuls. A history of special collections in popular culture is yet to be written, but it is certain that this will prove to be the origin of many collections of broadside ballads, chapbooks, recipe books, dime novels, labor tracts, comics, theatre handbills, Valentines, picture postcards, restaurant menus, nudist magazines, matchbook covers, community-sing books, high-school yearbooks and heaven knows what other ephemera that have gone to make up the texture of human lives.

With such a long and interesting history of popular culture in museums and libraries, it might be asked why this book is limited to the twentieth century. One answer is provided in several of the essays, in that the increase of mass-produced, electronically mediated, disposable and commercialized consumer products, entertainment, communication, transportation, and political and social institutions has been geometric or even exponential since 1900. Popular culture *is* twentieth-century American culture. But the other reason is that insofar as museums and libraries are concerned, the popular culture of earlier centuries is secure. Distance lends enchantment, and the rarity and remoteness of the everyday lives and the commonplace things of earlier times guarantee their value in the minds of the moment. Everyone respects a pioneer log cabin, an Abraham Lincoln campaign banner, a colonial recipe book, and an early edition of the *Sacred Harp* hymnal, but a Winnebago recreational vehicle, a *Who Can Beat Nixon?* board-game, a Cuisinart food-processor manual, and an Anita Bryant Christmas album do not win our reverence, however much they may be parts of our daily lives. The degree to which both museums and libraries have ignored our popular culture is appalling when one thinks of documents and artifacts whose value for the future is unquestionable. A mere handful of libraries have complete files of *Playboy, TV Guide* and *Schwann* record guides. Only the Library of Congress has a file of *Young America*, a World War II elementary school national newspaper, and this, on wartime newsprint, is crumbling. Only the Museum of Man in Ottawa has developed a rational plan for collecting packaged foodstuff, including regional canned goods. Few, if any, museums have purchased Monopoly games for their archives, or Barbi-dolls, or GI Joe. Videotapes of local news personalities may be held by the stations, but these tastemakers and interpreters are rarely archived in their regional libraries and museums. And even such responsible new approaches as oral history programs overwhelmingly emphasize exceptional but acceptable people, ignoring "the people" themselves as well as the minority fringes. No doubt about it, it is contemporary popular culture that is the endangered species.

However, the articles in this collection do not merely "view with alarm," nor do they wink at gigantic problems of developing institutional policy or at problems of cost—fiscal, human, energy and space—or problems of process and technique—in personnel training, in acquisition, cataloging and dissemination. But one thing is certain, this book is no last word. Nor, for that matter, is it the first word, although it may be the first attempt to view the situation comprehensively.

One more question has surely occurred to the readers. Why museums *and* libraries? Why not one or the other? To answer this, it must first be said that it was no accident. Museums and libraries are both cultural archives. All museums have libraries; many started by sharing the same building, as with the British Museum and British Library. Libraries of all kinds have exhibit areas, both of a permanent nature and for loan collections. Furthermore, in recent decades the lines of distinction have been dissolving, most particularly because of audio-visual popular culture. Photographs, films, disc recordings, tape recordings, and video belong exclusively neither to the world of print nor of the material artifact. Many public libraries circulate art objects, and some circulate toys, tools and dress patterns. Thus, as cultural archives, as research service centers and as providers for public recreation, education and inspiration, museums and libraries are strikingly similar institutions.

Such was the editorial rationale for combining museums and libraries. As the contributions arrived, several common themes emerged as well. One is concern for problems of *selection* in the field of popular culture, "connoisseurship of the future," as Edith Mayo names it. Questions of choice, of specialization, of representativeness are discussed throughout this volume. Another theme is the need for *sharing* by loans, cooperative collecting, national and regional indexing, and computer networking. A third theme is that of going *directly to popular culture* where it is, withal its unprofessional commercialism. There is a certain amount of grubbiness in this sort of opportunism, but there is also a bouyant sense of adventurous discovery that is not found by touring the national convention exhibits of the American Library Association or the American Association of Museums. Related to this is a common theme that could be called *populism*, a sense of dedication to silent or vociferous majorities and minorities, not only to preserve their culture for people of the future but to reaffirm our institutional commitment to serve the whole public today with respect and understanding. One last common theme is somewhat negative, but it is familiar to anyone who has become involved in popular culture: it is a feisty *opposition to the forces of conventional traditions* in our professions. The tone is never bitter or angry, but rather is expressed with good-humored irony that covers over the pitched battles in committees, the steady sniper-fire from neighboring colleagues, the devious strategies to circumvent bureaucratic restrictions that are inescapable for those who carry the popular culture banner into our cultural institutions. One consequence of this is that *Twentieth-Century Popular Culture in Museums and Libraries* is refreshingly different from most professional literature in that it is not an unrelenting rhapsody of success stories; readers will find more realistic almost-successes, not-quite-complete programs and partially-solved problems, along with authoritative practical information based upon extremely knowledgeable professional experience.

Thanks are due to the editors of *American Libraries,* the *American Studies Association Newsletter, History News* and the *Popular Culture Association Newsletter* and to Edith Mayo, Ray Browne and Russel Nye for their assistance in locating contributors. Many more potential contributors might have been identified, most certainly, because twentieth-century popular culture in museums and libraries is not exclusive to a few professionals, but is a major movement that is involving a large number of dedicated and responsible persons in institutions both large and small. I have borne this in mind, and the contributors have been selected to represent a wide range of examples and varied experiences and points of view.

"I believe the museum profession
must see the gradual emergence of
a new breed of curator, and a
change in emphasis from
collecting of the past to a
connoisseurship of the present
and the future: a connoisseurship
of anticipation."

*Edith Mayo, "Connoisseurship of
the Future"*

II

Our collection of articles begins with two selections that most particularly look toward revision of practices and goals to prepare our cultural repositories for the twenty-first century. This is not the only keynote that Edith Mayo sounds in the first article. The themes of cooperative sharing, data-base networking and of going directly to the people for popular resources are introduced here and recur throughout this book. On the theoretical level, Mayo discusses the tremendous problem of the sheer bulk of popular material culture: always ephemeral to a greater or lesser extent, a large amount of today's cultural artifacts are disposable, planned for obsolescence or responsive to whimsical fads and daily current events. Selectivity is not to be thrown to the winds; on the contrary a new kind of connoisseurship is urgently needed. On the practical level, Mayo recounts some of the procedures she and other members of the Division of Political History have employed in recent years to prepare two of the more popular exhibits at the Smithsonian Institution.

Edith Mayo graduated with honors from the George Washington University (B.A. in History, M.A. in American Studies, 1970). She joined the staff of the Division of Political History at the Smithsonian as a research assistant in 1969, and became Assistant Curator in 1975, and now holds the post of Associate Curator. She has been actively engaged in collecting, research and exhibition relating to women's history, political reform movements, voting rights, black civil rights and the anti-war movement. She produced the 1972 exhibition, "The Right to Vote," and the Petition and Voting Rights section of the Bicentennial exhibition, "We the People."

Edith Mayo

Connoisseurship of the Future

COLLECTING CONTEMPORARY HISTORICAL artifacts for the museum of the future requires a great "leap of faith"—the faith that the museum will remain a vital and viable institution of the future, and that the profession will retain a philosophical commitment to the concept that objects will continue to be worth collecting. If we wish to retain the primary essential in the definition of museum we must continue to maintain the object as central.

The great proliferation of material culture, currently and in the future, forces upon us the realization that additional storage facilities are a critical need, that usable computerized data retrieval systems are only around the corner, and that collections cannot be built with the same thoroughness in the future. These facts will necessarily alter the philosophy of collecting, as we know it.

Since the middle of the 20th century, there has been a discernible trend toward objects which are easily disposable, made to become obsolete; objects which could be classified as ephemeral. This trend is pervasive in many areas of our physical culture. Nowhere is it more evident than in the field in which I work, political history. The ephemeral nature of political objects, and those in many other areas of traditional history collections, must necessarily affect the philosophy and techniques of acquisition.

Today's disposable culture places a lesser value on physical objects, a trend likely to continue with the increase of mass-produced, mass-disseminated materials. Cultural historians who have often discovered historical treasures preserved in layers of earth, or even in privies, will not be so fortunate in the future. Even our trash is disposed of differently—usually obliterating any traces for cultural retrieval.

Such facts lead us to question how best to deal with collecting essentially short-lived cultural artifacts. I believe the museum profession must see the gradual emergence of a new breed of curator, and a change in emphasis from collecting of the past to a connoisseurship of the present and the future: a connoisseurship of anticipation. Curators must be trained to assess what trends can be discerned in today's mass culture which will be historically significant, and collect to reflect those areas. This training should in no way mean a lessening of historical scholarship now required of the curatorial function, but should be based on the same grounding in historical discipines, with additional emphasis on training in

13

projected historical and cultural trends.

Such an emphasis on contemporary collecting, on a connoisseurship of anticipation, presents real challenges for museums. This is so for more than the obvious reason that one has to make decisions on what is and will be important. It is a challenge because it is incumbent upon the collecting curator to establish the necessity and rationale of collecting in a particular area, or of acquiring a particular object.

Despite cultural changes already evident, a perusal of the published museum literature reveals that scant heed has been paid thus far to such evidence. A few professionals such as L. Thomas Frye, Curator of History at the Oakland Museum, and G. Ellis Burcaw, Director of the University of Idaho Museum, have dealt with the legitimacy of contemporary collecting. Mr. Frye, in writing of a 20th century collecting project at Oakland, stated, "The ... present can be interpreted ... and indeed should be handled as systematically by history museums in research, collections, exhibitions and interpretive programs as the more distant past." But he adds, "Most history museums have not actively acquired contemporary materials."[1] At a conference of the Popular Culture Association in 1978, in a session on Contemporary Collecting, Ms. Barbara Riley, Curator of History at the Museum of Man, Ottawa, Canada, outlined a model program of contemporary collecting conducted by that museum.[2] Efforts such as these, however, are still the exceptions within the museum community. Mr. Burcaw, in writing of collecting activities in history museums, described "...a failure to look ahead, to appreciate that what a museum ought to have in its collections a hundred years from now might not be there simply because such objects were not acquired when they were available." He continued, "There is little likelihood that collecting objects of today would be a waste of time and space."

Other projectors of the museum's future, however, have not seen a like necessity. Dr. Wilcomb E. Washburn, Director of the Smithsonian Institution's American Studies Program and former head curator of the Division of Political History, has asked, in view of the rapid increase of collections and the increasing inability to retrieve historical information amassed, "Are Museums Necessary?" He proposes as one possible solution "... whether, in the future, the museum object will not be converted into information that is as satisfactory for human purposes in this case primarily historical scholarship as the object itself?" He poses "... the prospect of seeing a representation of the thing and not the thing itself" and suggests "... saving a small sample of any class of objects directly." He asks if "Objects can be translated into the machine language, into visual description, into scholarly analysis ... need one save objects at all?"[4]

These provocative and legitimate questions should not be dismissed casually. With the proliferation of objects, with data retrieval systems becoming easily accessible, with storage areas increasingly overtaxed, is this a valid course to choose?

It appears to be the current consensus among professionals that the real object should remain central to the museum. The object is likely to become even more important in the future. In an age which promises increased mass production, mobility, rootlessness, computerized impersonality, rapidity of change, and attenuated experience, the real object will continue, as Joseph Veach Noble says, to "... exude an ethos which no replica can possess."[5] As Dr. S. Dillon Ripley, Secretary of the Smithsonian Institution, has written, "Museums will need to provide immediate encounters with authenticity.... In this brave new world of ours, perhaps only objects which inherently possess truth can teach truth."[6]

It also appears probable that museums will continue to play an increasingly dominant role as a cultural institution in this society. We must see that the museum finds the language of communication to speak meaningfully to its audience.[7] This is unlikely to happen without real objects.

I suggest, therefore, that there are other alternatives to Dr. Washburn's suggestion which could retain the object as central and yet combine the best features of contemporary collecting and of the data retrieval methodology of which he speaks so highly.

Why should contemporary collecting be a pivotal part of the alternative? It would ensure preservation of increasingly ephemeral cultural objects. It would assure the unquestioned authenticity of an object in an age when technology will be able to produce forgeries and frauds with increasing ease and accuracy. It would ensure that increasingly mass-produced, mass-disseminated cultural artifacts are saved on a representative basis. The greater the use made of mass media and mass production, the greater the "mass culture," and the greater the possibility that objects of the upper classes will be increasingly unrepresentative of the society as a whole. Preservation of such mass culture will probably result in less of an "elite" collection than exists today in most museums. That will necessarily be the case if we truly wish to preserve that which is most representative of the culture and its value system. Custom-designed-and-executed objects will be more rare, exorbitantly expensive, and will not be representative of the general culture. Contemporary collecting would provide the museum with the authentic object before either its rarity or its destructibility drove the price out of reach of museum purchase. With rapid change, time is increasingly telescoped, and collecting of mass culture would ensure a "democratic" representation of culture and a continued relevance to current museum displays, as well as the preservation of vital historic cultural documents for future scholarship.

Having established a rationale and a necessity for contemporary collecting, what procedures can be adopted for the building of an effective and legitimate collection? Establishing the legitimacy of contemporary collecting does not provide an escape from the challenges and dilemmas which it presents. Without

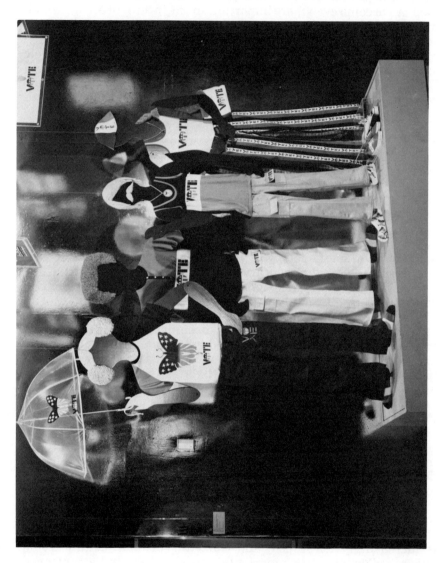

Fig. 1 Display of "Youth Vote" clothing in the 1972 Election Year Special Exhibition, "The Right to Vote," Museum of History and Technology.

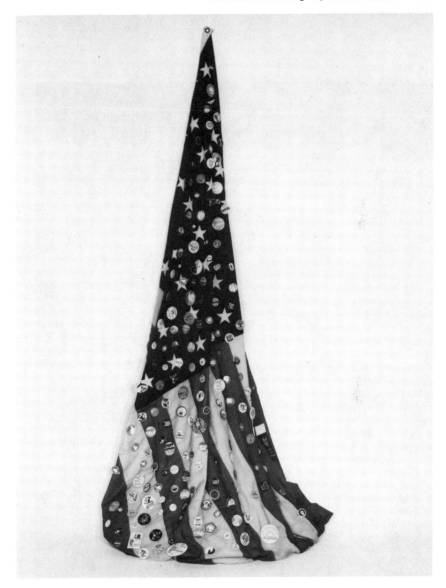

Fig. 2 American flag and anti-war buttons used in anti-Vietnam war demonstrations of the late 1960s and early 1970s. These items are currently displayed in the Bicentennial exhibition, "We the People," Museum of History and Technology.

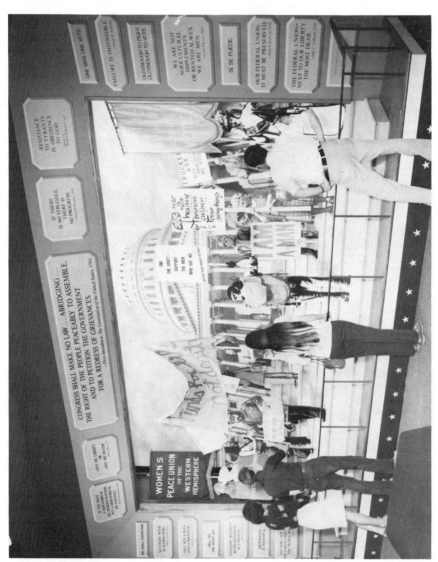

Fig. 3 A portion of the Right to Petition section in the Bicentennial exhibition, "We the People," Museum of History and Technology. Contemporary collecting supplied items on anti-Vietnam war protests, civil rights, the truckers' strike, veterans' protests, and the Equal Rights Amendment.

historical perspective as a guide, how does one know what to collect?

As with collecting of the past, the curator collecting for the future gradually "develops an instinct" grounded in sound historical training. The curator must assess the thematic types of objects within the museum's existing collections and establish the rationale for a contemporary acquisitions program by building on the base of the old collections. It is incumbent upon the curator, therefore, to determine the themes of the collections and to project them forward to the future; to demonstrate an integral relationship between the currently-collected objects and the already-existing collection or collecting field. If museums have an Acquisitions or Review Committee, this committee, as well as the museum administration, must become sensitized and attuned to the acceptance of currently-collected objects.

The experience of the Division of Political History of the Smithsonian may provide helpful examples. This Division has, for many years, been a repository for collections of Presidential, First Ladies, political campaign, and Inaugural objects. Our contemporary collecting programs came into existence from the need to add to these collections on an on-going basis. We found that when we did not follow this course, the materials quickly became unobtainable.

Since the base on which our collections rest is the maintenance of holdings which reflect political activities in this country, it became evident that we would fail to meet this goal if we did not assess what trends could be discerned in current political activity and collect to reflect them. If they were to retain legitimacy, our collections must reflect the politics of the time. In our view, the single most important manifestation in the political field, other than the use of modern technology by the candidates to reach the public, is the rise of coalition, "cause," or "movement" politics.

Several of the most obvious movements were those of petition and protest by blacks and other racial minorities, the women's movement, peace activism and citizen and consumer lobbying activities. The Political History Division maintained already-existing collections on political reforms, women (suffrage), and black rights (abolition). These holdings enabled us to develop a rationale on which to extend our collecting to current politics.

In the last fifteen years, therefore, the Division has expanded its contemporary collecting program beyond the conventional campaign, Presidential, and White House collections. We have begun serious collecting in the fields of civil rights, voting reforms, youth and activist politics, anti-war activism, the women's movement, black elected officials and minority politics. The Division now has the nucleus of a good collection in each of these fields.

Once the curator defines the field of collecting, he or she tries to determine what groups or organizations represent that area. We try to collect from several similar groups, if possible, to reflect differing approaches or philosophies of a given movement.

Because we have found the most effective contact to be the personal one, our collecting is often begun by attending a rally or protest, or by observing/participating in the activity. Most objects collected to date have been acquired through personal contacts of the curatorial staff, either by attendance at rallies and demonstrations, attendance at conventions or meetings of the various groups, or by making the acquaintance of a member of the organization.

The Smithsonian has a particularly fortunate location for such collecting, as Washington is the focus of many protest marches and demonstrations petitioning for some type of redress. On many occasions the members of the Division have attended such rallies and demonstrations to collect. It is somewhat hazardous to collect at such demonstrations, but from such collecting forays have come our most valuable "movement" materials. Among these are huts, posters, organizational materials from the Poor People's Campaign at Resurrection City; posters, literature and banners from anti-Vietnam War demonstrations; American Indian Movement demands and literature from the occupation of the Bureau of Indian Affairs, and Nixon impeachment materials.

If it is not possible to attend the activity personally, contact the organization or group by telephone. A follow-up letter on museum stationery is a "must" to proclaim your legitimacy. If you are fortunate enough to establish rapport with someone in the group, zero in on the items you want, and explain why.

With each contact, whether in person or by telephone, it is important to ask for additional names and contacts in the field who might be interested and helpful. Ask permission to use the first contact's name as a reference. That will often bring immediate results. Continue asking for additional contacts and you will soon find yourself on an "informal grapevine" of a movement. That is when you know you have "arrived" and when you can hope to achieve maximum results in terms of material objects.

Assuming that your contacts are successful, what should you request? We seek materials which demonstrate the following:

> the membership of the group
> the political and fund-raising tactics used
> objects which convey the "personality" of the movement
> good, three-dimensional objects for display
> hand-made or hand-painted materials which reflect the personal commitment or "gut reaction" generated by the movement. (Most political materials today are mass-produced and mass-disseminated and, therefore, have "plastic" personalities).

If you are working on a specific exhibition for which objects are needed, you can offer the contact the prospect of imminent display of his or her material, a kind of "historic publicity" which most groups find flattering and valuable.

As a special exhibit for the election year 1972, the Division of Political History produced an exhibit entitled, "The Right to Vote," which traced the history of an expanding electorate in the United States from the early Republic through the first "youth vote" cast that year. That exhibit utilized many contemporary materials, and numerous groups were contacted to provide objects relating to the voting rights of black citizens gained through such activities as voter registration campaigns, the Selma Voting Rights March of 1965, and the Voting Rights Act of 1965. Clothing and flags worn and carried on the Selma March were displayed, as were materials from groups specializing in black voter registration in the South. "The Right to Vote" also featured clothing, posters, promotional literature, and gimmicks produced in 1972 to encourage the first "youth vote" in our nation's history.

A current exhibition produced for the Bicentennial by the Division, "We the People," contains a section on the Right of Petition. The theme of this section made it necessary for the Division to attempt contacts with such groups as the Black Panther Party and the American Indian Movement.

The process of contact itself, in the case of radical activist groups, is a difficult maneuver. Once accomplished, it is even more difficult to persuade the leaders or members of such organizations that your request for materials is not a "put-on," a "put-down," or, worse yet, that you are not a spy for some law enforcement or intelligence-gathering arm of the establishment.

Although we were ultimately successful in reaching the leadership of both the Black Panther Party and the A.I.M., and were given a cordial and respectful reception to our requests for objects and materials, nothing was forthcoming. Whether the lack of contribution was due to dislike of the "establishment," or whether activist groups are too involved in their day-to-day organizing activities to contribute to something so "peripheral" as a museum display is impossible to say.

Radical activist groups are correct in realizing that they have not seen themselves or others like them in museum exhibits to date, and they are quite rational in questioning why they should believe that they can expect a change in the future. This lack of historic credibility on the part of museums presents a formidable obstacle to collecting which should be dealt with more seriously by the museum profession if we are to document contemporary political movements or attempt to display and interpret them. I would hope that once displays dealing with contemporary political movements become part of the museum scene, and activist groups and the public alike become aware that we are attempting to build collections of this type, it will become less difficult to collect.

It is easier by far to collect from reformist groups who still operate within the political system, that is, established civil rights groups, most women's movement groups, and citizen lobbyist groups, than from organizations who operate generally outside the system, or whose origins are outside the system. The Division of Political History has been very fortunate in receiving excellent cooperation and collections from citizens' lobbying groups, voter registration organizations, women's and peace activists, and black elected officials.

The need to "sell" the rationale for contemporary collecting to museum administrations cannot be overstated. Often the curator or Division involved in contemporary collecting is ahead of the museum administration's policy along collecting lines— particularly along activist political lines. We need to develop the legitimacy of collecting in this area—and pursue it actively without the need to be defensive or apologetic about our collecting. Once such a legitimacy is established in the minds of the museum administration and the public alike, one of the great obstacles—the fear of embarrassing or adverse publicity to the museum—would, in my view, be largely eliminated. A museum could announce its intention to collect on a broad range of political activity, across-the-board, and that the collecting and preserving of movement materials for historic purposes does not constitute an endorsement of the institution.

By its very nature, the saving of objects and the preserving of cultural artifacts, the museum is a "conservative" institution. With contemporary collecting, curators must continue to stress the museum's preservation aspects—we are still conserving—even if it is for the future instead of the past. Objects generated by political movements today, mass-disseminated media, are "expendable" and quickly become unobtainable. In the future they will be almost unavailable, unless they are saved by collectors. In that case, the museum will not "inherit" them for many years to come—and only at a great price.

Having achieved acceptance by the museum administration of the collecting activity itself, the hurdle of financial commitment to support such collecting remains. Collecting without funding doubles the problems of acquisition of objects. It usually takes great persuasion to convince individuals or groups to part with objects for which they feel personal attachment, or which embody a commitment central to their lives. It is doubly difficult not to be able to purchase the object to compensate them. To avoid problems of paying money to a particular cause, arrangements should be made with groups or individuals similar to paying a dealer or owner of an antique. Currently, the most we can offer is historical preservation and a possible exhibition.

Obviously, the sheer physical volume of materials would preclude collecting everything. We must go with what capable and trained curators feel is relevant. Inter-museum cooperation must be greatly accelerated. Since no museum will be able to collect everything, representativeness will be a must, and we must make careful efforts to preserve geographical, class, ethnic and other balances. To complement contemporary collecting I propose the creation of collecting consortia of museums and universities set up along topical or subject lines, linked by a computerized data retrieval network with central computer banks of objects and descriptions, which would permit quick access to information and objects in other collections. Within this consortia there should be planning conferences to determine which institution will collect which aspect of the topic. This would permit a topic, such as political campaigning, to be well documented, but each institution collecting objects in that field would not have to store objects for every aspect of the field. Perhaps an institution would preserve particular geographical, class or ethnic variations of a particular genre. Objects may be kept in their original setting where they retain their ambience and validity. The data retrieval link within the consortia would enable future curators doing research or exhibitions to have access to various phases of the subject and a wide range of original objects without having had to destroy the originals or to store every one in his or her own museum.

Such an arrangement would also mandate accelerated cooperation in the borrowing of real objects and true historical selflessness in object dispersal. If one museum's collection of materials became taxing to its storage space, some of the items could be deposited in smalleer museums within the consortium for preservation, with the knowledge that the information and the object could both be retrieved through the computer retrieval system. There must be a discontinuance of the spirit of exclusivity and one-upsmanship which pervade many museums today which has been referred to as "the maintenance of our own splendid empires."[8]

Museums must develop a flexible accessioning and holding policy for current collecting with the ability to review collections at 25 or 50 year intervals. Such a review of materials "currently collected" would allow for a reflective re-examination to determine what has retained historical value and importance, what no longer retains significance, what has become merely peripheral. There are pitfalls here. History, like other disciplines, has vogues and cycles of interpretation. Materials which curators wanted to "dump" twenty-five years ago are seen as critically important today. More flexible de-accessioning policies would also be in order so that with vital storage space being filled, materials could be deposited in smaller or local museums without being altogether lost.

The evaluation of curatorial performance would have to be changed from how many and how valuable were the objects brought into the museum's own collection to how much was done to assist in preserving historic artifacts in as broad a sense as possible.

Finally, in tomorrow's world as in today's, the central mission of the museum will be as a conservator of culture. This function of the museum will be of paramount importance in maintaining a sense of self within change, and maintaining democratic control within an increasingly impersonal society. With rapid change and the further development of technology, we must not become victims of the process. Museums must continue to serve as conservators of culture. We must keep alive a sense of time, of history, without which there can be no real future. In doing so, museums must play the vital role: they must record and give shape and ordering to our experience; interpret the human condition. The museum must not permit the death of the past but must, in a mass culture, be the key to communication which preserves a sense of reality, not detachment, which sees and portrays life as significant, which preserves the human element, the humanity of man.

Notes

[1]L. Thomas Frye, "The Recent Past is Prologue," *Museum News,* LIII (Nov., 1974), 24.

[2]Barbara Riley, "Contemporary Collecting: A Case History," *Decorative Arts Newsletter,* IV (Summer 1978), 3-6.

[3]G. Ellis Burcaw, "Active Collecting in History Museums," *Museum News,* XLV (March 1967), 22.

[4]Wilcomb E. Washburn, "Are Museums Necessary?" *Museum News,* XLVI (Oct., 1968), in the column "Opinion."

[5]Joseph Veach Noble, "Museum Manifesto," *Museum News,* XLVII (April 1970), 20.

[6]Alma Wittlin,"Foreward," *Museums in Search of a Useable Future* (Cambridge, 1970), pp. xi-xii.

[7]American Association of Museums, *Museums: Their New Audience,* Co-Chairmen James Elliott and John Kinard (Washington, 1972). See also: Otto Wittman, "Museums at the Crossroads," *Museum News,* XLIV (Sept. 1965), 15-19.

[8]Michael Spock, "Museums in Collaboration," *Museum News,* XLVIII (April 1970), 23.

"Energy—or the cost of it—
directly affects a museum. It takes
a lot of green stuff to fill a
dinosaur. How many chattering
squirrels could live on the lettuce
intake of a dinosaur?"

*Kenneth R. Hopkins, "Let's
Chatter in the Trees"*

III

Small is beautiful was the title of a book of the Sixties whose message has not yet been heeded to the extent that the energy crisis of the late twentieth century demands. In this essay, Kenneth R. Hopkins applies the concept to the museum world. In a pungent style reminiscent of Emerson, Hopkins telegraphs a message of hardhitting realities for facing the future. Part of the problem for many small museums, Hopkins insists, is one of identity. Rather than striving to emulate the major museums, they need to define their roles as active, responsible participants in their own communities. The popular culture of Hopkins' essay, therefore, is populism. However, he does not envision the small museum's independence as one of provincialism and alienation, but of sharing and cooperating through self-help programs. In many of the articles that follow on both museums and libraries, remarkably creative specific instances of such programs can be seen. The articles by David Orr and Mark Ohno, by Richard Hurst and by William Schurk and B. Lee Cooper are to be particularly recommended in this light.

Kenneth R. Hopkins has been Director of the State Capitol Museum in Olympia, Washington since 1965. An incorrigible gadfly on such institutions as large museums, universities, museum associations and federal agencies, Hopkins has an impressive record of experience with a rich variety of museums, including serving as Director of Explorers Hall at the National Geographic Society in Washington, D.C., as Historic Preservationist with Bethlehem Steel Company, as Curator at the Buffalo, New York Historical Society and the Wisconsin State Historical Society and as Art Director at Old Sturbridge Village. Hopkins' first love is sculpture, and his latest self-help project is manufacturing reproductions of Washington State furniture for the purpose of raising funds for the programs of the State Capitol Museum.

Kenneth R. Hopkins

Let's Chatter in the Trees

ON THE WALL OF MY STUDIO is a drawing by a friend who happens to be my daughter.

The drawing is of a dinosaur and its verse goes like this:

> In evolution, simplicity is always linked to complexity
> Huge dinosaurs lumber into extinction
> Tiny mammals chatter in the trees.

What matters is not the source of these words, but the understanding a young 30 year old) artist has about the veritudes of our confused times.

I couldn't imagine working or living in a place in which one or more of this now adult offspring's works were not integral.

Her spirit is fresh and her understanding is real. I wish it were as easy for me to understand the confusions of the museum world.

I see huge urban institutions lumbering into extinction. I see tiny museums chattering in delight at what is possible.

I have lumbered with some and chattered in others.

The longer I gambol in the latter, the more monstrous seem the former.

There is not the slightest doubt I am biased. I am biased in favor of the small community museum. Obviously, my bias about dinosaurs is heavy.

I think about the questions of our time. Nearly all answers return to the problem of energy.

Energy—or the cost of it—directly affects a museum. It takes a lot of green stuff to fill a dinosaur. How many chattering squirrels could live on the lettuce intake of a dinosaur?

I favor squirrels. The dinosaur seems to be extinct and I watch a squirrel from my window. His energy is infinite. I chose wisely.

Energy will continue to plague us, possibly forever. Museums— or other institutions that produce nothing—will continue to be the complacent victims of inflation.

Forever? No. Because we simply will not survive forever.

The costs of mammoth physical plants that consume vast amounts of energy without producing anything in return will escalate until those costs will consume every other available asset.

The financial ability to bring together a professional staff, millions of visitors, millions of artifacts, housing all in a mammoth structure, at the expense of overburdened taxpayers will eventually

27

collapse as an economic impossibility.

The pressures on the reduced funding by available foundations will increase until only the barest fraction of museums will find it worthwhile to apply for grants. (Almost the case now.)

The support of operating costs will overburden the foundations. Operating costs are the Achilles heel of fund raising. Once foundations—or government—get into this bottomless pit, the result will be our extinction. HEW presumably is beginning with such a program. Where else would a bottomless pit be happier?

I have heard university administrators ask each other, how can we continue to bring thousands of individual students from all points of the compass, to one location, house and feed them for the better part of four more years, provide all of the complex of physical facilities we believe necessary to provide a modern educational process, provide for expensive people to do the instruction and even more expensive administrators, provide changes and growth and do all of this and more, with decreasing attendance and increasing costs? The traditional sources of funding, even now, are insufficient.

If the energy crisis is real,then the simple, or not so simple, fact of the transportation of thousands of students back and forth each year, many times, simply does not make economic sense, in case it ever meant educational sense.

Bring the kids to the place where the teachers are. This is simplistic nonsense in an energy burdened society. How about bringing the teachers to the students?

As realistic or unrealistic as this may sound, depending upon your position in the game, the answer to an energy crisis in universities must be found by turning the traditional process around.

Just as I believe, as an observer, that universities must go out to the community, so do I believe that museums must also go to the people instead of depending almost wholly upon the people transporting themselves to the museums.

Obviously, there are contrasts with the plight of academia in the future role of the country's museums.

Students do not have to be housed in a museum. There are other contrasts. But the basic problem remains. A large museum must have a massive physical plant, that is, by its very nature, outrageously expensive.

Nowadays the technical requirements of professional talent in a museum can be expensive.

The costs of some museum basics—insurance, freight, maintenance—seem to be exploding.

It is a fact that in the economics of any business, or museum, the cost that will hurt the quickest, that once set in motion cannot be reversed, that breeds on itself, that will always be most vulnerable to economic pressures, is the the cost of labor.

Labor, in any business, is the cost most difficult to control and when out of control, business fails.

Fig. 1 As a first step toward potential financial self-sufficiency, the Washington State Capitol Museum has established Museum Enterprises, Inc. to market reproductions such as the rawhide-seat "Historic Tumwater Fancy Chair", first made in 1869 in Steilacoom, Washington. This enterprise was preceded by a careful feasibility study by an independent consulting firm. (Photograph courtesy Museum Enterprises, Inc.).

I believe that museums must assess costs in a way museum administrators have never felt necessary.

I am in favor of business trained museum management. But where do the small museums find Wharton grads?

(I hear about seminars for better museum management. For a few hundred dollars some of us—there is always a grant proposal to be submitted and a committee to make selections—may attend. To do what? To hear the museum establishment propound its own antiquated ways to those of us lucky enough to be chosen.

I recently received an announcement of a non-profit organization management seminar conducted by a large midwestern university that offers to help me:

> "increase team spirit in my organization"
> "avoid internal communications problems that waste time and money"
> "get useful feed back from staff about my abilities as a manager"
> "reduce conflict between staff and volunteers"
> "deal with uncomfortable evaluation situations"

Non-profit organizations are always ready to help other non-profit organizations, for a fee.)

If we do not already have them, we must make projections into a distant future. In 1985 what will be possible in our museum? In 1989? In 1999?

Will it require a doubled, tripled, quadrupled budget to remain solvent in 1985?

The energy-induced inflation does make one budgetary fact clear.

Since labor remains the most volatile cost with which we will always contend, we know that the cost of the physical plant is the cost we can project more fairly. The increase will disturb us, but it can be projected.

The costs of equipment and supplies can be adequately estimated. Utilities and energy costs begin to introduce us to our world of economic fantasy. Labor costs, however, afford us not even the luxury of fantasy.

The day of the $100,000 associate profesor is on its way, if not already here. There may even be million dollar contracts for a chair of this or that (grant funded, of course).

Faculty, administrators and staff people will demand, and receive, increases that more and more will be tied to the cost of living. This means 20% a year. This means doubled salaries every five years.

Every time you double a salary, you more than double fringe benefits.

The budgets of almost all museums are overly balanced toward labor. Labor is the single major cost. For most museums it is also the only variable major cost.

When crises arise, the labor force will be cut back before anything else. You cannot reduce storage, insurance, utilities, curatorial processes—but you can reduce secretaries and groundskeepers and curators and assistant curators.

The public must be able to visit, so your restrictions are well camouflaged behind the facade. Programs are cut back. Pet curatorial exercise is eliminated. Publishing, printing, new exhibits are reduced or eliminated. But the plant is maintained. The guard force is continued. The public is satisfied.

There are museums that, in face of crisis, have reduced hours, or even closed their doors. Some have profited from scare tactics. But the result is often cloudy, with clear resentment by the public.

Since museums are public institutions, the public is easily alerted to the awkward situation of high priced curators closing up a museum, then accusing the public of non-support. A little of that goes a long way.

The taxpayers' revolution of the late '70s and early '80s has only begun as this is being written. It seems predictable that taxpayer unrest will accelerate, at least briefly, and will continue in a number of as yet unexpressed forms.

There is no question at all that government, particularly at the federal and state levels, has become its own kind of behemoth, ceaselessly growing and growing until the frustrations of the public bring uninhibited lashing out.

It is reality that those who suffer first will not be political bureaucrats, but the poor and the disenfranchised of our country. But it is also reality that massive and lasting changes will be wrought in our political society as the unleashed power of the taxpayer overwhelms many long held political notions.

What does this mean to museums? It means that governmentally subsidized museums, being some of the weakest segments of political bureaucracy, will suffer the earliest budget cutting. Political bureaucracy will tend to protect itself first. Self protection in such cases is not a long suit of most museum directors.

Government can absorb tremendous economies, when the issue is forced. But, at first, the economies will be those that will capture headlines.

It will take time for bureaucrats to understand that the public is really fed up with the high cost of government.

We will never see the New Deal liberal again. He is gone. There are entrenched politicoes who seriously believe that government can and should right all wrongs, feed all hungry, charm all unfortunates and that taxpayers will endlessly subsidize every new worthwhile project.

It is clear that this part of our heritage is over. To the degree that public museums are a product of this thinking, we are going to be victims of the changes, unless we ourselves change, and quickly.

A museum rarely merchandises its assets—i.e. collections.

Antiques journals carry some ads for auctions of museum collections. Museums do cash-in collections, usually justifying this as being for the good of the collection, et al, but in some cases, clearly the motivation is the need for operating funds.

It is a delusion that any organization can survive, much less succeed, by reducing capital assets. It is a bookkeeper's approach that none of us would relish.

Museums must, therefore, reconsider collections. Collections, by their nature, should be inviolate. We must reconsider the concept of collection and assess what it really is that we own. Are our collections a conglomerate bank account?

A museum has no "right to exist." It has the privilege of existing. It exists exactly to the degree that its community finds it desirable. Without belaboring how you get to that point, a museum can only represent its community.

If a museum expects its community to support it, forever, *carte blanche*, it will lumber—no—it will probably jog—on to extinction. I see no future for the dinosaurs in our museum world. I see a beautiful future for the small museum.

The small museum can and will exist. There should be no real problem in this.

The small museum by its very nature can "chatter in the trees." Perhaps chattering in the trees is not as earth-shaking as a lumbering footstep, or a roar of dragon fire, but neither is it sinking in a tar pit.

The small museum is not a miniature dinosaur museum. The small museum is an entity unto itself, valid, real, lively and significant. A squirrel, after all, is not a dinosaur.

There is no reason for people in a small museum to believe they are poor cousins of that large urban neighbor.

The small museum can be an important statement in its own way. There is a place for a beautifully designed functional small car and such cars exist. A Porsche can be more expensive than a Cadillac and more fun. Each has its place. (Cadillacs are getting smaller!)

It is possible for a staff in a small museum to relate to the people in a community directly and personally.

I liken this also to the "feel" of a sports car. The small museum experience gives you the opportunity to "feel" your museum's programs. You are directly involved. You can shift, move about, reflect, react, respond—in short, you can do all of the intelligent things that are needed to produce effective community interaction.

Community interaction is the password to a successful small museum. Obviously, most small museums have small (in number) collections. Hasn't it dawned on you that the "large" museums in our country never get around to showing more than a tiny proportion of their extensive collections?

I won't even deal with the question, "Why?" I've always wondered, well, a little wonder, at the fact that our large museums rarely initiate any sharing of their stores.

No matter. I believe it is a fact that we small museums don't need basement hand-me-downs from the dinosaurs. Nor do most of us desire them.

On the other hand, we do resent the dinosaurs lumbering into our town and spiriting away treasures from local collections.

Our society is clearly heading in the direction of reduced energy consumption via the reduction of the large energy consumers.

Almost everything that a large museum does can be done, if one wishes, in a series of small museums. I would argue all could be done more easily, simply and economically in small museums and at a saving of energy.

This is not an argument for decentralization. Nor is it a dull reflection of the concept of "intermediate technology."

The small museum is not a $100 institution. Nor are we the product of a poor (uncultured?) society. We do not evolve from an unsophisticated environment, nor from poverty stricken multitudes.

We exist because the communities of which we are a part wish to have us in their lives.

This does not come from any outside paternalistic goodwill. It occurs through the nature of people to want to understand a little more about what it is we all are, were and will be.

All of this takes more than one generation. It is in a small museum that we understand this. Thus, the small museum becomes more than a Sunday afternoon visit, or a school tour, or a glamorous King Tut exhibit.

There is a good question about the "ownership" of a museum. Who "owns" a museum? Does anyone in New York City "own" the Metropolitan? Of course not.

Then, who owns it?

The "people" of the city? The "people" of the state of New York? of the United States? Do I "own" a piece of it?

There are legal answers to this question. But IRS regulations and corporate law and miscellaneous state statutes don't answer the thrust of the question, "Who owns a museum?"

I ask this because any attempt to answer it must bring to mind a good many questions about a museum, questions we rarely consider. A New York resident must accept the fact that he or she has nothing at all to do with the policies of the Metropolitan.

You may be proud of it. You may derive exceedingly appropriate intellectual returns from experience within it. But, you must also be aware that you are only one person out of millions in any personal identification with it. Are you an "owner?"

I look at the small community museum and I see the "owners," every one, people in the community, on the street, in the museum, in the schools, and they are real, they exist as individuals, and if you want respect you must earn it and they will give it, but not without consideration.

Since this interaction with a local citizenry has nothing, or very little, to do with the size or the quality of your museum collection, since the response of your community is to what you do together, not what you collect and show to them, questions about the validity of extensive collecting do arise.

This returns us to the dinosaurs.

Dinosaurs consumed vast amounts of energy in day to day living. They also required considerable territory, territory that had to be continually expanded simply to provide for existence.

The large museums in our society lumber on, with expanding collections required simply to justify existence; expanding collections mean expanding buildings, expanding buildings mean expanding staff, all mean more energy consumed, ad infinitum.

The chattering squirrels who are their neighbors need to be quick to evade rapacious jaws or crunching tails.

As energy sources dry up the dinosaurs will turn on each other. As this occurs it will do well for the squirrels to join forces. Not to become mini-dinosaurs, but to establish and secure new ways of living in cooperative success.

A number of predictions are possible. Small museums must develop individually and in new ways to relate to their communities. If they do this, they not only will survive, but will prosper.

Small museums can and should develop self-help, self-supporting programs, utilizing free enterprise processes. By doing this, small museums can provide mutually for economic survival outside of government.

Small museums must disassociate themselves from the gifts, grants, government, creative writing syndrome that has traditionally replaced self initiative in most cultural fund raising. By developing new endeavors in a free enterprise system, by working together, small museums will not need governmental funding.

Indeed, it may well be that government funding will not only not be needed, but government funding as we have come to expect it, will simply not exist.

If we have actually reached a watershed level in cultural funding, as a result of the effect of "taxpayer's revolt" there would be no alternative to museum engagement in increased outside business.

Unless small museums move rapidly into self-help cooperative programs we are all vulnerable to reduced government funding.

It is time not only to assess our assets and determine new policies for the exploitation of them, but for original and creative thinking about museums, what we are and where we intend to go.

We cannot sit back and suffer in silence, if suffering is our game. We cannot allow a confused political society of economizers, right wingers, radicals and opportunists who may take over government also direct our museum future.

Let us be the directors of our own future. To do this will mean all of us must devote a vastly more effective effort toward determining our own destiny.

Self-help. Self-regulation. Creativity. Cooperation. Unselfishness. Whatever. Independence is the word. We must become independent of a confused government buffeted on all sides by the whirlwind of unhappy taxpayers.

I like unhappy taxpayers. I am one. Having been a part of government for more than thirteen years, I am well acquainted with unhappy bureaucrats. It always seems as if everyone likes a museum. On occasion they even like museum directors.

But, when I compete head to head with frightened bureaucrats for reduced tax money, my position of weakness becomes painfully apparent. No one likes me.

The advantage I have, if I care to use it, is my ability to be creative. Since I am unconcerned with sheer survival, I can afford to take chances. Since I can imagine doing something else in life, my life is not wedded to a Civil Service wheelchair.

Small museums have no traditions that straitjacket new ideas. Therefore, new ideas are the heart of everything the small museum can and should be. It is in the small museum that imagination breeds in fertile ground. If small museums break the traditions that have been handed down from the dinosaurs, a new kind of institution can evolve, whether or not it is called "museum" is immaterial.

We'll call it something else. We'll probably not be operating in a marble hall. But we will be relating the old realities of living to the new. And somewhere along the line the community will discover that a museum works because everyone is a part of it.

"Critics have accused us of plying our material as 'instant nostalgia' aimed at thousands of demonstration 'veterans' for their particular self-gratification and ego trip. Nothing could be farther from our own basic desires."

David G. Orr and Mark R. Ohno, "The Material Culture of Protest: A Case Study in Contemporary Collecting"

IV

Popular Culture work brings together strange bedfellows, and nowhere is this made clearer than in the following three case studies that chronicle the techniques, tribulations and triumphs of creating museum exhibits on popular culture. Edith Mayo has in an earlier article demonstrated the problems that emerged in America's largest museum; in the following article, the authors explain what happens on a smaller scale, when Professor David G. Orr and student Mark R. Ohno set forth to prepare a smaller exhibit without outside assistance or institutional sanction. The result was not only popular but populist as they developed a viewer participation program that might serve as a model for other museums. Starting with a theoretical discussion of the rationale and need for contemporary collecting, the authors note the ironic fact that provenience and attribution of current materials is at least as problematical as it is for remoter artifacts. Readers will want to compare Orr and Ohno's collecting methods with those in the later essays on libraries by B. Lee Cooper, Maurice Crane and William Schurk.

David Gerald Orr currently serves as Regional Archaeologist for the National Park Service Mid-Atlantic Region in Philadelphia. Formerly he was an Assistant Professor of American Civilization at the University of Pennsylvania where he was also Curator of American Historical Archaeology at the University Museum. His interests include vernacular architecture, folk ethnographies, industrial archaeology, Roman religion from preclassical times to the present and American popular culture. He has published articles in all of these subjects. Mark Ohno holds B.A. and M.A. degrees from the University of Pennsylvania. Both authors are developing an expanded "cause item" exhibit for 1981-1982 and will welcome leads to obtain further items, trade proposals and comments, particularly anti-war and ecology.

David G. Orr & Mark R. Ohno

The Material Culture of Protest: A Case Study in Contemporary Collecting

THE IDEA THAT MOST of the visible products of culture are by nature fragile and impermanent is forcefully driven home when one glances casually around at the amazing physical shroud which ephemerally covers most of contemporary America's expressive statements.[1] We have embodied most of our civilization in paper, celluloid and plastic. We have a culture powerfully molded from constant image bombardment and yet we preserve or consciously strive to preserve little of it.[2] America is a world power where ideas are lodged in forms whose shapes are transitory and whose physical lives are doomed at their very genesis. Iconically and intellectually our environment is verbally and non-verbally short lived. All this has been argued elsewhere in many ways. But still the critical issue in the discussion and recording of our era is one of serious threat; the menace of irretrievable loss of both datum base and cultural value. Somewhere in the early stages and discussion of our little exhibit all these spectres were faced and addressed. Certainly the imperative of high wastage was our concern. The second concern involved the simple process of selection, that mysterious process which creates great museums for elitist collections of art and form, that process which decides what building is to be measured, drawn and even saved and what building is to crumble back to the earth. In our zeal to accept the clarion call to preserve and interpret the ephemeral world, that "we have lost" we paused to ponder over the broader issue of what worlds were being preserved. Where are our efforts, financial and material, being directed? What types of historical forms are being isolated for survival? Abodes of great men and women, sites of important historical events, unique and progressive works of art, battlefields and significant artifacts of technology and science make up the lion's share of preserved forms in America today. Vanguards of change have recently added a small group, but hopefully growing collection, of different genres of buildings and objects; occasionally collected under new assemblages possessing cryptic titles like *vernacular architecture, folk* and *naive art, industrial archaeology* and so on. Many students of ethnography and other holistic approaches to human history and behavior have already accepted the simple truth that the study of material culture is *all* material culture. In such simple concepts the true energy of past and present cultural activity can be studied.

Contemporary collecting, i.e., extracting from our most recent past coherent groups of data, is a response aimed at alleviating the illogic suggested by the problems of selection based on the vagaries of ethnocentric involvement. Our dilemma is often the fact posed by our surrounding world; it is the most familiar, commonplace, and intimate, and as such it is usually the part of culture which can be lost to future generations first. Our own knowledge of domesticity in early America, for example, in eastern urban areas in the eighteenth century, is largely fabricated from material analysis of the most basic sort. Historical archaeology produces a real contribution in this area largely because of the fact that most people did not precisely record that they ate from tin-glazed plates and drank from local fired earthenware tankards. Neither did they stop to write in detail how they built a simple one room house and what exactly did they furnish it with. Material culture study undertaken in close harmony with primary written sources strives to answer these questions. Yet the problems of connoisseurship are immense. Additionally, archaeologists are still working with a comparatively narrow data base and many conclusions must consequently rest on the slimmest of evidence. We have learned from the hard lessons postured by the availability and survival of tri-dimensional evidence. Therefore, many students have sought to avoid this situation by extracting the material from our society now for the benefit of future generations.

Programs recently instituted by the National Museum of History and Technology's Division of Political History[3] and the Canadian Museum of Man[4] are solid commitments to archive and to interpret an ephemeral data base extrapolated from an historical economy of abundance. It is not too bold for us to assert that the future accuracy of our present cultural nature may rest upon such programs. Moreover, we need many such programs before we have really met the challenge of contemporary archiving. Our own little exhibit of protest material and our subsequent attitudes and goals rested on a similar, albeit more modest, desire. Our teleology was elementary indeed; it consisted of merely isolating a well defined group of contemporary objects, ephemeral by nature and firmly documenting them for exhibit. We discovered early on that cultural memory was both fragile and transitory.

It is difficult to believe that the highly charged emotional content of the objects we chose to study could ever be neutralized or even lost. Yet the material which formed the heart of our visual essay, anti-war buttons and related items from America's experience in Indo-China just recently concluded, was extremely difficult to document and identify. Indeed, there is probably, at the present time, no firm possibility of ever documenting such things as issuing organization, manufacturer, designer, year and number produced.[5]

Such data are not readily available even for the most recent material. Another of the great lessons learned from our exhibit was even more striking than the above. We found that much of the sloganry and visual material utilized on the anti-war buttons of the late sixties and early seventies was alien to our college audience. Ten years had "cooled" the ardor from events we had thought had burned more deeply than what our viewers' reaction had suggested.

Sometime in September of 1977 our exhibit and interest in protest materials was initiated. Both of us had been participants and collectors in many anti-war demonstrations. Our nucleus was roughly 200-300 items mostly selected from our numen-charged demonstration artifacts. We decided that we would create an exhibit which would use these kinds of materials to convey a visual message of the peace demonstrations of the sixties and seventies. From there we made an additional decision which involved us ultimately with protest organizations of all kinds and of practically all issues. The result was an extremely popular campus exhibit of about fourteen hundred items which was on view in the Van Pelt Library of the University of Pennsylvania in November/December 1978. The exhibit required about fifteen months of effort and cost us about $1500. It was supported financially by no outside agency or person and no organization or academic department sponsored it in any manner whatsoever. It was a professor/student exhibit; it was barely mentioned in university classes that it related to in some theoretical or substantive way. Most of our academic colleagues looked at our enterprise as a harmless antiquarian exercise; few took it seriously or saw any large issue. Yet it was received by the campus community warmly and positively; its success can be measured in part by its wide popularity in West Philadelphia. Major newspapers and TV stations interviewed us and broadcast our efforts to the public. It has propelled the authors into what is assuredly a lifetime interest and involvement in its subject matter. Critics have accused us of plying our material as "instant nostalgia" aimed at thousands of demonstration "veterans" for their particular self-gratification and ego trip. Nothing could be farther from our basic desires. Our exhibit sought, more than any other single aim, to document a large and fast-disappearing genre of material culture. Our framework was our most recent past; a dangerous area for the scholar. The result was mixed, as we shall see, but our methodology was successful. Since our purpose, in the exhibit, was to illustrate this methodology, we shall describe it at some length. Acquisition of the exhibit was very cost-effective, as we will now discuss in some detail.

In designing a direct mail solicitation campaign to obtain protest objects, we wrote to 328 currently existing movements, worldwide, gleaned from telephone books, movement lists and directories, private referrals and other written sources of various kinds. This formed the most important part of our exhibit since this material was well documented and otherwise identified. Some were sent gratis, others required minimal payment, but all material was well provenienced. Exceptional material (for example a fine group of objects from Tasmania) was sent free of charge in many instances.

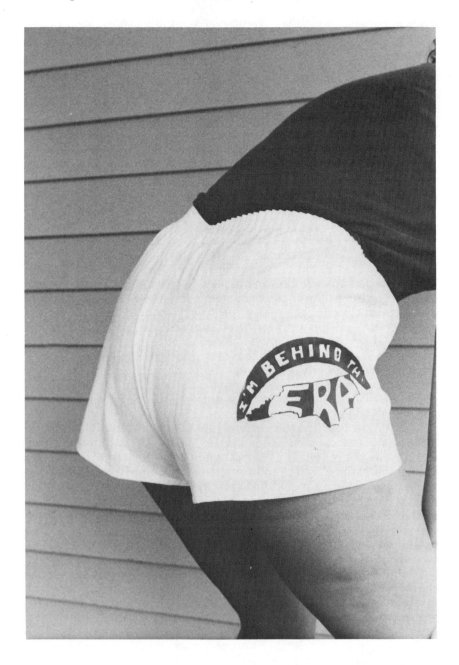

Fig. 1 "I'm Behind the ERA" shorts made by Durham, North Carolina Chapter members, National Organization for Women (ca. 1977) in support of state referendum. (Unless otherwise credited, all photographs are from the Ohno-Orr collection).

Fig. 2 Ecology

Fig. 3 1961 Peace March

Fig. 4 Civil Rights lynching imagery: British anti-apartheid movement 1978; Black United Liberation Front, Philadelphia, 1976.

Fig. 5 Danish *Kvindefronten* "Womenfront" 1977; Gay Rights, 1977.

Fig. 6 Anti-Viet Nam: AFSC (American Friends Service Committee) with place to write prisoner of war name, 1973; WRL (War Resisters League), 1977.

Fig. 7 Civil rights: CORE (Congress on Racial Equality); SSOC (Southern Student Organizing Committee); NAACP (National Association for the Advancement of Colored People, college division). All early to mid '60s.

Fig. 9 Genre photograph of the late 1960s and early 1970s demonstrations from the Swarthmore Peace Collection.

Fig. 10 Genre photograph of the late 1960s and early 1970s demonstrations from the Swarthmore Peace Collection.

"Famous protestors" and organization leaders were less responsive to our missives for a large variety of reasons. Some anti-war types would write us saying that they were "not into buttons but ideas." Unfortunately little could be done to mitigate this attitude. A generation of hobbiests' collecting almost everything had prepared them for our letters. Many looked upon our letters as self-serving, petty and a thinly veiled rip-off designed to milk rare ephemera from the anti-war movements.

Learning quickly, we resorted to psychological ploys, similar to those used previously by our charity solicitation comrades, to overcome suspicions and even ennui. Many of the organizations we wrote to did not possess an established mechanism for routinely answering mail. Since we never sent anything remotely resembling a form letter (each organization was asked particular sets of questions), this meant that our letters travelled around the office until interest in our project was either stimulated or snuffed. Authority for the removal of posters, for example, was generally broad-based and the more often our letters could reach this base the better our chances were for a successful reply. Whenever possible, we tried to arrange personal interviews with local groups in order to assure them of our sincerity and of the merits of our exhibit. The degree of success in this program was solid; seventeen percent of all groups contacted responded by giving us material of one kind of another. It should also be remembered that many of our letters (about ten percent) were returned to us by the postal service because the group had either disbanded or moved to an unknown forwarding address. Many of the groups replied that they never issued the types of material we were asking for. Add to all this the facts that we solicited materials from groups on all continents and that a fair number of organizations responded by sending more than one item (twelve groups sent more than ten buttons) and one can easily measure the success of our mail program. Even when one also considers the problem of duplication of material it was always welcome to receive large packages of items. These were then traded off for examples of material not represented in the collection. Although all letters were individually written, most of them did follow a general pattern. Their variability depended on perceived motivations on the part of the groups solicited. Buttons and materials were received occasionally from members of organizations who were interested in our project and who responded unofficially; many persons so contacted sent material unrelated to their own group.

Parts of our letters also targeted the core leaders of these groups. These people have a strong sense of history and possess the self-image that they are a vanguard of some sort of special future. They responded positively to the sections of our letter which stressed the documentation process. They seemed to appreciate the preservation of fragile links with their movement that our exhibit would achieve. Most wanted to save these material memories for future examination and edification; a process which they knew was part of an ongoing series of important historical events.

All solicitations emphatically stated that materials received would be acknowledged in the exhibit. Of course this was done, and both individual and group donations were prominently identified. Some letters offered financial remuneration for objects we might receive, since the sale of such material does represent an important funding source for many of our target organizations. When requested, we promptly reimbursed groups who responded and accompanied our payment with a *Thank You* note which oftentimes aided in mollifying opposition to our future dealings with them. We should also mention one way in which we solicited material from diametrically opposed political organizations. Taking innocent advantage of such political dualisms, we would inform one group that we had received material from their arch-competitor and that the material was excellent. Then, we would casually mention that if they would respond in kind we could project a more "balanced" presentation in our exhibit. Some will attack this method as Machiavellian at best, but in our defense such balanced material *did* fulfill one of our main goals in staging our show in the first place. Our tactics merely enabled us more effectively to achieve this very desirable aim.

Another way in which we could tap a responsive chord was to stress the attendant publicity our labors would attract. Our audience would be numerically large and generally unversed in the complexities raised by particular issues. We discovered later that many of our donors seriously desired to communicate with what they perceived to be an "unprejudiced" audience. Thus the publicity generated by the exhibit was mutually welcomed by both the donor and the sponsor.

Finally, some of our letters emphasized the message that failure to contribute to our exhibit was, in a sense, to be "left out." We stressed the diversity of our materials and described how they represented such a broad spectrum of political and social beliefs. The implication was that if they sent material they could join this marvelous assemblage of political thought. Again, such a ploy sincerely depended upon our desire to get the greatest number of groups and objects for our exhibit. Slightly mercenary, quite manipulatory, our mail solicitation program was not cavalier or unselfconscious, but was carefully orchestrated and executed. Its detailed methodology was structured to achieve a maximum yield of objects. It was tempered by our limited budget and it was fueled by our desire to attempt individually tailored approaches for each of our projected exhibitors. It was by far the single most important factor in the exhibit's subsequent success.

Three other methods were used to acquire material for our exhibit and these should be summarized below. None of them could offer the qualities of provenience, unquestioned authenticity, etc., possessed by our mail order campaign. Purchasing objects from both dealers and participants resulted in a large amount of excellent material. Our sources were direct purchases from activists who "had been there," button dealers usually found at button conventions, flea markets and antique shops. Low mail bids executed in large button auctions occasionally netted some fine objects. Also in the bargain category were damaged objects (still of exhibitable quality) since these are generally rejected by the cognoscenti of protest collecting. It should be added here that the types of objects sought by us for our exhibit already had possessed a rather fine and active market, and interest in these kinds of objects is growing rapidly. One example of this interest is the Cause Chapter of the American Political Items Collectors which among other activities has recently published its own profusely illustrated journal.[6] We also discovered that advertising to purchase or even trade buttons in movement newsletters was totally ineffective. Several important loans were arranged for our premier exhibit and we feel very strongly that our upcoming major show will depend very heavily upon this method of acquisition. Trades have also been reasonably effective for us (more so at the present time) as we acquired a large pool of duplicates and irrelevant material. In the course of the past two years we have built effective trading relationships with six major American and international collectors.

Our first protest exhibit did not involve a major interpretation effort on our part. We traced the brief evolution of the American Political button from McKinley's 1896 campaign down to the present. We illustrated material from the Spanish American War to argue this early involvement of cause espousal groups in button, banner and stickpin manufacture.

Another small portion of our exhibit illustrated the current technologies involved in button manufacture. Here we were immeasurably aided by the assistance of Mr. Edward Horn of Philadelphia, a prominent producer of buttons and other related material. The great bulk of the exhibit was made up of panels illustrating the enormous variety of themes present in protest organizations. Over half of the material displayed directly concerned itself with America's experience in Vietnam. Our next exhibit will present this material in an interpretative manner, emphasizing the relevant sociological and historical aspects.[7] Special sections of the exhibit concentrated on minority and civil rights, suffrage and feminism, ecology and environment, abortion, labor, gay rights, national liberation struggles, prohibition and other forms of narrowly defined political activism. Although the exhibit traced the twentieth century flowering of such groups it clearly focussed on the movements active in the 1960s and 1970s.

One of the most popular sections of the exhibit allowed for viewer participation in two main ways. Spectators were invited to identify buttons displayed on a large white panel which were labeled from A to Z. These buttons were totally unknown as to provenience or message. Any help, therefore, from our audience was greatly desired. By using a plexiglass "participatory box," viewers could write their guesses and deposit them in the box. We then checked with the box every week and removed material identified by the audience and added new "unknowns" to the panel. It was an extremely popular feature of our exhibit and did assist us by identifying correctly several previously unknown buttons. This box also encouraged participation through "donation of protest buttons, miscellaneous information, written comments and criticisms and feedback." All of the above was accomplished at one time or another during the run of the exhibit. Viewers' comments came by the hundreds. The great percentage, over 97%, were favorable to our efforts. Yet, the adverse remarks were extremely interesting and we feel should be presented in this essay. Many of them commented on the "cooling" effect our eclecticism had on the fervor and ardor of the issues. The activists didn't like it. Secondly, many objected to the idea of presenting these items as "nostalgia" and as an "antiquarian exercise." Some thought us enemies of progress and change. Others deeply suspected our motives. A few accused us of aesthetic elitism! None of our more controversial items, i.e., Nazi armbands and anti-semitic buttons, etc., provoked any discussion whatsoever. We benefited very much from the two-way forum provided for us by our participatory box.

The process of precise documentation has been one of our most cherished aims throughout our collecting during the past two years. At the time of our exhibit only about 40% of the material we displayed also had some definite provenience and/or identification. Of the remaining 60% we had knowledge of only a portion of the artifact's total content; either the organization which produced the item, some aspect of its symbolic message, or some detail of its design or statement. In the approximately fifteen-month period since the close of the University of Pennsylvania exhibit we have gathered about four hundred additional items. The percentage of complete documentation for this group is gratifyingly higher; about 80%. Most of the newly acquired material has come from contemporary sources and is correspondingly well identified. We have carefully retained all correspondence which has accompanied buttons and stickers, these letters being crucial to our collection methodology. Some organizations, for example, have assisted us greatly in our research by providing as much existing information about items as they have on hand in their offices. Two organizations, the National Organization for Women (NOW) and the United Farm Workers (UFW) stand out as exceptional in this respect. The Chicago office of NOW sent us individually typed index cards with full details of manufacture, etc., which identified all material sent to us before our first exhibit at the University of Pennsylvania. The United Farm Workers patiently identified material at their local office in Philadelphia for us. Fortunately their kind of cooperation was mirrored by dozens of other groups. In our current quest for anti-nuclear power material, the Clamshell

Alliance, for example, has provided us similar services. Many of our early anti-war buttons were tracked down in archives; the Swarthmore Peace Collection, for example, furnished us both documents and photographs for the exhibit. Yet the individually preserved object, sometimes saved almost like a Victorian keepsake or memento, was usually the most powerful bearer of content and message. A Delaware friend gave me a battered wooden sign carried in one of the Pentagon marches; its faded blue script reading thus: "Stamp Out War in the World." Many of our buttons were firmly documented as relating to individual marches and rallies. All of this led inexorably to an honest depiction of material. We eliminated for the most part artifacts which were sold at outlets cashing in on marches and other events. The great majority of our material was produced by organizations to raise funds and to broadcast ideology.

Why were such steps taken in order to document what many scholars and commentators have termed as "insignificant and trivial"? The answer to this question was the real *raison d'etre* for much of what we did. Perhaps it was precipitated by one particular comment directed at Dr. Orr by a distinguished member of the History Department of the University of Pennsylvania. When he saw what Dr. Orr was carrying, a box of buttons, he shook his head. "Why don't you study something significant?" he sneered. Both of us felt, of course, that we were. The main idea that he seemed to miss was that the study of material culture is *all* material culture. Maybe we should have entitled this essay, "Learning from Protest Buttons." It would take a separate essay to fully dispute this in the language of all who labor in the world of material culture at the present time. Yet, some of the main points should be underlined. We documented these materials because they are ephemeral statements of our culture and contain valuable expressive connotations concerning our era. They act iconically; that is to say that they are instantly recognized by other "true believers" and they become icons of reform and change. They represent to their wearer the outwardly communicative kernel of some special force or tenet which is of great personal and group value. They identify and classify; they sort and cull for us as we witness groups wearing and carrying such items. Since few agencies or individuals were taking adequate steps to insure their preservation and to provide for the mandatory annotation with eager hearts we accepted the task. Many of our readers are undergoing a similar process of frustration and non-support from academic and professional colleagues. Self-effacing as it may seem externally the rewards for such efforts are legion. Protest buttons are tangible memories of violent political events; their langugage and design cut to the viscera and their compositions often are painfully delineated. Yet they entomb the power of the age that created them. They act as tridimensional catalysts for those seeking to interpret the twentieth century. They still forcefully remind us of visions and wars, won and lost.

As artifactual *comparanda* the protest buttons we exhibited possessed an additional valuable quality. Many of their designs inconographically related to the aesthetic trends of their contemporary society. David Levine, Alexander Calder, Gary Turdeau, Jules Feiffer and Peter Max have all created designs for the *tondos* of buttons. Much of their artistic content vividly connects art created as non-political in terms of participation with major political and social events. They advertise all sorts of messages. They act as purveyors of shifting social values. In sum, we documented these mass produced items because they were rapidly drawing away from their context. Scholars in the past have dreamed about such foresight. Why didn't that Windsor chair maker in Philadelphia in the late eighteenth century fill his notebooks with room furnishing plans, reasons for color changes, public versus private content aspects of Windsor Chairs, detailed comments on why such chairs were desired, etc., etc.? Alas, in most cases he didn't. Yet, we study them with great zeal and energy.And so we should, since the Windsor Chair is an important testator on American values and contexts in that period. Does the protest poster, button or sticker merit attention also? Obviously we hold that it does indeed.

One of the greatest statements that protest buttons and like material express about our culture is the simple truth that you can say on lithographed metal (or plastic) those things you really can't express to people directly. Such rather implicit messages as "Lesbians Ignite," "Hell No We Won't Glow," and "Sick of the War" can be worn without bothering to orally confirm their strident nature.

Our little exhibit tried to accomplish much of what is contained in this essay. We hope that our larger and more substantive foray into the world of popular material culture will be more successful. As a case study our exhibit presents itself as a lesson in the effectiveness of contemporary collecting. Data banking the physical ephemera of our age is surely one way in which the future will become aware of cultural elements not presented elsewhere. We can only argue that the most intimate is often the first to perish. We can only stress that the most abundant often is the last to be studied.

Notes

¹Several people should be acknowledged at the onset of our essay as major stimulators and contributors to our work. They are: Edward Horn, Philadelphia; Edith Mayo, Washington; Robert L. Harned, Philadelphia; Kate Ohno, North Carolina; Linda Orr, Delaware City; Marshall Fishwick, Virginia; Jo Freman, New York; Albert Feldstein, APPA; Marshall Levin, New York City.

We would also like to thank the University of Pennsylvania's Van Pelt Library for staging our exhibit, all of the contributors mentioned in the first panel of that exhibit, all of the groups who donated and/or made available materials, and all of the people, particularly those at the university, who helped us put the exhibit together. One portion of this essay was presented at the Popular Culture Association's National Meeting in April, 1979.

²For example, see Cooney, Robert and Michalowski, Helen. *The Power of the People: Active Non-violence in the United States*, Peace Press: 1977, for illustrations of the kinds of materials not

saved.

¹Edith Mayo, "Contemporary Collecting for the Future," paper presented at the Popular Culture Association National meeting, April, 1978.

¹Barbara Riley, "Contemporary Collecting: A Case History," paper presented at the Popular Culture Association National meeting, April, 1978.

³Mark Ohno, "A Display of Cause Items," *The Cause*, Vol. 1, no. 3, April 1978.

⁶See also the useful series of publications published by the Association for the Preservation of Political Americana.

⁷Our last exhibit was well reviewed. See for example: Anthony Lyle, "Buttons," p. 2., *Pennsylvania Gazette*, Feb., 1978; Melody Kimmel, "Say it With Buttons," *The Daily Pennsylvania*, Vol. XCIII, no. 1, 114.

"Throughout the meetings, the
four fan representatives...
laughed at, became indignant,
and generally protested any labels
that implied a social significance
to popular culture..."

*Richard M. Hurst, "Impossible or
Improbable? Popular Culture in a
Regional Historical Society"*

V

To most of us, popular culture is by definition national and international, but in this article, Richard M. Hurst chronicles the development of a major exhibit on popular entertainment that reflects the regional contribution of Buffalo and Erie County, New York. It is an approach that could be replicated in other museums, and Hurst provides a careful account of each step in the preparation of the exhibit which effectively drew in an entirely new museum patronage. Of particular interest is the unusually frank story of diverse cultural groups—nostalgia fans and collectors, academic scholars, local history enthusiasts, and professional museum personnel—working together in a sometimes uneasy alliance to develop an exhibit program that touched a responsive chord among patrons from many walks of life. Richard M. Hurst holds degrees in history and folklore from Indiana University and a Ph.D. in history from SUNY at Buffalo. He was a research associate with the Bureau of Public Discussion at Indiana University from 1962 to 1964. After two years on the IU staff he moved to the Illinois State Historical Society where he served as Historical Markers Supervisor. In 1967 he went to the Buffalo and Erie County Historical Society, one of the leading regional historical societies in the country, as Chief of Resources, and in 1979 he returned to Indiana as Assistant Director of the Indiana State Museum at Indianapolis.

Hurst, a proponent of the philosophy that history is not only valuable as an educational force but also as an instrument of entertainment, has published and delivered numerous papers and articles in such diverse fields as American history, popular culture, folklore and museum/historical society functions. In addition to his administrative duties he has taught in the fields of museology, popular culture and historic sites at SUNYAB and SUCB. He serves on various local and national seminars and consultant projects, and is a board member of various folklore, popular culture and film study organizations. His dissertation on the effects of Republic Studio on the American social scene from the late Depression to the McCarthy era was published by Scarecrow Press in 1979.

Richard M. Hurst

Impossible or Improbable?
Popular Culture in a
Regional Historical Society

IN SOME QUARTERS,the idea of a popular culture group and a historical society working together not only on general continuing programs but also on a specific project such as a major exhibit seems a contradiction in terms. So frequently the typical historical society stereotype is that of a conservative, tradition-bound institution which collects, preserves, and interprets the history of its geographical or subject area only in terms of political, military, economic and, occasionally, limited social history. At the same time, popular culture organizations are thought of as some combination of suspect academicians, who are attempting to find significance in the pleasures of the past, and nostalgic fans, who are collectors viewing popular culture as a hobby and openly resenting anyone approaching it as a scholarly pursuit. While these descriptions may well be simplifications, the fact remains that there are elements of truth in all three categories—historical societies *do* emphasize the traditional, academic popular culturalists *are* positively defensive about the importance of their discipline and fans *are* critical of attempts to find meaning in their entertainment.

Nonetheless such a coalition did occur when in 1974 the Western New York Popular Culture Society, with both fans and scholars represented, was founded in conjunction with the Buffalo & Erie County Historical Society. The WNYPCS has undertaken several projects on its own and in 1978 created in cooperation with the interpretative staff of the Historical Society just such an exhibit. Moreover, the exhibit was created with the support of a grant from the Arts Development Services, Inc., regrant program with funds from the New York Council of the Arts and the City of Buffalo, thus giving the project an aspect of legitimacy and recognition within the arts community. The exhibit, which cannot really be called a culmination because both sponsoring organizations see it as a stepping stone to other popular culture and historical society joint projects, went through many stages of development but eventually became an overview of popular culture on the national scene with regional vignettes emphasizing Western New York contributions to the subject especially in the area of entertainment. But we are getting ahead of ourselves. Both the affiliation and the exhibit were the results of much deliberation.

In truth the Buffalo & Erie County Historical Society is indeed an old line large regional historical institution. However, it has benefitted from innovative leadership and has a full spectrum of programs covering historical society/museum functions from the traditional to the experimental. The main building of the Historical Society was originally the New York State Building at the Pan-American Exposition in 1901. Turned over to the Society the following year, the building became the site of major collections and exhibits pertaining to American history in general and the Niagara Frontier specifically. In 1929 two wings housing a library and auditorium were added. Situated on Mirror Lake in Delaware Park near the edge of Buffalo proper, the white marble building presents a panorama of US and Western New York heritage, through its period galleries, changing exhibits, and collections offices. The Society is also responsible for the Buffalo Lighthouse, an 1812 cemetery, and has a close relationship with the Theodore Roosevelt Inaugural National Historic Site.

The collections consist of predominantly Western New York materials with special collections emphasizing such subjects as military history, museology, Presidents Millard Fillmore and Grover Cleveland, Niagara Falls and the Erie Canal. The library consists of over 50,000 volumes, microfilm runs of major area newspapers, and appropriate journals and periodicals, while the vertical file adds another 40,000 pieces of Western New York ephemera. The manuscripts department has over one million documents and other primary materials. The iconographic section is the department responsible for two-dimensional collections. It has over 500,000 photographs, as well as paintings, architectural plans, maps and other visual materials so important in our audio-visual oriented era. This includes a major collection of local television newsfilm from three stations dating from 1962. Finally, the museum department has over 40,000 artifacts from which are serviced the Society's own exhibits department, loans to other cultural institutions, and serious researchers utilizing study collections.

The Historical Society also maintains a full schedule of educational services through its educational department. In addition to loan kits on Western New York history for school use, panel shows are provided for use in banks, shopping malls, and educational institutions. Building tours—both school and adult groups—average around 350 to 400 per year. For many years the Society published scholarly publications such as *Museum Notes*, the hardcover *Publications of the Buffalo Historical Society*, and the *Voyager* newsletter for school groups. It later expanded its program to publish the *Niagara Frontier*, a quarterly journal; a monthly *Newsletter*, and *Adventures in Western New York History* and *Storyteller* booklets for school and general use.

The Society has twelve exhibit galleries in the building—nine of which are long-term major installations illuminating important eras or facets of Western New York history, and three are devoted to temporary exhibits drawn from its collections, loaned by other institutions, or created as two-dimensional panel shows. Some of these, particularly panel shows, are retained and made available as traveling exhibits throughout the region. The Society also contributes ideas and substantial assistance to the exhibit programs of other area historical, cultural and civic agencies.

It operates with a wide range of support. The operating funds come primarily from Erie County government but the Society also receives assistance from the City of Buffalo and the State of New York through agencies such as the New York State Council on the Arts and from the federal levels through the National Endowment for the Arts, the National Endowment for the Humanities, the National Museum Act, and the Institute of Museum Services. It is nonetheless a private organization and has over a thousand members. To encourage memberships, the Historical Society has implemented several special activities including film series, workshops and cooperative courses in area universities.

Among these activities is the sponsorship of six affiliates—the Landmark Society of the Niagara Frontier, the Military History Chapter, the Civil War Roundtable, the Lower Lakes Marine Chapter, the Western New York Medical Historical Society and, of course, the Western New York Popular Culture Society, each having a variety of meetings, events and publications. Of the six affiliates, the WNYPCS is perhaps furthest removed from the mainstream of Historical Society activities. Its creation was in fact somewhat sub-rosa, which is to say that it did not come about through the approach of an outside group to the Historical Society for support. Rather it was created from the inside.

A staff member, completing a Ph.D. in American history, was working in the area of popular culture. He also had a personal interest in the influence of the entertainment media on American society and taught an adult education course on popular culture at an area university. Because of his contacts, he realized that there was a great diversity of people interested in the subject and felt there was the nucleus of an organization if they could be brought together. As a result, in November 1974 an organizational meeting was held at the Historical Society and the benefits of affiliation were discussed—basically the use of the Society facilities including the auditorium and the "legitimacy" of an existing sponsoring cultural institution. Officers were elected and affiliation was officially requested.

The Historical Society Board of Managers hesitated on granting the approval for six months although the proposal was presented as a routine matter. It finally accepted the WNYPCS as a means of reaching yet another section of the community. In the meantime, the WNYPCS continued to meet on a monthly basis at the Historical Society with two staff people as members/liaisons.

Fig. 1 Introductory panel of the Buffalo and Erie County Historical Society's Popular Culture Exhibit. (Photographs courtesy Buffalo and Erie County Historical Society).

Fig. 2 1920s case.

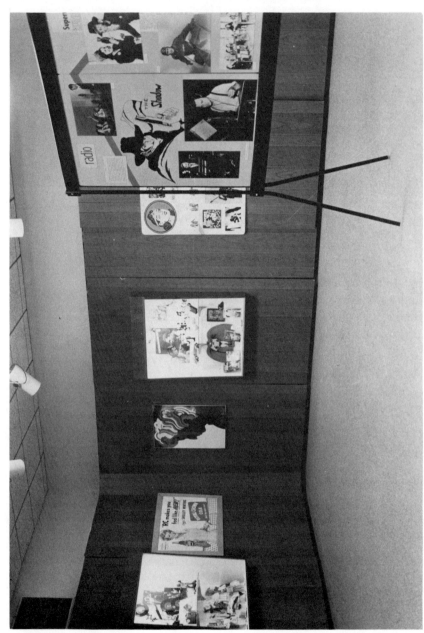

Fig. 3 Representative corner including cases, panels and single "flavoe of an era" original items.

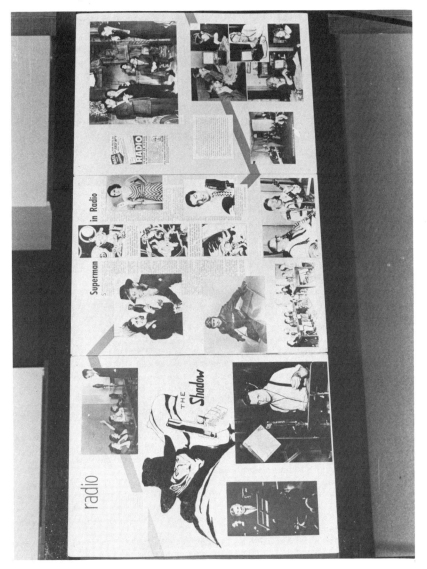

Fig. 4 Converting audio into visual: the radio panels.

During those first months, radio interests dominated the membership, although scholars, movie fans and other areas were represented. Programs tended to be an equal mix of radio and film. Eventually the radio people broke off amiably and formed their own groups (the Old Time Radio Club of Buffalo). Some remained members of the WNYPCS and look upon it as the radio group's founding organization. The radio group, relying predominantly on a newsletter and a national mail membership, became quite large while the WNYPCS stabilized at between 30 and 50 members.

A flier created to promote the WNYPCS illustrates the direction it has taken:

The Western New York Popular Culture Society (hereafter WNYPCS) was established in November, 1974, as an affiliate of the Buffalo & Erie Historical Society. Since then, the group has held monthly meetings (minus July and August, the traditional summer break) plus "specials" on various subjects, such as the *Captain America* and *Shadow* movie serials in 1975; the feature films *Gunga Din* and *Rock Around the Clock* in 1976; the *Spy Smasher* serial in 1977, as well as our first annual POP CULTURE FLEA MARKET in August of '77. The members of the WNYPCS have many interests which are reflected in their various personal collections. This has resulted in fine, exciting programs for the group. Although some programs are based upon these various interests, the emphasis has always been focused on the visual media (movies, television, etc.). Each and every member is welcome to present his/her own particular field of interest in a prepared program, formal or informal. The group has been treated to many individually prepared programs, such as a lecture/discussion on comic books; a discussion on violence in media; and even an audio-visual presentation on streetcars.

The WYNPCS publishes a monthly magazine entitled IT'S NOT JUST NOSTALGIA, which strives to inform members about upcoming meetings, as well as publishing articles and comment by club members concerning popular culture, past and present. The club also publishes an annual journal, featuring longer articles or fiction by WNYPCS members. All members are urged to contribute material, although it is not compulsory.

Although it has always been informally a non-profit organization, early 1978 brought the WNYPCS official status as a non-profit organization. All dues and monies raised by the group are channelled into its treasury, for use in club projects. According to its by-laws, the purpose of the WNYPCS "shall be to study the popular culture of America, especially of the period 1900 to 1960, to promote interest in it, to commemorate its events and to assist the Buffalo & Erie County Historical Society in collecting materials relating to it."

Popular Culture is concerned with that part of human culture that relates to the *people* as a whole, instead of to just a few select critics and reviewers. Quite probably, more people know that Superman's secret identity is Clark Kent than know "The Thinker" was sculpted by Auguste Rodin. And no doubt more people have misquoted Bogart's "Play it" line from *Casablanca* than Hamlet's remarks about poor Yorick.

Popular culture belongs to everyone. Its study includes movies, television, comic books, old time radio, bubble gum cards, pulp magazines, animation, political cartoons, nickel libraries and dime novels—to name but a few.

Why do we bother with it? For one thing, it can be reasonably argued that all the movies, comics, TV or radio shows we had contact with as children, had a great effect on our development of ideas ... some of us are concerned with building a deeper understanding of this effect. Of course, some of us belong to the group mainly to enjoy and relive these experiences of the past, or to catch up on some of the newer ones. There are even those who attend to learn about them for the first time.

Perhaps this sounds a bit nostalgic. The fact remains that "grass roots history," consisting of popular culture, folklore, and oral history as it relates to the media and to the common man is an inadequately explored and valuable aspect of our history.

The last two paragraphs make clear the fact that a dichotomy of viewpoint has developed within the WNYPCS. Its very strength—

that of appealing to all varieties of individuals interested in popular culture—has also proved to be one of its biggest continuing areas of contention. The Newsletter of the WNYPCS has from the very beginning been controlled by the nostalgia fans, although at least one academic contributes to it regularly, and most of the programs have been strictly entertainment-oriented with the exception of a few slide presentations and roundtable discussions. At the same time, the current president is a university professor and, of those individuals guiding the group, one of the most outspoken is a scholar who is interested in keeping the image of the WNYPCS "mature and serious" in order to continue the support of the Historical Society and area cultural grant agencies. Nowhere is the division of opinion seen better than in the attempt to obtain grant funding and the creation of the exhibit resulting from a successful grant proposal.

In its third year of existence, the leadership and especially the founder of the WNYPCS felt that, while the monthly meetings and newsletter were varied and interesting, the group was getting into a rut and not showing potential for development. With this thought in mind the WNYPCS, with the assistance and guidance of the Historical Society staff person in charge of development, sent tentative letters of inquiry to several local foundations and other sources of cultural support. It was decided not to approach national grant agencies at this time because it was felt that WNYPCS was not ready for a major program, the membership was relatively small, and the Historical Society had limited resources to commit to an affiliate in providing matching personnel and services. The exploratory inquiry focuses on two potential projects of reasonably limited goals. While several local agencies expressed interest in the concept of the WNYPCS, one came forth with encouragement for these specific proposals.

The New York State Council on the Arts is one of the largest and most successful of such agencies in the nation. Among its programs is a regrant format wherein it distributes funds to regional cultural agencies for redistribution to small organizations. The Arts Development Service in Buffalo is one such center for both the NYSCA and the National Endowment for the Arts. Both proposals were submitted to this program. In order to qualify for a grant the WNYPCS was required to obtain a Charities Registration Certificate from the State of New York as proof of its non-profit status.

The first proposal for a grant of $1500 (to upgrade the newsletter and expand its circulation) was rejected on the grounds that the publication was of limited appeal, circulated only to members and through resale in a few stores, and that its content lacked professionalism. The criticism was entirely valid in that, in its first 28 issues, the newsletter had taken a fanzine editorial stance and the proposed plans for expanded circulation were not fully developed.

However, the second proposal for an exhibit on popular culture emphasizing Western New York wherever feasible had the cooperation of the Historical Society, the support of a professional staff, and had appeal as a tangible project which would benefit the community. The original proposal described the project thusly:

> An exhibit on popular culture in Western New York as it relates to the national scene is being prepared in conjunction with the Buffalo Historical Society utilizing the expertise of the WNYPCS. Actual construction of the exhibit will be handled by the Buffalo Historical Society staff. Tentatively scheduled for December 1978, as a major temporary exhibit at the Historical Society, the end product would hopefully become a panel show of twenty to thirty panels for distribution throughout the region.
>
> Utilizing the talents and knowledge of Western New York Popular Culture Society members who are experts in their areas of interest, the entire spectrum of Western New York popular culture would be covered. Included are two university professors, a free lance writer, two book store managers, and several private film collectors. Sample areas of subject emphasis and their WNY relationship include 1) theatre, Katherine Cornell and Michael O'Shea, nationally known theatrical pioneer, 2) radio, Fran Stryker and the Lone Ranger; 3) film, actors James Whitmore and Reed Hadley; 4) books, author Taylor Caldwell; and 5) newspaper comic strips, Buffalo is a leading publishing center and Bruce Shanks of the Buffalo Evening News was a Pulitzer Prize winning political cartoonist.
>
> The local/regional treatment would be enlarged to give the exhibit national significance. Pictures of the common man in work day activities with appropriate quotations would be integrated within the panels on related entertainment subjects. Readily recognizable popular culture icons would be juxtaposed against period newspaper headlines or "letters to the editor" columns. Artifacts of entertainment and everyday life might be utilized in comparison with the major political events of the period. The exhibit should be an exciting and thought provoking program but assistance is needed to provide the best effort.

Amazingly, the end product was quite close to this description in most respects although several changes were made to accommodate available material and the original exhibit was expanded to include three-dimensional material in cases. The project was budgeted originally at $2850 but reduced to $1750 by the grant agency, resulting in a cutback on all expense lines and the elimination of an exhibit catalog which was replaced by the idea of covering the exhibit extensively in the newsletter. $1000 was allocated to exhibit and related photo supplies and the remaining $750 to modest honorariums for the consultants. The number and mix of the consultants provided for varied input and not a little contention. Herein was illuminated the basic dichotomy of interpretation—fan versus academic. Four were fans: a bookstore manager expert on comics and current newsletter editor; an ex-comic book store manager, collector, and past WNYPCS president; a teacher and film dealer/collector; and a free lance writer, radio authority, and past newsletter editor. The scholarly viewpoint was represented by two professors from each area university, one the current president of the WNYPCS and recognized film authority and the other a well known American historian and popular culture advocate. These two were frequently supported by the founder/liaison of the WNYPCS and acting Chief of Interpretation for the Historical Society. The consultants meetings were rounded out by the Historical Society curator of exhibits, an art trained researcher/designer who by her own admission knew little of popular culture, and the preparator, the man who would build the panels, refurbish the cases, and help put the exhibit together.

There were eight such meetings between August and December, and given the short schedule, the too large number of "cooks," and the basic differences of opinion, surprisingly a workable plan was developed and executed. The consultants provided leads and contacts, information on areas of emphasis, some research, a few labels, and much loan material. The exhibits curator and preparator submitted projected layouts and alerted the consultants to suggested areas needing more material or special attention. The liaison/coordinator provided a loose overview outline based on a chronological arrangement with the addition of appropriate subject areas emphasizing the popular culture of the region. The final outline, eventually approved by the consultants, was as follows. This "game plan" was published in the newsletter with appeals for membership assistance and, while the final exhibit differed in details, the overview remained intact.

Popular Culture Exhibit jointly sponsored by the WNYPCS and Buffalo & Erie County Historical Society. Projected Format: 10 cases and 20 panels (later convert to 30 panels for traveling panel show).

1) Early popular culture (Colonial Period to 1900)—2 panels—Broadside reproductions; pioneer toys, tavern art and games; Erie Canal scene; Fillmore political cartoon; dime novel reproductions (Horatio Alger, Frank Merriwell, Western and Adventure covers); turn of the century theatre; minstrels; *Harpers* or *Leslies* related illustrations; circuses and wild west show posters. During this period modern popular culture was unformed and popular culture was very close to folklore and grassroots history which will become apparent in the introductory presentation.

2) Prelude to popular culture explosion (1900-1920)—2 panels and 1 case—Teddy Roosevelt and the "Teddy" bear; Pan-American Exposition posters (perhaps Midway); growth of the silent film, WWI (movie serial, perhaps Irene Castle chapter vehicle, flying pulp cover); end of the dime novel; rise in sports activities; coming of the "wireless," (early radio shots). In this era modern mass media developed and the wedding of the media and entertainment for profit through wide distribution and popular appeal was a philosophy which gained ascendency. The potential blossoming of popular culture as it is currently defined will be emphasized in this section.

3) The Jazz Age (1920s) —4 panels and 2 cases— Rise of the pulps; the silent era and the coming of sound; radio becomes a force (Buffalo contributions); theatre and the decline of vaudeville; social games (mahjongg, bridge). This was the period when popular culture as we know it really developed with the fortuitous combination of the mass media and the entertainment industry, more leisure time, the rise of the automobile, and the general social giddiness of the country masking serious economic and political undercurrents. This and the next three categories will be the focal points of the exhibit.

4) The Great Depression (1930s) —4 panels and 2 cases—Hollywood helps out (series films and serials); the age of the comicstrip; the birth of the comic book; mystery fiction and the popular novel (A.K. Greene); the heyday of the pulps; burlesque thrives; the incubation of television. The 1930s represent a period when the popular media gave an appearance of the country pulling together as well as providing the much needed escapist entertainment. The musical number "Shuffle Off to Buffalo" in a well known Warners musical is a prime example on several levels. It could be used here or in a Buffalo subject panel. The group effort theme will be highlighted in several ways.

5) The War (1940-1945) —2 panels and 1 case—Radio, movies, pulps, comics all reflected preparedness and preparation; paperbacks became important. The media were influenced by and at the same time contributed to the war effort and environment. This and the preceding period represent what most people identify as representing popular culture. Patriotism will be a major motif in this section.

6) "Back to Normal" (the late 1940s) —2 panels and 1 case—Radio begins to decline; television

gains a foothold; comic books enter a fallow period; Hollywood crests in 1946 and slips; sports and the popular novel thrive (Taylor Caldwell). The period was represented best by the Bomb, the growing Red Scare, and the loss of a unified militant enemy resulting in an aimlessness and lack of purpose reflected in much of the media and entertainment formats. While it was back to normal on the surface, the confusion and hesitation in much of society and popular culture will be accented.

7) The Eisenhower Years (the 1950s) —2 panels and 1 case—The rise of noncommitment; the "death" of dramatic radio; the comic purge; media reflect the car culture and the expansion of suburbia; the beginning of rock and roll; the re-emergence of the horror movie. The 50s generation as the "silent generation" were not as portrayed in the current pop culture "Happy Days" television motif. The youth cult was a major force however and the real vs. nostalgic popular culture will be seen. The complacency of the era will be emphasized.

8) Camelot (The 1960s) —1 panel and 1 case—the Kennedy contribution; television as a major force; rebirth of radio; re-emergence of comic books in the late '60s; sports (the Bills); growth of the paperback; the music scene (Elvis and the Beatles); student unrest and revolts (how related to pop culture); decline of downtown districts including movie palaces; movies fight back. This was a confusing decade with a growing dichotomy between the maturity/success orientation of much of the country and the youth/unrest movement. Pop culture reflected this situation but the era is too close to cover analytically. The questioning of traditional values as shown in popular culture will be a major theme in this section.

9) The Present and Beyond (the 1970s) —1 panel and 1 case —A potpourri; suburban theatres; downtown developments (Studio Arena, auditorium events); Rich Stadium; the changing musical scene; re-emphasis on leisure time activities (recreation vehicles, camping, return to native theme); escapist movies return; television falters. No theme *per se* will be developed in this section because of its subjectivity. It will be an overview of the accelerating changing scene as well as, conversely, a nostalgic re-emphasis of the traditional values.

Where possible, subject panels will be integrated with the above rough chronological format. Potential subjects include:

    1) WNY in the media—Niagara Falls movies; Captain Marvel in Buffalo; Fu Manchu; the Avenger; movies in the 1970s.

    2) WNY contributions to the media—Michael Shea; James Whitmore; Franchot Tone; Reed Hadley; etc.

    3) Fran Stryker—creator of the Lone Ranger, The Green Hornet and Sergeant Preston.

    4) Popular Culture industries in WNY—Comics Greater Buffalo Press, kazoos, M. Wile Co. and Johnny Carson clothes, Fisher Price Toys, etc.

    5) Separate subject panels on pulps, comics, radio, television, movies.

Throughout the meetings, the four fan representatives who, although quite knowledgeable in their areas of expertise, styled themselves as "non-violent Hells Angels," laughed at, became indignant, and generally protested any labels that implied a social significance to popular culture or any juxtaposing of entertainment icons with artifacts representing political events of a period. They felt that the exhibit should emphasize nostalgia, fun, and the pleasures of the past. The two academics steadfastly and quietly offered examples of popular culture mirroring culture. The coordinator served as a "tie breaker" and ultimately tried to give the exhibit a feel of nostalgia through the choice of material used and an air of academic respectability through the labels. In terms of viewing it is definitely a popular "crowd pleaser." When one takes the time to read the labels, and connect the objects with historical references to the period, however, the point is made that popular culture is a valid method of viewing American society and an alternative approach to American historical analysis. While both viewpoints are represented, the fan approach dominates on the surface and the academic theme is obvious upon reflection.

Perhaps the introductory label on the title panel as created by the coordinator summarizes the situation:

Elite culture is considered art. Popular culture is considered entertainment. Both have been with us from the beginning of time and will be with us as long as humanity needs relaxation. From the campfire raconteur to television, popular culture has always been based on the need and desire to reach the largest possible audience. With the development of the mass media (print, radio, movies, television), larger audiences were available and the profit motive became a major consideration. The major era of modern culture proved to be from the 1920s to the 1940s. But throughout modern history, the tri-cornered foundation of popular culture has been entertainment, large audiences and profit. Therefore, popular culture, be it literature, film, sports, music, or other forms, has often been downgraded by historians.

However, more and more scholars are finding popular culture significant. While nostalgia buffs sometimes find this approach uncomfortable, popular culture is created to appeal to mass society, it is dependent upon society, and thus it often reflects that society and frequently influences it. Popular culture is yet another dimension of our lives—a way to study ourselves and enlighten our history.

Whether you are an historian, a fan, or a curious viewer, what follows is a sampling of how we spent our leisure time in America. Enjoy it.

Given that a museum exhibit, especially one that is designed to be converted into a community outreach, traveling panel show, must be attractive and entertaining as well as educational this exhibit seems to have hit a happy medium. The consultants and the Historical Society staff, after extensive discussions, compromised and concurred.

Another example was a panel devoted to Fran Stryker, Western New York author and popular culture figure. The panel itself is festooned with the various incarnations of the Lone Ranger and related items while the label discreetly and briefly makes a point:

Fran Stryker: During the 1930s and 1940s, Western New York author Fran Stryker was involved in the creation of three major popular culture figures—the Lone Ranger, The Green Hornet and Sergeant Preston of the Yukon. While all were heroic and influenced several generations of youths, the Lone Ranger is the most famous and was adapted to all media. As an influence for good, the Ranger was both persuasive and pervasive. The Green Hornet was the Ranger's great nephew thus providing continuity between crime fighting in the Old West and in the modern city.

Two problems occurred during the creation of the exhibit. All the consultants—fan and academic—were rather easygoing by nature or involved in several other projects. Despite continual warnings from the time of the first meeting, the advisors were unable to realize that the project was working with a short lead time and that, in most cases, exhibit materials should be on hand two months in advance to allow time for reproduction, selection and any necessary additional interpretative research. This meant we had time for one month of preliminary research; one month of gathering materials from our own collections, area media sources and private collectors; and two months to prepare the exhibit and organize the opening. The preparator and exhibits curator impressed upon the consultants that this seems a long period but that this type of work is exacting and time consuming. Nonetheless the consultants declined to be hurried or show concern—leading the exhibits curator to frequent despair over working with non-professionals.

Secondly, everyone was alerted that, while the Historical Society had more popular culture materials than many museums because of the interest of the WNYPCS and a broad collecting policy, there would undoubtedly be major gaps to be filled either by the consultants, other donors or purchase and that these areas should be pinpointed early. Because the exhibits curator did not know popular culture and the consultants did not always make clear genre priorities, in the final exhibit there were indeed some uncovered aspects of popular culture both national and regional. Availability and time became the deciding factors. Still, in the last analysis, we worked with what we had, obtained what we could, and, given the immense spectrum of popular culture and the uniqueness of the exhibit, ended with a credible and entertaining survey of the field in a limited amount of time and space.

The Historical Society chose to make the exhibit their Christmas event and gave it a big play in their December newsletter. Under a large photograph of the television Lone Ranger and Tonto, the Historical Society newsletter said:

The Society's holiday exhibit is "How We Entertained Ourselves," a nostalgic and entertaining look back at what is now called popular culture but had far less importance attached to it when it was new.

Popular culture items such as comic books, dime novels, Mickey Mouse wrist watches, and Wonder Woman toys will be treated as the historical forces they are in a new exhibit at the Buffalo & Erie County Historical Society which opens on December 14 and continues through April.

Popular culture is an alternate method of observing and understanding our society and its history, which has been gaining greater acceptance during the last decade.

Included in the exhibit is popular culture as it developed from the Colonial period through the Turn of the Century and into its most notable periods of the Jazz Age, the Great Depression, and World War II. The postwar period, the Eisenhower Years, and the Kennedy Years will be included along with items from the current media to bring the story up to the 1970s. Special emphasis will be given to Western New York contributions to the media, such as Fran Stryker's creation of the Lone Ranger and Tonto, Sergeant Preston, and the Green Hornet. There will be separate panels devoted to the pulps, comics, radio, television, and the movies.

This exhibit is a cooperative project between the Society and one of its chapters, the Western New York Popular Culture Society. It was made possible in part with $1,750 received from the Arts Development Services, Inc. Re-grant Program with funds from the New York State Council on the Arts and the City of Buffalo. It will be a traveling exhibit after April and will be available on loan throughout Western New York. Bookings may be arranged through the Society's education program.

Consultants for the exhibit are: Dr. Milton Plesur, Dr. Frank Hoffmann, Brad Becker, Charles Seeley, Kean Crowe, and Gary Evans.

A reception will be held from 5:30 — 6:30 on December 14 for Society members and their friends to preview the exhibit. In the spirit of the holiday, hot toddies will be served.

In addition to the publicity received in the two newsletters—WNYPCS and Historical Society—an invitation to the opening was sent to all members with a striking drawing of Captain Marvel, comic hero of the 1940s revived under the title *Shazam* in the 1970s. Press releases were sent to the media and coverage was very good both in the newspapers and on television.

In contrast to the usual openings of either full dinners or wine and cheese receptions, the Historical Society with the concurrence of the WNYPCS opted for hot toddies, hot chocolate and "junk food" (popcorn, potato chips, pretzels) during the 5:30—7:00 hour to attract children as well as adults. As it turned out, the group attending the membership opening was predominantly young adults of the modish variety who contrasted nicely with the few traditionally dressed members and youngsters. However, the exhibit itself was the star of the evening.

What the museum patrons and popular culture advocates saw on that opening evening was quite different from the shows usually exhibited at the Historical Society. As they entered the gallery they were confronted with a framed poster extolling the WNYPCS and membership therein. Created for an earlier project, the poster highlighted King Kong threatening Batman and Robin while various popular culture figures looked on. Proceeding into the room the viewer saw the title panel on the center post. Under the title "How We Entertained Ourselves, Popular Culture in America," was the label, quoted earlier in this article surrounded by several ads and pictures including a color drawing of Superman and Mammie Yokum.

Extending out from the pillar were four sets of three panels each devoted to the movies, comics, radio and television. Each panel had five to seven photos, drawings or color poster reproductions pertaining to the subject. Each of the fours sets also had an extended label (approximately 250 words) physically broken up into two or three paragraph sections giving a capsule history of its subject and attempting to identify its importance to the American social scene.

Around the periphery of the gallery was the chronological interpretation of subject materials. Short descriptive labels (in addition to brief identifications) were included to act as guideposts but were deliberately general in order to let the patrons develop their own assumptions and insights into the relationship between popular culture and historical events.

Two wall cases and one panel were devoted to the early years and included such combinations as a photo of immigrants with a panel from a Katzenjammer Kids comic strip with "ethnic"dialogue. A magazine illustration of child labor was combined with an early candid photo of children grouped around a neighborhood hurdy gurdy man. A woman suffrage banner was juxtaposed with an early *Life* cover lampoon on men's rights. Several other objects and visuals, including a Lotto game, a Nick Carter weekly, and a Horatio Alger novel, were worked in. The two descriptive labels stated:

Early popular culture — prior to 1900 popular culture was very close to folklore and grass roots history. While the dime novel was prevalent, most mass media formats lay in the future. Our entertainments reflected the relative simplicity of the country.
Prelude (1900-1920) — the first two decades of the 20th century saw the development of modern

mass media. The profit motive quickly gained ascendancy in the alliance between the media and entertainment for the country. Popular culture as a social factor was on the horizon.

The first subject "island" followed and consisted of an early colorful Buffalo theatre poster and a panel devoted to area theatres. The 1920s received one case and one panel and had a variety of materials such as a mahjongg game, an early radio, various "personality" toys (an Orphan Annie stove, a Jackie Coogan candy tin), and *Captain Billy's Whizzbang.*

Two cases and one panel were given over to the 1930s and obviously related the Depression to popular culture. A picture of a man with a sign requesting work was highlighted with a cartoon about tramps stealing food and a copy of Disney's *Three Little Pigs.* Examples of other items include the Sunday Funnies (Buffalo printed), a Fisher-Price Popeye pull toy (Buffalo made), a Busby Berkeley scene, two Tarzan *Big Little Books*, Bingo and Winnie Winkle dreaming of success in Hollywood.

The two cases on the 1940s brought in the war and its aftermath by the use of such artifacts as a *Time* magazine war effort saluting the three services, a color poster devoted to women workers and the homefront, a Wilkie campaign poster, Chaplin as *The Great Dictator*, lesser known heroic comic figures fighting spies, a Gene Autry lunch box, some sports programs, and a record case from *Oklahoma.* Two labels differentiated briefly the war period and the post-war-period.

Following an "island" devoted to Fran Stryker and the Lone Ranger, two cases and one panel on the 1950s emphasized reality versus memory with a Civil Defense bomb shelter construction manual, a CD "example" newspaper on the atomic destruction of Buffalo, and a *Life* magazine story on Korea. The lighter side was represented by a variety of items including a Dick Tracy strip emphasizing television, a complete Barbie doll set, a model of *The Creature From the Black Lagoon*, autographed major league baseballs, Lucy on the cover of *TV Guide* and Hopalong Cassidy.

One case and one panel on the 1960s and beyond included two labels emphasizing confusion and acceleration. The final label made the point:

The Present and Beyond (1970s) — with an increasing return to leisure time activities, popular culture is frequently emphasized. Television is pervasive. Sports are a major industry. Recreation vehicles are popular as is a "return to the native" theme. Escapist movies have returned. Nostalgia is Big Business. Does the future hold an electronic dominance over entertainment and Society? In this era of accelerated changes, the answer is unknown.

Whatever happens, popular culture and entertainment will continue to fill human needs in a variety of ways.

Some of the materials representing the 1960s and 1970s were a shot of Woodstock (the festival, not the bird), newspaper coverage of the moonwalk, a Feiffer cartoon, Martin Luther King, Wonder Woman's return to popularity, a *Star Wars* "sandpeople" mask, a Hulk model, the Beatles and Elvis, a menu sporting psychedelic art and finally a framed poster of Bob Dylan.

While there was no deep interpretation or surprising revelation in the exhibit and the hoped-for regional emphasis suffered by comparison to the more plentiful and recognizable national material, the end result was a good surface treatment which was colorful, entertaining, and, (with deliberate intent in the labels and combinations of material), thought provoking. Within the limited perimeters of what an exhibit can be expected to achieve, the popular culture exhibit met its goals. As proof in the week after the opening, the floor guard reported that patrons "stay with the exhibit, follow clear through, and examine each panel closely." Here's hoping they also read the labels.

Was it all worth it? Well, aside from several spirited discussions, a couple of bruised egos, and a few sleepless nights by the exhibits curator, no harm was detected and everyone seemed to have benefitted. The Buffalo & Erie County Historical Society obtained one of its most colorful in-house exhibits and future traveling shows with only the commitment of staff time. The Historical Society also received the donation of additional popular culture material which it might not otherwise have obtained and which will be useful in future exhibits. The exposure of the Society to a segment of the community which normally does not patronize the Historical Society was perhaps most valuable from the Historical Society's point of view. An estimated 75% of the guests at the opening were new faces to the institution's events. While the youthfulness and clothing styles of this group raised a few eyebrows among some of the older members attending, it was definitely a healthy experience.

For the WNYPCS, the event was a crowning success. The newspaper publicity, the membership information distributed, and the recognition of a most active affiliate were all to the good. Internally it broadened the outlook of the WNYPCS from a newsletter, monthly program, flea market mentality to a feeling that the group could and should attempt new projects and consider funding sources other than membership. As a fine example of community educational outreach, the exhibit project benefitted both organizations.

As for the individual viewpoints and philosophies within the WNYPCS the results are less clearly defined but nonetheless positive. The fans still have control of the newsletter and annual journal while the academics seem to be having more voice in the running of the monthly meetings and the general direction of the WNYPCS. It is possible that a rupture may come in the future, but, at this point, both groups seem to recognize that each has valid ideas and that they can co-exist in the same organization. Most importantly, both have discovered and proved that they can compromise and actively work together with the WNYPCS and with the Historical Society to create successful projects like the popular culture exhibit.

"...the selection of a fad item—a *Star Wars* T-shirt, for example— may mean that one has passed up the opportunity to preserve a Fahrenheit thermometer, a box of disposable diapers, or a set of spark plugs, which may become more significantly obsolete because of metric conversion, ecological crises, or abandonment of internal combustion engines."

Fred E.H. Schroeder, "How to Acquire, Accession, Catalog and Research a Popular Culture Collection for Your Museum of History, Technology or Art for $97 per Year"

VI

Practical measures for the implementation of programs for collecting and exhibition are part of many of the articles in this book, as are more general proposals toward self-help, independence and exploitation of local resources. Yet, as Kenneth Hopkins has argued, museums tend to think in terms of procuring major grants. Small museums, in particular, are dismayed by the costs in money and expertise that are implied in museum literature and in the exhibitions of exemplary institutions. In this article, Fred E.H. Schroeder proposes a program that at first glance seems absurd. The program, which he maintains is infinitely adaptable to different museum missions, utilizes mail-order catalogs as a source for popular artifacts, selected with care for current exhibits and for cumulative resource collections.

Biographical information about the author will be found in the preface to the first chapter.

Fred E.H. Schroeder

How to Acquire, Accession, Catalog and Research a Popular Culture Collection for Your Museum of History, Technology or Art for $97 per Year

THE PROMISE IMPLIED by the title of this article is quite serious. Moreover, the program is so simple, so inexpensive, so responsible and so flexibly adaptable to different museums that it would be shortsighted for any museum not to initiate the program immediately. The crux of the program is the mail-order catalog. All mail-order houses will regularly issue free catalogs to customers who place a minimum number of orders during a reasonable time-period. Specific policies vary, but Montgomery Ward currently requires three orders each "season," that is, from the Spring-Summer and the Fall-Winter catalogs, or from concurrent sale or special catalogs, while Sears, Roebuck will sell the current catalog with the purchase price refundable with the first order. The mail-order catalog, as historical museum personnel will know, is a rich research tool for identifying and classifying an immense range of material artifacts from the late nineteenth-century to the present day, and consequently the acquisition and maintenance of a complete file is in itself a worthy investment for the research library. Although this article is proposing the use of catalog orders to build a collection of popular artifacts, it should be emphasized that the minimum orders can be made for immediately usable museum materials and equipment, including office equipment and supplies, hand and power tools for the shop, building supplies, exhibit materials such as fabrics, lamps and light bulbs, wall coverings and the like, and even personal items for staff members (who would, of course, reimburse the institution).

The mail-order catalog also provides a readymade cataloging system. Any item ordered will have a catalog number, and most will have an illustrated description in the book. Although accessioning and labelling for this program could be incorporated into current procedures at each museum, if this is to be a planned, regular program of acquisition, it is common sense to key these artifacts to the catalog by date of issue, page number and catalog order number. Moreover, the mail-order catalog uniquely provides the cultural context of a given artifact. At very least the artifact is located in a list of comparable items, but in many cases such things as household furnishings are pictured in a setting that in the future would provide an accurate indication of the "ideal" environment in which the artifact would have been viewed.

The reasons for initiating such a program are implicit and explicit throughout *Twentieth-Century Popular Culture in Museums and Libraries.* Popular artifacts are ephemeral, and if they are within the realm of fashion and fad, or are in what George Kubler calls a "formal series" that is currently subject to rapid technological change, they are doubly vulnerable to being discarded. Kubler, in his thought-provoking little volume *The Shape of Time: Remarks on the History of Things* states that "The decision to discard something is far from being a simple decision.... It is a reversal of values. Though the thing once was necessary, discarded it becomes litter or scrap. What was once valuable is now worthless; the desirable now offends; the beautiful now is seen as ugly." Later he states: "An object made for emotional experience—which is one way of identifying a work of art—differs from a tool by this meaningful extension beyond use. Because the symbolic frame of existence changes more slowly than its utilitarian requirements, so the tools of an era are less durable than its artistic productions. It is much easier to reconstitute a symbolic facsimile of medieval life with a small museum of manuscripts, ivories, textiles and jewelry, than to attempt to describe feudal technology."

These statements are quoted because the question of which artifacts to select from the catalog is a complicated one, and the selection of a fad item—a *Star War* T-shirt, for example—may mean that one has passed up the opportunity to preserve a Fahrenheit thermometer, a box of disposable diapers, or a set of spark plugs, which may become more significantly obsolete because of metric conversion, ecological crises or abandonment of internal combustion engines. Clearly this sort of program of selection and acquisition is not child's play; it is an urgent matter of what Edith Mayo calls connoisseurship for the future.

How then do we select what to order? A partial answer is provided by the mission of your institution, and this will be refined by practical considerations of cost and space. Thus, although one could hardly reconstruct popular middle-class American life of the 1970s without an electric refrigerator, a power lawnmower and wall-to-wall carpeting, both cost and size may render such artifacts out of the question. But here we can borrow a poetic device, synecdoche, according to which the part stands for the whole. An ice-cube tray, a spark plug, a carpet remnant exhibited before the open catalog of the whole item could be at least suggestive, although none of these examples is likely to be taken as a recommendation. The point to be taken, however, is that creative selectivity can build a significant collection without major investment or storage requirements.

Before discussing relating the selection process to the mission of the museum, it is worth remarking that selection need not be only for the future. An annual exhibit of the artifacts selected in that year could be an exciting, provocative program. "This is what *we* selected as the most (representative or popular or expressive or timely or desired or vulnerable—or whatever—). What would *you* have chosen?" Or the artifact or artifacts might be incorporated into a regular "today and yesterday" exhibit with historical artifacts from your permanent collection. In any event, museum personnel should never forget what power there is in the placing of *anything* on exhibit in a museum. To the public, display in a museum is a statement of validation and significance. This is important in view of the humanistic function of a museum, for the potential danger of popular culture to morality is not in the material things but in the values that we assign to them. The mere act of focusing public attention upon a commonplace thing by exhibiting it in the context of a museum is a means of helping people to find meaning in everyday life, and to look more clearly into their own values. Old things are no more good because they are rare than current things are bad because they are abundant.

Several specific examples of how to collect popular artifacts in relation to a museum's mission are in this volume. The political and protest collection of which Edith Mayo writes is directly relevant to the mission of the Division of the Smithsonian for which she is Assistant Curator, while Richard M. Hurst's account of northwestern New York State materials is appropriate and indigenous to his regional institution. It is significant that neither of these collections could be developed from the mail-order catalogs which continue to be as they have always been, apolitical and nonregional (with some subtle exceptions). The culture of the catalogs is national, majority and popular, not local, minority and elite. Its representativeness is not total, therefore, but it falls in line with one of the most common missions of county and state museums and reconstructions; namely, the preservation and exhibition of *typical* lifestyles. The question of selection and the most frequent basis of criticism for most reconstructed buildings or rooms that are not "association" reconstructions (i.e., those associated with a specific personage such as a governor, president, magnate, etc.) is whether or not a given artifact would have been *typically* consistent and *representative* of the majority of persons.

For the museum with such a collection, marked, for example, by a "pioneer room," a "Victorian room," and a "roaring twenties room," it would be entirely reasonable to embark on a five to ten-year catalog-purchase program for room of the 1980s. The time-span of this program would in itself replicate the normal mode of accumulation in the American home. While it is fairly typical for a young married couple to start out with a "five-piece living-room suite"—the "pieces" incidentally, are not exclusively major furnishings, and may include two throw-pillows or a hassock and an ashtray—typical rooms are not furnished completely, at once, and then set for all time.

Among such factors as several moves, increased income, replacement of worn or broken items, and inclusion of craft projects, any living room is likely to contain a decade of family history. The statement seems obvious, but many museum reconstructions (as well as domestic "period" rooms) imply that people of the past had consistent decors that were flushed every ten or twenty years to be replaced by another set of furnishings, equally consistent with a new aesthetic. This is simply not the case. Examination of our own homes will indicate a greater or lesser mixing of styles today, while close study of interior photographs of the nineteenth-century rooms will bear out that "Victorian" usually meant a conglomerate of the current decor style plus all those of the previous two or three decades. Thus, the better reproduction furnishings that are ordinarily purveyed today as Victorian, are indeed Victorian, but quite specifically 1850-1860 in a mass-produced heavily-upholstered eighteenth-century French court furniture revival; yet these styles are almost entirely absent from photographs for the whole nineteenth century. Moreover, where they do appear, they tend to be mixed with earlier Empire styles or with later Gothic, Arts and Crafts, colonial and art nouveau styles.

These remarks apply particularly to *popular* history and *typical* lifestyles; certainly the consistent, rationalized stylistic models did and do exist, but they are the products of professional architects, decorators, tastemakers, of their clients, and of those persons who, while lacking sufficient money to hire a professional, are sufficiently wealthy and sophisticated to be able to imitate the models. Exhibits based on such ideal or elite models are appropriate to a museum whose mission includes design history of the cultivated tradition, but for most historical museums, large or small, catalog purchases over a decade will come closer to reality than anything designed to reflect the ideals in *Better Homes and Gardens, Architectural Digest* or even *Woman's Day*.

Which all seems to suggest that the mail-order catalog is not an appropriate resource for the *art* museum. Art museums are by definition not in the business of preserving and exhibiting cross-sections of culture; they are in the business of selecting that which is regarded as the best. However, it has been a long time since *best* has been limited to certified individual works of the academy or to works whose function is unadulateratedly aesthetic. Since the great international expositions of the nineteenth century, good industrial design has vied with beaux artes in aesthetic matters. Since World War II popular entertainments such as dance bands, musical cinema and comics have been carefully re-evaluated as art forms, and it is a rare museum today that has not brought Hollywood film, journalistic photography, magazine illustration and advertising, fashion, and some pop music into its galleries. Furthermore, the Pop Art movement of mid-century (a "high culture" phenomenon) often went beyond satire into bouyant celebrations of mass expression. In short, there are legitimate connecting links between fine arts and popular arts in all but the most staid museums.

From 1928 to the mid-1960s, John Cotton Dana of the Newark Museum prepared exhibits of inexpensive objects of "good taste." These included not only Bauhaus design (which, incidentally, was *supposed* to be mass-produced), but more traditional ornamental designs such as Blue Willow dishes and prints "suitable for framing." Many of the objects exhibited at Newark were in a price range of ten to fifty cents. A revival of this type of exhibit would seem entirely appropriate for today's art museum, most particularly since the funding of art museums has so dramatically shifted from private patronage to more widely-based low-priced memberships and tax dollars. The art museum need not surrender its qualitative, normative, judgmental mission, but its democratization of art ought to be able to go beyond doing television specials on the Treasures of Tutankhamen. Either "art" and "good taste" can become part of everyone's life, or we should give in finally and honestly to the separation of the museum from everyday reality. An exhibit of "good taste" in inexpensive objects from the mail-order catalogs would be controversial because it would require curators to take a stand publicly. Unlike the selection of one-of-a-kind pieces of Milanese Renaissance painting, or a piece of Frank Lloyd Wright furniture for which the patron is unaware of the pool of possible items from which the choice was made, this sort of acquisition is made from a public storehouse whose contents can be viewed and judged by the patron as easily as by the curator. Once more let it be emphasized that the cost is so negligible that there is no excuse for not embarking on this modest program today. The selection of a Ming jar for your ceramics collection could be a matter of thousands of dollars in addition to being a matter of informed good taste; the selection of an oven-proof casserole dish is hardly a matter of money, but it is no less a matter of informed good taste. The Ming jar, on exhibit, can enrich our aesthetic experience, but the casserole dish, on exhibit, can enrich our everyday lives by providing direct guidance in selection of commonplace commercial objects.

For the art museum, strict adherence to the mail-order catalog may not be so necessary as it would be in the historical museum where the total material environment is significant, and where the accumulation of semi-annual catalogs as research volumes is a desirable by-product. That is, the accumulation of a reference library of mail-order catalogs is important to a historical museum for later research into such non-aesthetic areas as prices, technological innovation, advertising psychology, physical context, and so on. A fine arts museum that is developing a "good taste in popular objects" program might prefer direct retail shopping in discount chain stores such as K-Mart, Pamida, Target, Woolworth's, and the retail outlets of Sears, Wards and Penney's. On the other hand, a fine arts museum may want to consider the mail-order catalogs of the upper-middle-class trade. It is doubtful that any library is making a conscious effort to collect the mail-order catalogs of the Horchow Collection, Gumps, Kaleidoscope or of the Neiman-Marcus, Marshall Field or Sakowitz department stores. These catalogs of gifts, housewares and clothing express unrelenting good taste of the moment, and yet they are a popular phenomenon of the later twentieth-century. Like the major mail-order catalogs, they are socially egalitarian. An order requires money and a zip-code, not a face-to-face encounter with a sophisticated salesperson or even the perilous journey of quest that brings one past forbidding doormen, over thick pastel carpets, through a glitter of objects whose pricetags are demurely hidden, and into a clutch of well-coiffed, murmuring salespeople, urbanely willing to assist. Some of us thrive upon these experiences, but for many others, the catalogs are a cozier route to the acquisition of elegant artifacts.

Moreover, these catalogs are as equally responsive to popular movements in the arts as the general mail-order catalogs. The rapidity with which Egyptian-motif jewelry, clothing, chinaware, games and puzzles came into these tasteful catalogs along with the "King Tut" traveling exhibit is quite parallel to the *Star Wars* T-shirts, pajamas and lunchbuckets that appeared in the major catalogs at the same time.

Popular styles need not be tawdry; "good taste" need not be expensive; fine arts need not be one-of-a-kind commissioned pieces; museums need not separate art from everyday domestic life. If these rather obvious principles can be accepted, it is clear that the art museum must exhibit twentieth-century popular arts. The catalogs are one way of doing this in an orderly way, and in a way that guarantees access to fine arts for all museum patrons. Without a program that requires reference to popular retail outlets, the temptation to drift into exclusiveness or into unrealistic assumptions about general availability could be a real hazard.

Before taking leave of fine arts museum exhibits of popular objects it should be reiterated that the idea is not new and that many museums have done things along these lines. During the late Sixties, in particular, a number of museums exhibited middle-class living rooms furnished in the current popular (non-decorator) style. These were Pop Art exhibits that were sardonic expression as much as they were honest reflection. At the extreme, these took the form of exhibits of "kitsch" artifacts. Selecting kitsch is an amusing activity, an easy game that is just about as urbane as visiting Bedlam Hospital to snigger at the misfits of society. Kitsch exhibits *are* fun, but provide nothing in the way of "elevating public taste," or refining techniques for discriminating choice.

At the other end of the scale are the exhibits of good industrial designs that have been part of some museum programs since the great world expositions of the mid-nineteenth century first brought attention to the aesthetic value of practical manufactured goods. At the periphery are folk art exhibits. Although most of these are "purist," insisting upon old rural traditions, some, such as the

Renwick's exhibit of elaborately decorated leather jackets and blue jeans, show folk arts as dynamically responsive to changing technologies. It is unlikely that any museum has paid tribute to the transmutation of folk arts and home crafts that has occurred as a result of craft kits, patterns in magazines, craft supplies stores and art training in institutions by professionals and amateurs. These may be more in the province of technological, historical and community museums.

Craft and hobby kits are among the ephemera that the mail-order catalog can help to identify. The needlepoint kits of today, woodburning outfits of two decades ago, the wooden airplane models of World War II are examples of fad items that are not collected because of their abundance and that disappear in their kit forms because the kits have been assembled. Yet all are woven into the fabric of American leisure life, as are the games, toys and puzzles of the Christmas "Wishbooks." A mail-order catalog acquisition program assures the orderly building of a mint collection. Forward-looking curators will buy duplicates and, where possible, extra material for tactile exhibits of the future. For example, yardgoods might be acquired and stored for use in exhibit backgrounds, or for a touch-rail in front of an exhibit. Wallpaper, drapes, table coverings, vinyl and formica sheets are some other ephemera that will not only be expensive to duplicate twenty years from now, but have high potential for use in exhibit designs. And they are easily stored.

These are indeed perilous times for museums. Inflation feeds upon every small gain made in the area of funding; the rises in energy costs neutralize the effect of every economy that we introduce to cut energy usage. One thing is certain as we face the new decade and the end of the century: the cures for our budgetary ills will not be larger doses of the old remedies. We must look alive for the wholly new concepts that are sure to emerge from the ever-fertile human imagination, but while we await such messianic deliverances, we will do well to look for the commonplace opportunities that surround us for partial remedies that might elude those whose eyes have been fixed too high. The mail-order catalog is one such commonplace; let us strive to uncover many more.

"There are many untold stories in the artifacts that exist in space past as well as in time past."

Thomas A. Schlereth, "History Outside the History Museum: The Past in the American Landscape"

VII

Connoisseurship for the future is not limited to material artifacts as we customarily understand them in museum terms. In this article, Thomas J. Schlereth takes us across the American landscape of the twentieth century, pointing out myriad examples of aspects of our culture that can only be fully appreciated *in situ*, at the same time acquainting the reader with a variety of the new approaches to historical study and museology that truly bring history outside the history museum. This is both a challenge to museum professionals to develop suitable interpretive and educational programs to utilize these artifacts, and an open invitation to exploit local resources—an invitation that carries with it an urgent RSVP in a time of shrinking budgetary and energy resources. Readers will also find that Schlereth introduces concepts that are explored more fully in later essays by Edward Green and Maurice Duke.

Thomas J. Schlereth is an Associate Professor of American Studies at the University of Notre Dame where he teaches American cultural, urban and architectural history as well as material culture studies. Prior to 1972, he taught at Grinnel College, Grinnel, Iowa.

Dr. Schlereth is the author of a biography of *Geronimo: The Last of the Apache Chiefs* (1974), a monograph on eighteenth-century European-American intellectual history (*The Cosmopolitan Ideal in Enlightment Thought,* 1977), a university history (*The University of Notre Dame: A Portrait of Its History and Campus,* 1976) and a contributor to the publication series of the American Association of Museums (*It Wasn't That Simple,* 1978) and the American Association for State and Local History (*Historic House Museums,* 1978). He has published major articles in *American Studies International, Journal of the Society of Architectural Historians, American Historical Association Newsletter, American Studies, The History Teacher, Journal of Urban History, Museologist, Chicago History, Southern Quarterly, Museum News, Environmental Review* and *History News.* He is presently completing a study of Chicago architectural history and a volume on material culture studies in America scheduled for publication by 1981.

He has taught as a Faculty Fellow in Newberry Library's Associated Colleges of the Midwest Humanities Seminar in Chicago and as a Visiting Associate Professor of the NEH Learning in the Museum Program at the Indianapolis Museum of Art, and has served as consultant to major historical societies. Schlereth also serves as an Associate Editor of *The Old Northwest: A Journal of Regional Life and Letters,* and as a member of the Editorial Board of *The Magazine of Indiana History.* He has held many major fellowships and is a member of the Indiana Committee for the Humanities, the Indiana Library Association Advisory Council and the American Studies Association Regional Studies Committee. Recently he represented United States scholars at the First International Conference on Material History held at the National Museum of Man in Ottawa.

Thomas J. Schlereth

History Outside the History Museum:
The Past on the American Landscape

THE WAYS IN WHICH single individuals or entire societies view their pasts are, to a considerable extent, reflected in those objects and places that they choose to preserve as reminders of themselves. Family photograph albums, attic trunks and assorted memorabilia in a chest-of-drawers inevitably contain artifacts of what we value in our individual lifetimes. History books and museums represent similar attempts at collecting and keeping communal memories.

Until the recent, expanded interest in genealogical "Roots," the present boom in the historic preservation movement, and what one observer calls "the democratization of the antique" among collectors,[1] most Americans considered their major contacts with "the past" to be two-fold: the history texts that they labored over in various courses during their classroom schooling; and the historical museums, monuments and sites that they occasionally visited on a weekend or an extended vacation. Both history texts and history museums often reinforced this perception by subtly suggesting that historical reality was only found between the covers of a book or within the glass cases of an exhibition.[2]

Historian Neil Harris has documented one possible reason why museums did so. He argues that they had to compete with two other settings where objects were exhibited indoors in great number and variety: the department store and the world's fair expositions.[3] Many history museums also owed their origin to a major benefaction of a single donor who, in addition to continuing to treat the collections as his or her private fiefdom, also often tended to reinforce the misconception among the general public that history was only what the wealthy or the eccentric collected and housed in imposing architectural monuments.[4] Finally, history museums frequently nurtured their claim to a type of institutional monopoly or accessibility to the past by portraying themselves as the only libraries and/or archives of the artifact. Of course, they were, and are, vital depositories of much of what we know about the material culture of the past. Nonetheless, the attitude (equally present in history classrooms at all levels of academe) that one can only know history when one is within the halls of marble or of ivy, has influenced a large segment of the American populace.

Fortunately, in the past decade, historians in both the academic and museum professions have begun to recognize and rectify this myopia. There is a growing awareness, for example, that there exists a historiography of museum exhibition as well as of historical literature.[5] Or, to put it another way, we are now beginning to realize that history museums have also had histories. Beginning with the eighteenth-century exhibits of Charles Willson Peale to the most recent installation at the Smithsonian, it is possible "to read" the historical museum just like any other artifact. Historical museums are cultural Rorschach tests, recording the hopes and fears, ambitions and ideologies of each generation of benefactors and curators who are associated with them.

Greenfield Village in Michigan, for instance, tells us as much about Henry Ford's perception of *his* nineteenth century midwestern agrarian boyhood as it does the historical reality of small-town life rural America.[6] Interestingly, the outdoor historic museum village such as Greenfield (opened to the public in 1927) is solely a twentieth-century phenomenon in this country.[7]

Fortunately, curators now more openly acknowledge the origins and development of their museums as part of both the history of American museums and American cultural history.[8] One cannot help but applaud this serious and sincere attempt of museum professionals to get outside their own institutional frameworks. It can be argued, I think, that historical museum interpretation might be pushed still further out the door into the city streets and along back country roads; that is, the history museum or historical society can go beyond its institutional perimeters out to Andre Malraux's "museum without walls." It can show its visitors and members how they can become, as Carl Becker always argued, "Everyman his own historian."[9]

Above-Ground Archaeology

How might this be done? One technique is what some call "above-ground archaeology."[10] Intent upon learning from the abundant material culture evidence that lies extant all about us, the above-ground archaeologist seeks to discover, justify, classify, decipher and interpret the surviving artifactual record of the past that exists largely outside the typical confines of the history museum. In this context, the rural agrarian countryside, the suburban tract development or the central city core can be examined as a mammoth artifact collection, an open-air museum and classroom wherein local and community history can be discovered in a personal and novel way.

The concept of above-ground archaeology is simple. Like the pre-historical, post-medieval or historical archaeologist,[11] the above-ground archaeologist concentrates on a) using material objects and physical sites as primary evidence; b) employing extensive fieldwork as a fundamental research tecnique; c) adapting anthropological explanatory concepts (e.g. typology, diffusion, etc.)

where feasible; and, d) acquiring historical knowledge about humankind as the principal objective of the investigation.[12] The above-ground archaeologist simply does his or her "digging" into the past "above ground."

In addition to its obvious debts to traditionally conceived archaeology, above-ground archaeology borrows much of its theory and practice from related fields such as art history, historical and cultural geography, architectural history, toponymy, history of urban and town planning, folkways, and the history of technology. Above-ground archaeology also goes by various synonyms: "landscape history," "material culture studies," "environmental history," "urban archaeology," "history under foot," "landscape anthropology."[13] A common denominator that unites these various approaches is their mutual interest in the history of physical things that are, for the most part, located beyond the walls of the usual historical museum or historical society.

Vernacular Building

The housing in which most of us live, for instance, is usually not the subject of major exhibitions in historical museums. The show "Signs of Life: Symbols in the American City," designed by Venturi and Rauch at the Renwick Gallery of the National Collection of Fine Arts was a notable exception.[14] Even historical house museums do not fully exploit their multiple historical meanings to the average visitor.[15]

To the above-ground archaeologist, however, vernacular architecture in its myriad of forms—the hall-and-parlor, the shotgun, the bungalow, the four-over-four, the row house—is a crucial primary source for identifying and interpreting the history of a community through its residential environment. Vernacular building is, in short, the material culture of the American Everyman. As Fred Kniffen, a historical geographer of such Americans building types and styles, insists, "there needs to be less concern for a house because some famous character lived in it and more concern that it is or that it is not typical of the houses of its time and place. The study of the unique normally adds little to the sum of our understanding of human behavior. The study of the kinds of things used by people during a given historical period reveals a great deal about them."[16]

Inasmuch as architectural historians have tended to concern themselves only with the so-called "high" or "academic" styles (e.g. a specialized building type designed and constructed by a builder following a pattern book or an architect working within a recognizable artistic vocabulary), the other ninety-five percent of the surviving American domestic buildings has gone largely uninvestigated and unappreciated. Fortunately settlement geographers, folkways experts, popular culture enthusiasts, and private citizens have become intrigued with how and where

Americans live.[17] The above-ground archaeologist freely borrows from their pioneering field-study and archival research in order to construct "working" definitions and tentative typologies.

The study of rural residential buildings, *in situ*, can still be done in many parts of the United States. Primers and guides to indigenous regional styles have appeared in this context which enable the careful observer to discover—often from his automobile window—trends, patterns and sheer aesthetic delight in residences formerly considered boring, inconsequential and certainly not art.[18]

Yet vernacular building—be it Mormon central-hall housing in the West; dog-trot homes of the South; cobblestone structures of the country's heavily glaciated regions; the upright-and-wing of the Midwest; or the ubiquitous prefabricated catalog architecture of mail-order houses such as Sears, Roebuck—remains a vital artifactual relic of a large majority of Americans. "When fully interpreted," argues Wilbur Zelinsky, these houses "tell us much, not only about the physical locale and the technology of the place and era, but also about the source and dates of the builder or renovator, the contracts and influences he experienced, his ethnic affiliation, and possibly also class, occupation and religion. In a very real sense, the house is the family's universe in microcosm, the distillation of past experience and a miniature model of how it perceives the outer world, as it is or perhaps even more as it should be."[19]

To be sure, the outdoor museum village movement has aspired to bring a portion of vernacular architecture within its circumference. Yet, with a few notable exceptions, it has not been able to duplicate, with genuine verisimilitude, the authentic historical context for its structures. In addition to their over-population of log cabins (an American archetypal structure venerated by the American citizenry and professoriate alike), the outdoor history museum, no matter what its geographical expansiveness, cannot capture the variations (regional and local) that the above-ground archaeologist finds upon the landscape. The outdoor museum village usually cannot adequately demonstrate the origins, distribution and migration of anonymous housing that scholars such as Pierce Lewis urge upon the careful observer of countryside and cityscape.[20] Heretofore the study of vernacular building focused primarily on rural environments. Now, largely because of a broader view by the expanding historical preservation movement, trends among self-proclaimed "new" social historians, and a faction within historical archaeology who are concerned with urban artifacts, there is an interest in nineteenth- and early twentieth-century tenements, worker cottages, apartment buildings and lower-class bungalows.[21]

Landscape Archaeology

Along with this fascination with all the historic houses of a community—not merely those so designated by a bronze plaque or by virtue of being one of the over 500 historic house museums in the United States—has come historical research and documentation of the physical sites of American buildings. Plant ecologists, naturalists and a few maverick scholars have long known that there is a corollary to the old saw ("What you eat is what you are") that translates into something like "What you plant is what you are." Elsewhere I have argued the validity of using vegetation as appropriate historical evidence that does indeed grow all around us.[22] The astute above-ground archaeologist can employ these techniques as well as those also developed by naturalists such as May T. Watts and others[23] to decipher any community's history through its extant plant life. Since I prepared that essay considerably more literature on the topic has emerged to help anyone to see his or her backyard, city street or local neighborhood as the natural history museum that it actually is.[24]

Of particular interest is the research that has focused on the typical American home and what we have planted outside, inside, and around it. Fred Schroeder, for example, has done a marvelous analysis of what he calls "the democratic yard and garden," its environs and its artifacts: plaster statuary, spring-necked flamingoes, plastic mushrooms, birdbaths and bleachbottle birdhouses that populate the landscapes of lower-middle class Americans.[25] Other investigators, particularly those working in urban folklife studies and in historical geography, have explored the social and communicative functions of the visual folk art of alley gardens, front-lawn plantings, roof-top gardens and the personal landscape habits and values of residents in various residential neighborhoods of varying economic, ethnic and social backgrounds.[26] Few museums and historical societies have paid much attention to collecting (at least in documentary photography) this kind of data or the popular culture artifacts that often accompanies the home garden: mail-boxes, fencing types and patterns, foundation plantings, front vs. back yard decorations, sign-name and light-posts, and house-number markers. If museum historians decided that this material culture deserved to be added to their collections, they would be working toward one aspect of what Edith Mayo and Barbara Riley call "the connoisseurship of the future."[27]

Fortunately, some historical preservationists have become more extensively involved in the restoration or reconstruction of botanical and pleasure gardens, parks and the preservation of natural forest preserves, forest wilderness areas and landscapes that are of outstanding historical and ecological significance.[28] Recently an entire conference devoted to "Historic Gardens and Landscapes" discussed the importance of historical landscape architecture and preservation.[29] John T. Stewart and others have developed techniques of what they call "landscape archaeology" in their research into existing plant material on historic sites as evidence of buried features and as survivors of historic species.[30] Now two texts (*Landscapes and Gardens for Historic Buildings* and *Every House a Home*) by Rudy J. Favretti and Joy Putnam Favretti assist the above-ground archaeologist in his or her quest for the cultural, social, economic and botanical history that survive on many parts of the landscape.[31]

Industrial Archaeology

As almost every American Studies scholar is wont to point out, Americans in the nineteenth century were often prone, in their literature and their arts, to embrace the cultural paradox that Leo Marx has labelled "the machine in the garden."[32] Thus it is no coincidence that the first great age of American industrialization took place in the same century that also witnessed the evolution of the country's public gardens and urban parks.[33] Park systems, arboretums, and pleasure gardens are therefore another important type of artifact significant to the above-ground archaeologist; so are the extant physical remains of American technology, transportation and industry.

At last count there were approximately sixty industrial and technological museums in the United States.[34] No single museum, however, has ever explored all the possible sites that do indeed document the various roles that industry has played in the nation's history. Moreover, the size and scale of many artifacts such as bridges, factories and mills usually prohibits their finding their way into museums.

Above-ground archaeologists who also call themselves industrial archaeologists work to rectify this situation. Using a variety of field research techniques—photography, mechanical drawing, plus a knowledge of the history of materials—they are interested in developing a comprehensive method of documenting and studying the physical shards which, for the most part, still survive above ground.[35] To the student of the American industrial landscape, the Silver King ore-loading station in Utah, the abandoned 1899 oil-rig near Volcano, West Virginia, the grain elevators near Hutchinson, Kansas, the 1868 Pejescot paper-mill in Topsham, Maine, or Colt's armory at Hartford, Connecticut, are all significant, physical documents of the American past. As R.A.S. Hennessey rightly points out, "Industrial archaeology has no objectively determined hierarchy of 'important' and 'less important' events or processes. Early Francis water turbines, Model 'T' Fords, Niles interurban cars, and the intriguing Lombard Street waterpipe truss bridge at Jones Falls in Baltimore (1852) are artifacts of significance in the democracy of industrial archaeology."[36]

The best general introductions to this relatively new way of exploring the history outside the history museum have been done in Britain, the progenitor of the Industrial Revolution in the west.[37] Handbooks and field guides by Kenneth Hudson and J.P.M.

Pannell can be supplemented by the work of an American, Harley J. McKee's *Recording Historic Buildings.*[38] Yet American industrial archaeology, largely because of its heretofore neglect by historians, is still practically a virgin research field for the professional and amateur alike. Railroad cuts, mine shafts, canal segments, relic trolley and street car lines, abandoned factories, previous sewer systems, water towers, quarries, workers' housing and numerous other artifacts lie about on the land waiting for identification, classification and interpretation in order to better reveal local community history and the history of technology, labor, business and government.

John D. Tyler has argued the case for a profitable alliance of industrial archaeology and the museum curator while Robert Vogel has made a similar proposal to American historic preservationists.[39] In any event, we are now getting a number of good typologies of industrial artifacts that make field identification easier for both the beginner and advanced student. For example, T.A. Camp and D. Jackson have done an excellent guide to "dating and identifying bridge truss types"; Fred Schroeder provides us with a detailed analysis on Victorian breweries; Larry Lankton has done the same for water supply systems; Ross Holland on lighthouses and Terry Jordan on windmills.[40] For the above-ground archaeologist's basic reference shelf, there is also Robert Vogel's comprehensive local community study of the Mohawk-Hudson river valley, Theodore A. Sande's pictorial survey, *Industrial Archaeology: A New Look at the American Heritage*, and Donald Sackheim's *Historic American Engineering Record Catalog.*[41]

Commercial Archeology

American technology and industry has produced all forms of material culture evidence but few of its progeny has had such a widespread impact as the automobile. The movable artifact has practically re-oriented the nation's countryside and cityscape. The horseless carriage has, in short, nurtured what historian James Flink calls "the American car culture." Or, as Marshall McLuhan puts it, "the car, in a word, has quite refashioned all of the spaces that unite and separate men."[42]

Part of this story is being told in the expanding number of historic car museums, transportation museums and private collections of vintage vehicles and antique car clubs that have proliferated since World War II. Soon, of course, there must follow museums of customized cars, psychedelic painted vans, as well as those mechanical/sculptural/mobile hybrids that Southern Californians call "truckitecture."[43] (In a state such as Indiana, where the mobile home and recreational vehicle industry comprise the second largest sector of the private economy, it seems inevitable that soon some museum attention will be paid to these artifacts.)

The commercial strip, variously referred to as the suburban

ribbon, the neon strip, commercial ribbon, string street, or simply "the strip,"[44] has, as Grady Clay demonstrates in an important primer for the above-ground archaeologist (*Close-Up: How to Read the American City*), existed throughout most of American urban history.[45] Yet the twentieth-century American addiction to the automobile has produced an unprecedented array of popular material culture close to and beside the strip.

Some historians, preservationists and museum curators may scoff at the American highway as a source of historical study and museum exhibitions but to anyone interested in probing the attitudes of the typical contemporary American who changes his address every five years, drives over 10,000 miles annually and eats every third meal outside his home, the omnipresence of gasoline stations, motels and drive-ins of all types looms as a significant cultural phenomenon. Should we not, therefore, give serious attention to the identifying and interpreting (perhaps even collecting?) of the pluralistic, eclectic, vernacular, regional, sometimes tediously similar—other times refreshing idiosyncratic—manifestations of the "neon culture" that has been with us since George Claude's invention was first installed on a theatre in New York in 1923?[46] On the commercial strip, where buildings are diminutive, neon or electric signs are gigantic and expensive. The huge graphic sign in space has become the monumental architecture of the American highway landscape. Should it not be saved and studied as we have eighteenth-century trade and tavern signs?

For the above-ground archaeologist seeking interpretive guides to the surfeit of artifacts that clamor for notice along the highway strip, Bruce Lohof and John A. Jackle have studied the American "service station as the evolution of a vernacular form";[47] John Baeder and Richard Gutman have studied diners.[48] On tourist camps and motels, the work of Reyner Banham and Warren Belasco is useful,[49] as is that of Neil Harris and William Kowinsky on shopping centers and malls.[50] The architectural firm of Venturi, Scott and Rauch, in addition to writing and designing the exhibition catalog (*Signs of Life*) mentioned earlier, also pioneered in showing us how to "learn from Las Vegas,"[51] the best primer currently available on how to analyze the mixed media (words, pictures, sculpture) of commercial strip signage. Venturi and Rauch willingly acknowledge their debt to Tom Wolfe who offers a mock typology of American signs: "they soar in shapes before which the existing vocabulary of art history is helpless," Wolfe admits, "I can only attempt to supply names—Boomerang Modern, Palette Curvilenear, Flash Gordon, Ming Alert Spiral, MacDonald's Hamburger Parabola, Mint Casino Elliptical, Miami Beach Kidney."[52]

The highway restaurant, be it a White Tower or a White Turkey, a Howard Johnson or a Frank-n-Stein, has its origins in American culinary and transportation history stretching back to the tavern and inn of the colonial period. Again, the coming of the automobile heavily influenced its further evolution and diversification. Physical evidence of this historical development survives all over the back roads, state routes and major U.S. highways built prior to the advent of the Interstate System which, incidentally, owes a great deal of its expanse to the Cold War (advocates of the system mustered considerable Congressional support for it because they insisted on its necessity as a network of evacuation routes out of American cities in case of a nuclear attack).

As Marshall Fishwick rightly claims, "the impact of fast foods, not only on our stomachs but on our psyches, has only begun to be realized and reported."[53] The impact of the fast food industry on the American landscape, likewise, has yet to be interpreted fully. Nonetheless, it is a veritable museum of popular culture, a fact recently demonstrated by some eighteen scholars who contributed essays about *The World of Ronald McDonald*,[54] an empire which has expanded from a single store in 1955 in Des Plaines, Illinois (now on the National Register of Historic Sites and Structures) to 4500 stores grossing an annual four million dollar business. There are other interpretive tools to the fast-food aspect of the built environment and Atlanta's Varsity (self-proclaimed as "the World's Biggest Drive-In") has even published its own history.[55]

Service stations, diners, motels and drive-ins have all become a ubiquitous fact of most city perimeters—a historical development now being documented and studied by an assortment of academic historians, museum curators, preservationists, and local history buffs who have banded together in the Society for Commercial Archaeology.[56] The potential of these outdoor data for exciting indoor museum exhibitions was recently demonstrated by a show ("Place, Product, Packaging") mounted by New York's Cooper-Hewitt Museum which assisted visitors in analyzing four popular American building types—fast-food restaurants, gasoline stations, diners and museum village restorations—"to see what they show about the art of design, and, from that, what they show us about ourselves, our pasts, and our futures."[57]

The Cooper-Hewitt's recognition that the "environment is a diary" is a major step toward understanding that history exists outside the history museum. It is also a timely and appropriate acknowledgment of Ada M. Huxtable's similar conclusion "that popular architecture is here to stay" and as such it "is the true democratization of the art of architecture in that it represents not just mass consumption but mass taste."[58] Dating back to the 1920s and the emergence of commercial building geared to the car culture, architectural historian David Gebhard contends that such artifacts (e.g. the hamburger drive-in in the form of a hamburger or the refreshment stand as an igloo or bottle) were the first forms of pop art.[59] American galleries have quickly collected and exhibited the work of Andy Warhol and Claes Oldenberg but have been strangely more reluctant to acquire Frank A. Gaw's "Big Red Piano" (Venice,

California) or "The Darkroom" storefront (Santa Monica, California).

The overscaled reproduction of a style or object turned into a building has some of its historical origins in the imagery of children's literature (Old Mother Hubbard did indeed live in a shoe-shaped dwelling) and in the extravagant claims of nineteenth-century American advertising graphics. Pop architecture since the 1920s has continued this tradition as well as functioned as an artifactual index to the changing popular mind, particularly as exploited by clever entrepreneurs who, in an increasingly consumer-oriented society, have long realized that even "history" is a growth industry.[60]

Many of today's commercial interiors aspire to be mini-history museums and are done in a "mood," "theme" or "period" architecture of the past. Redwood and Ross is an eighteenth-century English clothier, Victoria Station is a reflection of the great train days. The Jolly-Ox, Win Schuler's, and the Steak and Ale harken back to Tudor England. Howard Johnson's Williamsburg colonial exteriors are now matched by McDonald's local history interiors. In Saginaw, Michigan, the McDonald's chain's drive-in exploits the city's "one-time-lumber-capitol-of-the-world" theme; in Kokomo, Indiana, the restaurant draws its identity from the early days of the local automobile industry; in South Bend, Indiana, within a mile of the University of Notre Dame campus, is a McDonald's interior with over five hundred photographs of former Saturday afternoon fever. Finally, in addition to all the just slightly less blatant pecuniary "History-Lands," "Ye Olde Colonial Villages," and "Frontier-Towns" on the American landscape, there are the purportedly historical "Magic Kingdoms" of Walt Disney and associates, creators of two of America's greatest storied treasures (Disneyland and Disneyworld) and their rapidly increasing imitators—theme parks such as King's Island and King's Dominion, Six Flags Over Mid-America, or Marriott's many Great Adventures.

Historical Sites and Markers

These "historical sites" also deserve the scrutiny of the above-ground archaeologist. Read carefully, they, like specifically designated historical monuments, are as revelatory about a culture's values and priorities as is any history textbook. Cultural geographer Richard Francaviglia and cultural anthropologist Mark Leone provide us with numerous clues for deciphering the various past "presents" that are embodied in the historical theme parks that now proliferate across the landscape.[61] Similar investigations can be done by any visitor—if he or she knows what to look for—when walking through America's numerous outdoor museum villages.[62]

In addition to considering the various types of self-proclaimed historical museums as institutional artifacts of a wider cultural context, there is an abundant display of historical markers, plaques, memorials and monuments strewn about on the countryside and the cityscape.[63] Such material culture, largely unstudied by art and history museums alike,[64] contains at least two significant messages to the above-ground archaeologist. Besides conveying factual historical information about the specific event, person or place they are designed to commemorate, historical markers also provide a great deal of information about what was important to the generation that first set them in place and to the people who continue to preserve and maintain them as civic totems. Historical museums need to make their public aware of this history that they encounter on an urban square or a neighborhood street.

To pursue such an inquiry, W. Lloyd Warner's interrogation of "the ritualization of the past" in a New England's town's historical monuments is one useful model to apply to any environment's communal symbols and shrines.[65] For instance, it might be suggested to museum visitors whenever they stop at historical markers they take careful note of:

a) where historic markers are placed;
b) which historical events or personalities are consistently noticed or neglected in an area's past;
c) who in the community designated and funded the landmarks;
d) when they were put in place;
e) if the events memorialized are spread evenly across the area's history or if they tend to cluster (e.g. at the Revolutionary War in the East or the Civil War in the South) at one or more historical periods.

What would such an investigation or exhibition reveal about American values? In a nation where the people have argued there is no military tradition, the overwhelming artifactual evidence would suggest a contrary interpretation. As Robin Winks notes, the greatest number of historical markers and sites in the U.S. are devoted to battlefields and war heroes.[66] A reverence for classical antiquity is another cultural trait revealed by American historical markers. Ever since Horatio Greenough scandalously suited (or so his contemporaries thought) a bare-breasted George Washington in the toga of a Roman senator, we have embalmed many of our heroes in classical formaldehyde.

The American Bicentennial, of course, yielded an enormous corpus of historical monumentality that speaks volumes (if properly questioned) about what we, as a civilization, deemed important to mark for posterity. The thousands of courthouses, railroad stations, parks, residences, churches, log cabins, and school houses historically restored, recreated or renovated for the Bicentennial now form a sub-genre of American material culture as widespread as that produced by the WPA in the 1930s.[67] The City of South Bend (Indiana), for example, created a novel historical marker for the Bicentennial landscape when it originated the idea of painting its fireplugs in the likenesses of Revolutionary War soldiers and other American heroes. Other American cities such as Columbus (Ohio) and Niles (Michigan) have followed suit. The fireplug troops now outnumber the combined forces of Washington's several ragtag, eighteenth-century armies, although they lack their prototypes' capacity for strategic withdrawal. Some day they will be studied by anthropologists, folklorists and popular culturists interested in their cultural diffusion and regional variation as they spread across the country. They may even merit exhibition in indoor museum galleries as a form of 1970s American folk art.

The numerous art artifacts of the Bicentennial landscape point up another cultural value that pervades the history outside the history museum and recently dominated the historic preservation move—a tendency that might be called the "colonial fetish." Only in the past decade have historic preservationists begun to consider a house or site as truly historical if the structure antedates the end of the eighteenth century. Assuredly the most popular revival architectural style in this country continues to be the colonial (English, French, Dutch or Spanish); as every observer of the American landscape well knows it is the one historical style in all modes of American artifacts that since the 1880s has never been out of style.[68] It would follow that there must be deep cultural, social and psychological needs (besides aesthetic delight) that are satisfied by the ubiquitous colonial facsimiles and facades we lived in or behind; by the abundant Ethan Allen or Pennsylvania House furniture with which we furnish such Cape Cods, Saltboxes, and Georgian I-houses, as well as the colonial wallpapers (complete with replicated faded colors and stains) and Williamsburg paint colors with which we cover their interior and exterior walls.

Colonial American lives on in all facets of contemporary America: supermarkets, churches of all vintages, taverns, funeral homes, restaurants and gasoline stations galore. Texaco's adoption of a "colonial" design in its service stations occurred in 1928, the same year J.D. Rockefeller, Jr., publicly announced his intention to support the restoration of Williamsburg, a one-time colonial capital of Virginia. So taken are we with the supposed simplicity, moral purity and political virtue of the colonial era and its monuments that we use its design motifs everywhere.

Yet few historians or museums have studied the cultural implications of the successive waves of colonial revivals in, say, the suburban tracts or in the commercial strips of a particular city or town. Few have traced the cloning of any number of archetypical structures such as the log cabin or national icons like Independence Hall, Monticello, or Mount Vernon. Nonetheless, the careful above-ground archaeologist recognizes that ersatz Independence Halls of every size and material have sprung up all over the country serving as banks, schools, libraries, courthouses, shopping centers, prisons and (at the Henry Ford Museum) even as museum exhibition halls.[69]

*   *   *

As is probably apparent by now, these suggestions for greater recognition by university historians and museum historians of the history that is outside the history museum have a strong populist flavor. Such is the avowed objective of above-ground archaeology, for this approach considers the entire "city as a museum."[70] I would like to see us value "people's history" as a primary agenda for history teachers and museum curators: that is, to show average citizens various ways of knowing themselves and their communities through an understanding of their own pasts and the past of others.

Many of those pasts remain unrecognized and unstudied. Yet local and community history can be read in stone and steel, asphalt and cast-iron, street sign and equestrian statue, theme park and suburban tract as well as in libraries, municipal record offices and museums; the past is visual as well as verbal. The assorted material culture of any built environment can tell us as much about a society's popular culture as does a novel, a newspaper or a Fourth of July exhibition. There are many untold stories in the artifacts that still exist in space past as well as in time past. I think that historical museums in particular should attempt to seek out ways to assist their visitors in acquiring a "visual historical literacy" with which to read any involvement he or she encounters. Such a perspective, I am persuaded, helps us to recognize and interpret the past as it survives in the present with a vividness and an intimacy that enables any of us to discover the delight of doing history on our own.

Notes

[1] See the new journal *Family Heritage* (February, 1978), I:1, pp. 1-2 for the avid interest in local and personal history; Charles B. Hosmer, "The Broadening View of the Historical Preservation Movement," in Ian M.G. Quimby, ed., *Material Culture and the Study of American Life* (New York: Norton, 1978), pp. 121-139; Hart M. Nelsen, "The Democratization of the Antique: Meanings of Antiques and Dealers' Perceptions of Customers," *Sociological Review*, 18 (1970), pp. 407-19.

[2] Thomas J. Schlereth, *It Wasn't That Simple* (Washington: American Association of Museums, 1978); Thomas J. Schlereth, "The Historic Museum Village as a Learning Environment," *The Museologist*, (Spring, 1977), pp. 10-18.

[3] Neil Harris, "Museums, Merchandising and Popular Taste: The Struggle For Influence," in Quimby, *Material Culture*, pp. 140-174.

[4] Thomas J. Schlereth, "Material Culture Studies in America: Notes Toward A Historical Perspective," in *Proceedings: Canada Material History Forum* (Ottawa: Canada National Museum of Man, October, 1979, pp. 89-98.

[5] James S. Smith, "The Museum As Historian," *San Jose Studies* 2:2 (May, 1976), pp. 46-57; Harold K. Skramstad, "Interpreting Material Culture: A View From The Other Side of the Glass," in Quimby, *Material Culture*, pp. 175-200.

[6] Roderick Nash, "Henry Ford, Symbol For An Age," in *The Nervous Generation: American Thought, 1917-1930)* (Chicago, Rand McNally, 1970), pp. 153-63.

[7] See Frederick L. Rath, Jr. and Merrilyn Rogers O'Connell, "Outdoor Museums," in *Guide to Historic Preservation, Historical Agencies, and Museum Practices: A Selective Bibliography* (Cooperstown, N.Y.: New York State Historical Association, 1970), pp. 29-31.

[8] Thomas J. Schlereth, *Historic Houses as Learning Laboratories: Seven Teaching Strategies* (Nashville, Tenn.: American Association for State and Local History, 1978), Section 7, "Museum Interpretation Analysis."

[9] Carl Becker, "Everyman His Own Historian," *American Historical Review*, 37 (1932), pp. 221-26.

100   Popular Culture in Museums and Libraries

[10]John Cotter, *Above-Ground Archaeology* (Washington: Govt. Printing Office, 1972); Thomas J. Schlereth, "The City as Artifact," *American Historical Association Newsletters*, 14:4 (February, 1977), pp. 7-9.

[11]Definitions of these three archaeological perspectives on three major chronological periods can be found in James B. Griffin, "The Pursuit of Archaeology in the United States," *American Anthropologist*, 61 (1959), 378-88; Douglas Schwartz, "North American Archaeology in Historical Perspective," *Actes du Congres International d'Historie de Sciences*, 2 (Warsaw and Cracow, 1968), 311-15; Gordon Wiley and Philip Phillips, "Method and Theory in American Archaeology, II: Historical-Developmental Interpretations," *American Archaeologist* 57, pp. 723-819; and Gordon R. Wiley and Jeremy A Sabloff, *A History of American Archaeology* (San Francisco, Freeman, 1974).

[12]James Deetz, "Archaeology As a Social Science," *Bulletin of the American Anthropological Association*, 3:3 (Part 2), pp. 115-125; Thomas J. Schlereth, *Discovering the Local Community's Past Through Above-Ground Archaeology* (Indianapolis, Indiana Historical Society, 1979); James Daliband, "Architectural Recording as Above-Ground Archaeology," *Abstracts*: Third Annual Meeting, Society for Historical Archaeology (Bethlehem, Pa.: 1970), p. 15.

[13]Bert Salwen, "Archeology in Megapolis," in Charles L. Redman, ed., *Research and Theory in Current Archaeology* (New York: John Wiley, 1973), pp. 151-163; Mark P. Leone, "Archaeology as Technology," paper delivered at Department of Anthropology Colloquium, New York University, New York, 1972; Paul Huey, "Some Technical and Cultural Implications in Urban Archaeology," paper delivered at the Third Annual Meeting of the Society for Historical Archaeology, Bethlehem, Pa.: January, 1970; David Weitzman, *Underfoot: An Everyday Guide to Exploring The American Past* (New York: Scribners, 1976).

[14]Venturi and Rauch, *Signs of Life: Symbols in the American City* (New York: Aperture, 1976)

[15]Thomas J. Schlereth, *Historic House Museums: Seven Teaching Strategies* (Nashville, Tenn.: American Association for State and Local History, 1978), pp. 1-4.

[16]Fred Kniffen, "On Corner-Timbering," *Pioneer America* 1:1 (January, 1969), p. 1.

[17]The best available discussion of the classification of house types is R.W. Brunskill, *Illustrated Handbook of Vernacular Architecture* (London: Faber and Faber, 1971). Another excellent discussion is Henry Glassie, "The Types of the Southern Mountain Cabin," Appendix C of Jan H. Brunvand, *The Study of American Folklore* (New York: Norton, 1968), pp. 338-70. and much useful information is in Henry Glassie, *Pattern in the Material Culture of the Eastern United States* (Philadelphia: Univ. of Pennsylvania Press, 1968). Most of the better known works on house types in North America are listed in the voluminous footnotes of John E. Rickert, "House Facades of the Northeastern United States: A Tool of Geographic Analysis," *Annals, Association of American Geographers*, Vol. 57 (1967), 211-38, but for some inexplicable reason Rickert omitted Fred Kniffen, "Folk Housing: Key to Diffusion," *Annals, Association of American Geographers*, Vol. 55 (1965), 549-77, and Fred Kniffen and Henry Glassie, "Building in Wood in the Eastern United States: A Time-Place Perspective," *Geographical Review*, Vol. 56 (1966), 40-56. An ideal model of the manner in which the manmade structures of a particular area should be studied is R.W. Brunskill, *Vernacular Architecture of the Lake Counties: A Field Handbook* (London: Faber & Faber, 1974).

[18]Fred B. Kniffen, "Louisiana House Types," *Annals, Association of American Geographers*, 26 (1936), pp. 180-85; Richard Pillsbury and Andrew Kardos, *A Field Guide to the Folk Architecture of the Northeastern United States*, Geography Publications at Dartmouth, No. 8, Special Edition on Geographical Homes (Hanover, N.Y.: Dartmouth College, 1970).

[19]Wilbur Zelinsky, *The Cultural Geography of the United States* (Englewood Cliffs, N.J.: Prentice-Hall), p. 88.

[20]Pierce Lewis, "The Geography of Old Houses," *Earth and Mineral Sciences*, 39:5 (February, 1970), pp. 33-37; "Common Houses, Cultural Spoor," *Landscape* 19:2 (January, 1975), pp. 1-22.

[21]Arthur A. Hart, "M.A. Dishbrow and Company: Catalogue Architecture," *Palimpsest*, 56:4 (July-Aug., 1975), pp. 98-119; Clifford E. Clark, "Domestic Architecture as An Index to Social History: The Romantic Revival and the Cult of Domesticity in America, 1840-1870," *Journal of Interdisciplinary History*, 7:1 (Summer, 1976), pp. 33-56.

[22]Thomas J. Schlereth, "Vegetation as an Index to Past Landscapes: A Historian's Use of Plants as Material Culture Evidence," *Environmental Review*, 9 (November, 1979).

[23]May T. Watts, *Reading the Landscape of America* (New York: Collier, 1975).

[24]Eugene Kinkead, *Wildness is all Around Us: Notes of an Urban Naturalist* (New York: Dutton, 1978); Alan and Sue McPherson, *Edible and Useful Wild Plants of the Urban West* (Boulder: Preuett Publishing Co., 1979); Phoebe Cutler, "On Recognizing a WPA Rose Garden on

a CCC Privy," *Landscape* (Winter, 1976), pp. 3-9.

²⁵Fred E.H. Schroeder, "The Democratic Yard and Garden," in his *Outlaw Aesthetics: Arts and the Public Mind* (Bowling Green, Ohio: Bowling Green Popular Press, 1977), pp. 94-122.

²⁶E.N. Anderson, Jr. "On the Folk Art of Landscaping," 31 (1972) *Western Folklore*, pp. 179-188; James P. Duncan, Jr., "Landscape Taste as a Symbol of Group Identity: A Westchester County Village," *The Geographical Review* 63 (July, 1973), pp. 334-55; David Lowenthal and Hugh C. Prince, "English Landscape Traits," *Ibid.*, 55 (1965), pp. 186-222.

²⁷Barbara Riley, "Contemporary Collecting: A Case History," *The Decorative Arts Newsletter*, 4:3 (Summer, 1978), pp. 3-6.

²⁸Meredith Sylles and John Stewart, "Historic Landscape Restoration in the United States and Canada: An Annotated Source Guide," *A.P.T. Bulletin*, 4:3-4 (1972), pp. 114-58; John Stewart and Susan Berger, "The Case for Commemoration of Historic Landscapes and Gardens," *Ibid.*, 7:2 (1975), pp. 99-123; David Streatfield, "Standards for Historic Garden Preservation and Restoration," *Landscape Architecture*, 59:3 (April 1969), pp. 198-200.

²⁹Dumbarton Oaks Research Library and Colletion, ed., *Preservations and Restoration of Historic Gardens and Landscapes* (Washington: Dumbarton Oaks, 1976).

³⁰John T. Stewart, "Landscape Archaeology: Existing Plant Material on Historic Sites as Evidence of Buried Features and as Survivors of Historic Species," *A.P.I. Bulletin*, 9:3 (1977), pp. 65-72; John Stewart, *Historic Landscapes and Gardens (Nashville, Tenn.: American Association for State and Local History, 1974);* Donald H. Parker, "What You Can Learn from the Gardens of Colonial Williamsburg," *Horticulture* 44:28 (1975). Stewart's use of "landscape archaeology" should not be confused with Michael Aston and Trevor Rowley, *Landscape Archaeology: An Introduction to Field Work Techniques on Post-Roman Landscapes* (London: David & Charles, 1974).

³¹Rudy and Joy Farretti, *Every House A Garden* (Chester, Conn.: The Pequot Press, 1975) and *Landscapes and Gardens* (Nashville, Tenn.: American Association for State and Local History, 1979).

³²Leo Marx, *The Machine in the Garden: Technology and the Pastoral Ideal in America* (New York: Oxford, 1967), pp. 73-226.

³³Galen Granz, "Changing Roles of Urban Parks: From Pleasure Garden to Open Landscape," *Landscape*, 22:3 (Summer, 1978), pp. 9-18; Albert Fein, "The American City: The Ideal and the Real," in Edgar Kaufman, ed., *The Rise of an American Architecture*, ed. by H. Hitchcock, et al, (New York: Praeger, 1970), pp. 51-105.

³⁴*Directory of Historical Societies and Agencies in the United States and Canada*, 11 ed. (Nashville, Tenn.: 1978), pp. 456; 466-467.

³⁵Harold Skramstad, "American Things: Neglected Material Culture," *American Studies International*, 10:3 (Spring, 1972), pp. 16-19.

³⁶R.A.S. Hennessey, "Industrial Archaeology in Education," *The History Teacher*, 9:1 (November, 1975), p. 39.

³⁷Kenneth Hudson, *Exploring Our Industrial Past* (London: Hodder and Stoughton, 1975); and *Industrial Archaeology* (London: University Paperbacks, 1965); Brian Bracegirdle, *The Archaeology of the Industrial Revolution* (Rutherford, N.J.: Fairleigh Dickinson Univ. Press, 1974).

³⁸Kenneth Hudson, *A Handbook for Industrial Archaeologists: A Guide to Fieldwork and Research* (London: John Baker, 1967), 1-77; J.P.M. Pannell, *The Techniques of Industrial Archaeology* (London: David and Charles, 1974); Hanley J. McKee, *Recording Historic Buildings* (Washington: Government Printing Office, 1976).

³⁹John D. Tyler, "Industrial Archaeology and the Museum Curator," *Museum News*, 47:5 (January, 1969), pp. 30-32; Robert M. Vogel, "Industrial Archaeology—A Continuous Past," *History Preservation*, 19:2 (April-June, 1967), pp. 68-75.

⁴⁰T.A. Camp and D. Jackson, *Bridge Truss Types: A Guide to Dating and Identifying* (Nashville, Tenn.: AASLH, 1977); Fred E.H. Schroeder, "Victorian Breweries: High-Rise in Industrial Architecture," Paper presented at meeting of the Popular Culture Association April 22, 1978; Larry Laukton, "Valley Crossings on The Old Croton Aqueduct," *Industrial Archaeology* (1979); Ross Holland, Jr., *America's Lighthouses* (Brattleboro, Vt.: Stephen Greene Press, 1972); Terry Jordan, "Evolution of the American Windmill: A Study in Diffusion and Modification," *Pioneer America*, 5:2 (1973), pp. 3-12.

⁴¹Robert Vogel, ed., *A Report of The Mohawk-Hudson Area Survey: A Selective Recording of the Industrial Archaeology of the Mohawk and Hudson River Valleys in the Vicinity of Troy, New York, June-September, 1969* (Washington: Smithsonian Institution, 1973); Theodore Auton,

Industrial Archaeology: A New Look at the American Heritage (Brattleboro, Vt.: Stephen Greene Press, 1976); Donald E. Sackheim, *Historic American Engineering Record Catalog* (Washington: National Park Service, 1976).

[42]James T. Flink, *The Car Culture* (Cambridge, Mass.: Harvard University Press, 1975); Marshall McLuhan, *Understanding Media: The Extension of Man* (New York: New American Library, 1964) p. 201; also see John B. Rae, *The Road and the Car in American Life* (Cambridge, Mass.: Harvard University Press, 1971).

[43]"Nomadic Truckitecture," in *Environmental Communications* (Venice, Ca.: 1976), p. 24.

[44]A useful definition of the commercial strip can be found in Gordon, "Cultural Implications of the Commercial Strip," pp. 21-22; also see Louden C. Hoffman, "A Case Study of Commercial Strip Development" (unpublished M.A. thesis, University of Cincinnati, 1968).

[45]Grady Clay, *Close-Up: How to Read the American City* (New York: Praeger, 1972), pp. 85-109.

[46]Kathy Mack, *American Neon* (New York: Universe Books, 1977); Dextra Frankel, *Neon Signs and Symbols*, (Catalogue Art Gallery, California State University at Fullerton), Feb., 23, 1973-March 15, 1973).

[47]Bruce A. Lohof, "The Service Station in America: The Evolution of a Vernacular Form," *Industrial Archaeology*, 2:2 (Spring, 1974), pp. 1-13; John A. Jackle, "The American Gasoline Station, 1920-1970," *Journal of American Culture* (1979); James B. Schick, "Vehicular Religion and the Gasoline Service Station," *Midwest Quarterly, 19 (October, 1977).

[48]John Baeder, *Diners* (New York: Harry N. Abrams, 1978); Richard Gutman, "The Diner from Boston to L.A.," in *Environmental Communications* (Venice, Ca.: 1976), p.24.

[49]Reyner Banham, "Unrecognized American Architecture: The Missing Motel," *Landscape* (Winter, 1965-66), 15:2, pp. 4-6; Warren J. Belasco, "Americans on the Road: Autocamping, Tourist Camps, Motel, 1910-1945" (unpublished Ph.D. dissertation, Univ. of Michigan, 1977).

[50]Neil Harris, "American Scene: Spaced-Out at the Shopping Center," *The New Republic* (December 15, 1975), pp. 23-26; William Kowinski, "The Malling of America," *New Times* (May 1, 1978), pp. 29-55.

[51]Robert Venturi, Denise Scott Brown and Stephen Izenour, *Learning from Las Vegas* (Cambridge, Mass.: MIT Press, 1972); for an extended review of this provocative book see Sigrid H. Fowler, "Learning from Las Vegas," *Journal of Popular Culture* 7:2 (1973), pp. 425-433.

[52]Tom Wolfe, *The Kandy-Kolored Tangerine-Flake Streamline Baby* (New York: Noonday Press, 1966), p. 8.

[53]Marshall Fishwick, "Introduction," *The World of Ronald McDonald* (Bowling Green, Ohio: Bowling Green University Popular Press, 1978), p. 341.

[54]*Ibid.*, see, particularly, Kenneth I. Helphand, "The Landscape of McDonald's," pp. 357-362 and David Orr, "The Ethnography of Big Mac," pp. 377-386.

[55]See Paul Airshorn and Steven Izenour, "Learning From Hamburgers: The Architecture of White Tower," *Architecture Plus* (June, 1973), pp. 46-55; H. Roger Grant, "Highway Commercial Architecture: Albia, Iowa's 'Dutch Mill' " *Palimpsest*, 58 (May/June, 1958); David Morton, "They Did it All for You," *Progressive Architecture*, 6:78 (June, 1978); *World's Largest Drive-In, The Varsity* (Atlanta: n.p., n.d.)

[56]Chester Liebs, "Remember Our Not-So-Distant Past?" *Historic Preservation* 30:1 (Jan/March, 1978), pp. 30-35; *Proceedings*, First Annual Conference, Society for Commercial Archaeology, Boston, November 15, 1977 (Burlington, Vt.: SCA, 1979).

[57]Cooper-Hewitt Museum—The Smithsonian's National Museum of Design, *Place, Produce, Packaging* (Exhibition Catalog, January 20-March 19, 1978, New York); p. 5, part of the catalogue is also reprinted in *Architectural Record* (February, 1978).

[58]Ada M. Huxtable, "Pop Architecture Here to Stay," in her *Will They Ever Finish Bruckner Boulevard?* (New York: Macmillan, 1964), 172-174; Dennis A. Mann, "Architectural Icons: The Best Surprise is No Surprise," in Ray Browne and Marshall Fishwick, *Icons of America* (Bowling Green, Ohio: Bowling Green Popular Press, 1978), pp. 35-56.

[59]David Gebhard, "One Hundred Years of Architecture in California," in exhibition catalogue, *Architecture in California* (Santa Barbara, Ca.: Univ. of California Art Galleries, April 16 to May 12, 1968), p. 7.

[60]See J. Meredith Neil and Marshall Fishwick, *Popular Architecture* (Bowling Green, Ohio: Bowling Green Popular Press, n.d.), Vittorio Gregotti, "Kitsch and Architecture," in Gillo Dorfler, *Kitsch—The World of Bad Taste* (New York: Universe Books, 1969), pp. 255-76; Reyner Banham, *Los Angeles: The Architecture of Four Ecologies* (New York: Harper & Row, 1971).

[61]Richard V. Francaviglia, "Main Street U.S.A.: The Creation of Popular Image," *Landscape*

(Spring-Summer, 1977) 21:3, pp. 18-22; "Small Town as Mythical Landscape: 'Main Street' and the Frontier Town in Popular Culture Perspective," Paper presented at Popular Culture Association meeting, Cincinnati, Ohio, April 21, 1978; also see Margaret King, "Disneyland and Walt Disney World: Traditional Values in Futuristic Form," Paper presented at the Popular Culture Association Meeting, Chicago, April, 1976; Mark P. Leone, "The Material Culture of American Utopias," unpublished paper presented at Society for American Archaeology, San Francisco, May, 1973.

[62]Schlereth, "The Historic Museum Village," pp. 14-16.

[63]Raymond F. Pisney, *Tombstones on Posts: U.S. Historical Markers* (Verona, Va.: McClare Press, 1976); Bernard Barber, "Place, Symbol and Utilitarian Function in War Memorials," in Robert Gutman, ed., *People and Buildings* (New York: Basic Books, 1972), pp. 327-33.

[64]Two outstanding exceptions are Marianne Doezeman and June Hargrove, *The Public Monument and Its Audience* (Cleveland: Cleveland Museum of Art, 1977), James M. Goode, *The Outdoor Sculpture of Washington, D.C.* (Washington: Smithsonian Institution Press, 1974).

[65]W. Lloyd Warner, *The Living and the Dead: A Study of the Symbolic Life of Americans* (New Haven: Yale University Press, 1959), chapter 4.

[66]Robin Winks, "Conservation in America: National Character as Revealed by Preservation," in Jane Fawcett, ed., *The Future of the Past: Attitudes Toward Conservation, 1174-1974* (New York: Watson-Guptill, 1976), pp. 141-146.

[67]Compare Phoebe, "On Recognizing a WPA Rose Garden or a CCC Privy," p. 309 and David Lowenthal,"The Bicentennial Landscape: A Mirror Held Up to the Past," *The Geographical Review* 67:3 (July, 1977), pp. 253-67; also see Thomas J. Schlereth, "The 1876 Centennial: A Heuristic Model for Comparative American Studies," *Hayes Historical Journal*, 1:3 (Spring, 1977), pp. 201-10.

[68]William B. Rhoads, *The Colonial Revival in America* (New York: Garland, 1977); *House Beautiful* (New York) has recently begun to publish a monthly magazine entitled *Colonial Homes* promising "the best of America's Past for you to enjoy." (promotional brochure, 1979).

[69]John Maass, "Architecture and Americanism or Pastiches of Independence Hall," *Historic Preservation*, 22 (April-June 1970), pp. 17-25.

[70]Laurence LaFore, "The City As A Museum," in *American Classic* (Iowa City, Ia.: Iowa State Historical Society, 1975), pp. 37-95.

"In the twentieth century, scholars of European folk culture have broadened earlier collecting patterns to embrace the term material culture and in the process have come to recognize the natural extension of their inquiry to popular culture artifacts."

C. Kurt Dewhurst and Marsha MacDowell, "Popular Culture and the European Folk Museums"

VIII

Modern America and Canada are dotted with "Old Town" museums, ranging from refurbished living neighborhoods to meticulous academic reconstructions, to commercialized amusement parks, to the shake-and-bake agglomerations of some local historical societies. In this article C. Kurt Dewhurst and Marsha MacDowell introduce us to the original Old Town reconstruction, in Denmark, and offer the surprising information that the earliest exhibition techniques were patterned after the popular mass entertainments of wax museums and World's Fair expositions. A basic difference between the American and European popular culture museums emerges as well; whereas the "culture of the people" in the United States has always been in large part rootless, mobile and commercial, European popular culture has to a greater degree evolved from local folk traditions, most especially in rural areas. These "deeper roots" make it entirely appropriate to approach popular culture by way of the *folkemuseum.*

C. Kurt Dewhurst and Marsha MacDowell are both curators for the Folk Arts Division of The Museum, Michigan State University, which is involved in the documentation, research and exhibition of folk arts from Michigan and the Upper Great Lakes region. In addition to their joint research for this article during a National Museum Act-sponsored trip to Scandinavia, they collaborated with Betty MacDowell on a book entitled *Artists in Aprons, Folk Art by American Women* (Dutton, 1979), and on an exhibit "Rainbows in the Sky, The Folk Art of Michigan in the Twentieth Century," for which Marsha MacDowell prepared the catalog. She is currently working on "Folkpatterns," a National Endowment for the Humanities project sponsored jointly by The Museum and Michigan 4-H Programs, designed to assist youth in the investigation of cultural history on the local level. Dewhurst is working on a book about religious folk art in America which will be published by E.P. Dutton.

Kurt Dewhurst & Marsha MacDowell

Popular Culture and the European Folk Museum

WHILE POPULAR CULTURE enjoys an increasing level of recognition as a distinctive and fertile field of inquiry for American scholars, collections of popular artifacts by American museums are scarce and rarely systematic. An examination of the European experience with popular culture artifacts provides some valuable insights into the understanding of the continuum of material culture (folk, popular and fine). Both folk and popular artifacts are found in numerous national, regional and local museum collections under the classification of *volkskunde, musee d'art populaire, musee folklorique, folkemuseum, landesmuseum, frilandsmuseet* and still others. In America, one finds the collection of popular artifacts primarily associated with historical museums; in many European countries the collections, cataloging and exhibition of popular artifacts has become the province of the folk museum. Fine arts museums and technological museums, while they may have some folk and popular materials, generally emphasize more industrial, academic or elitist aspects of man's cultural experience. In the twentieth century, scholars of European folk culture have broadened earlier collecting patterns to embrace the term material culture and in the process have come to recognize the natural extension of their inquiry to popular cultural artifacts. Concern for the purity of the folk artifact has necessitated a developed understanding of the ways in which popular culture has eroded the fabric of folk culture in European countries. And yet, while the popular artifact initially seems beyond the realm of the folk museum, popular culture artifacts have been collected by many folk museums in recent years—and this process has been carried on with sensitivity and with a sound philosophical basis.

M. Henri Focillon has provided a valuable summary of the "elevated tone" that folk museums have assumed in France and other European countries" in his "Introduction to Art Populaire:" "In certain regions of Europe, wars and their consequences augmented the value of folk arts in their role as historical witnesses. As they prolonged the poetic and political thrust of Romanticism, folk arts became a public institution. ... The taste for folk arts and their processes of manufacture were propagated at the level of primary education, thereby assuring their force in the more profound depths of national sentiment. ... In nations where the peasant element dominated and charmingly preserved old-time talents, sophisticated spirits judged that it was possible, by calling to mind indigenous habits and handicrafts, to profitably compete with the banal, interchangeable products of mass production, and thus, by wedding folk art to the business life of the nation, to save their most precious heritage."[1] (See Fig. 1 and 2) A sensitized cultural conscience is one facet of the character of the European approach to the folk and popular artifact as they fall within the same fabric of material culture. Focillon stresses that the methodology that equips the scholar of folk culture also allows him to analyze popular culture. Focillon explains, "The duty to compare is the foundation of every science of observation, perhaps of all scientific disciplines. It is well known what development the comparative method has undergone during the past two generations; no longer a secondary technique, it is almost an art of thinking. To define is not to separate: even in order to isolate a phenomenon or a fact, one must compare; by reconciling differences, one arrives at specificity. Our goal in investigating folk art has been to show that objects can be set in series, not in discontinuity."[2] This approach, "objects set in series," lends itself toward understanding the interrelationships of art of the folk group and art for popular audiences. When objects, especially those produced by a relatively homogeneous folk group are analyzed in terms of this typology, research has demonstrated that art styles become valuable "cultural cognitive maps."[3]

Development of the Folk Museum Concept

The history of the folk museum concept deserves consideration in order to understand the emergence of these European museums in the twentieth century. Artur Hazelius is generally credited with formulating the idea of the folk museum in Sweden that has led to what is known today as the *Nordiska Museet* in Stockholm. In his earliest museum exhibit work, Hazelius "arranged his exhibits as stage sets with one side open facing the public, the figures arranged in highly emotional tableaux similar to the way it is done at a waxworks, and on which Hazelius has in many respects modelled his display."[4] Bernard Olsen, founder of the Danish Folk Museum, was said to have found Hazelius' method of exhibition "unsatisfactory" when he saw it at the World Fair in Paris in 1878. He preferred the approach that the Dutch had employed utilizing a complete room which one could walk into and where "each single thing came from old houses and stood in its accustomed position."[5] Olsen later recalled, "In contrast to the Swedish manner the effect was stirring, and from the moment I entered the old room, it was as if one were in another world—far away in time and space from the crowded, modern exhibition, and it was clear to me this was how a folk museum should be."[6] (see Fig. 3) The vision of Hazelius should not be overshadowed though, for in the words of Norwegian archaeologist Professor Haaken Shetelgib, "it [the folk museum] is a museum-type whose roots spring from the national romanticism of the North, conceived and developed through the genius of a single man, Arthur Hazelius, the founder of the *Nordiska Museet* and the great example to all who followed after, in fact the source of a totally new stream of cultural research in the North."[7] Later, in 1891, *Skansen,* the first open-air museum, was founded in Stockholm where old buildings were saved and then re-erected. Both the *Nordiska Museet* and *Skansen* provided the impetus for other nations and smaller community-oriented efforts in museum development. In the United States, museums as large as the Henry Ford Museum and Greenfield Village or the complex of buildings at Colonial Williamsburg, to small regional outdoor museums such as the Iron County Museum and Historical Society in the Upper Peninsula of Michigan, have been founded based on the guiding principles that originated with Hazelius and were pioneered at the *Nordiska Museet* and *Skansen.*[8]

Other notable efforts included private museums and combined publicly and privately supported museums. The Historical Museum of Bergen, Norway, now linked with the University of Bergen, was originally a private museum. The Sandvig collections at Lillehammer, Norway, were founded by a dentist, Anders Sandvig, in 1887 as a private foundation in receipt of grants from the state, county and town of Lillehammer. Established with a more limited mission, "to trace the development of the dwelling-house as far back as possible on the basis of contemporary knowledge of architectural history, Sandvig wanted to show the growth from the simple to the composite, from the primitive to the advanced; he paid less attention to chronology, and was more concerned with interpreting varying levels of culture."[9] Peter Holm, founder of *Den Gamle By* (The Old Town), was first elected head of a committee in 1907 whose task it was to organize an historic section of the National Exhibition in Aarhus, Denmark, in 1909. This exhibit, first housed in an old Aarhus building, formed the nucleus of what was in later years to become "The Old Town." The Museum of Tyrolean Folk Art was initiated in 1888 during the 40th anniversary of the reign of Emperor Franz Joseph I. In Norway, as in most northern European countries, many local museums evolved out of various jubilee or fair exhibits of local materials. This interest in local history is reflected in the introduction to a *Guide to the Museums in Norway*: "museum policy therefore aims at stressing the importance of specialization among folk museums, so that each shall as far as possible interpret the cultural character of its own particular locality."[10] After the first late-19th century wave of romanticism which spawned the first exhibits and museums of local folk culture, the founding of new museums slowed down considerably in the twentieth century. A new flood of interest in ethnicity, nationalism and local history—partly promoted by the Sixties' back-to-earth movement and more recently shaped folk museum policy has been ethnology. This emphasis has helped to expand the role of research activities beyond the mere collection of old artifacts of folk peoples—attention is given to the role these material objects play in man's life, how they are made and what they tell us of the cultural life of a people in a particular place in time. The questions now are how and why rather than which and what.

In order to more fully illuminate early objects of material culture, museums of folk culture in Europe have attached great importance to other documentary evidence and have emphasized these areas as critical to their collecting or acquisition activities. Photographic archives, questionnaires, taped interviews and careful studies of on-going traditions all are considered essential to museum interpretation of artifacts. Photoarchival activity is a logical undertaking for the folk museum and the collecting of photographs attempts to record the traditional life of the people through time. As early as 1940 in Denmark, questionnaires to record oral traditions were widely used throughout the country by voluntary workers under the guidance by the staff of the Danish Folk Museum. Developed by the National Museums Ethnological Surveys Department, the aim was to specialize in rural source material. Later efforts turned toward recording regional building customs and recording local traditions. This technique has been coupled with the use of photographs and filming for recording folklife and working methods. Scarcity and the high cost has contributed to the inability of most museums to continue the collection of early folk materials and has further prompted the folk museums to collect the popular artifacts of today to compare with the earlier folk artifacts. By incorporating a systematic method of acquisition, museums are gathering objects *and* documentation concurrently. The *Nordiska Museet* in Stockholm has been utilizing a model program entitled *"Foremal, Bild, Data,"* (Object, Photo, Data) that was developed at a symposium in 1973 at the Century Jubilee. Typical objects of popular consumption and/or use were identified and collected. The goal is to acquire objects with data and photographs. The folk museum thus takes on the role of repository for today's popular culture—a cultural "saving" institution for future public consumption. Working with five other museums in Sweden, this program selected a typical family (or families) in five areas of Sweden and has recorded through photographs, film and interviews their attitudes, values, customs, activities and the belongings for future use. Donations of popular objects of material culture are also sought from the selected families. This new approach to collecting has been widely cited for its thorough methodology and other museums have attempted some facet of this system. Obviously, though, only the most well supported museums could undertake such a program because of the research costs and the inevitable need to provide storage for the contemporary popular objects.

Museum acquisition programs have embarked on a more public-spirited plan to gain material for their collections. A museum in Detmold, Germany, has advertised in local papers requesting donations of particular artifacts to fill certain gaps in collections. This is a far cry from the "courting of collectors" that had absorbed the time of curators not long ago. Part of the attempt to demythologize the museum as a mere depository of artifacts can be demonstrated by the efforts of European folk museums to keep in touch with the "folk." The *Schweizerisches Museum fur Volkskunde* frequently develops its exhibits around social problems and attempts to illustrate man's ways of coping historically with these problems.

Museums such as the Altonaer Museum in Hamburg, Germany, now develop exhibitions in conjunction with local trade unions for both the museum building and other appropriate sights around the city. Another popular approach has been an open exhibition of naive art on particular subjects. A recent exhibition was planned to jury the work of German artists' representation of "ships and ports." Hundreds of entries poured forth and selection was difficult but the entries provide valuable insights into the collective consciousness of society toward this aspect of man's experience. At the *Museum fur Deutsche Volkskunde* in West Berlin, a handsome acquisition budget is used for purchasing objects of both popular and folk nature for specific exhibit development. As themes for new exhibitions are developed, the curators begin to collect the necessary materials. If an object is not in the collections, then it is purchased. This, though a highly unusual circumstance, allows the curators great freedom in portraying a well-rounded picture of the cultural use of an object.

Classification Systems for Material Culture

In the early days of the development of folk museums, simple listings of the items displayed in room settings sufficed for archival purposes. Soon, however, as collections increased and the programs of the museums expanded to include accelerated research/collecting missions, more complex systems of information retrieval and cataloging systems for objects were demanded.

In *Extractum ex Ethnologia Europaea*, Holger Rasmussen clearly identifies the difficulties inherent for the folk museum in developing classification systems for the heterogeneous collections of objects, and the supplementary material which puts it into perspective. And, he states, "it is important to remember that folk museums are by no means a uniform group, for they reflect the great divergencies that lie concealed in the term "folk"."[13] Whatever the differences in the interpretation of the term 'folk,' European museums initially based their archival systems for material objects primarily on the structure of classification employed in linguistic research. The Gothenburg Museum in Sweden took an early lead in publishing a classification guide "the main purpose of which was to provide a general survey of the material from an ethnological point of view."[14] The dominating principle used now in classifying objects is to base its category on its function, irrespective of its appearance or material. A comprehensive classification for the Danish Ethnological Museums developed in 1940 provides for not only the sorting of material objects, but also parallel headings for photographs and oral traditions.

With the contemporary emphasis on field collecting, any of the problems in retrieval of information on objects are being eliminated. Field researchers are able to bring objects into museum collections that are more fully documented. Projects such as *"Foremal, Bild, Data"* at *Nordiska* underscore the concerted effort to provide as much information as possible with an object. Occasionally, however, an innovative acquisitions effort such as a recent project at the *Norsk Folkemuseum* in Oslo, Norway, will provide unforeseen complications for the cataloger. In accepting the entire contents of an early twentieth century room, a wonderful addition in terms of contemporary popular culture materials, the museum staff was faced with the time-consuming task of cataloging the mountain of material contained therein. Not every museum has the staff or storage space to entertain the expansion of collections in more contemporary object areas.

Keeping up with the classification of incoming materials is a never-ending task for any museum. It was interesting that during World War II, the *Nordiska* Museum received an unexpected boost to their cataloging efforts. Unemployed musuem professionals in Scandinavian and European institutions were given work at the *Nordiska* and during this period *Nordiska*'s collections and documentation of those collections swelled with the result that the information on objects is both thorough and accessible.

Although the classification system based on the cardinal rule of function dominates the designation of objects in most European folk museums, the collections of each museum reflect the regional, geographical and ethnic influences on material object productions and sometimes demand special categorization. Pockets of specialized production such as rosemaling in Norway, carving in Germany, rya rugs in Finland, Appenzeller painting in Switzerland, etc., are regional variants that are often featured in their respective local museums. Sometimes a local toy or folk art form will become a popular artifact, manufactured in volume for popular consumption or distribution. (see Fig. 6) This in turn might demand a reclassification of an object, but usually designation by function remains consistent and the most predictable means of classifying objects.

Approaches to Exhibits: Three Models

1) Self-Directed Experiential Model

European folk art museums while influenced dramatically by the Swedish models of Artur Hazelius have varied their courses in representing folk culture in museum exhibitions. While most folk museums attempted to convey information about their collections through labels or guided tours, some museums developed philosophical policies that prohibited a formal didactic approach to exhibitions. The *Frilandsmuseet* in Denmark declares that "the purpose of the museum is to portray the living conditions of the countryman; to show the houses and homes and the farms equipped with the implements that would have been used. (see Fig. 7) There are, therefore, no displays or showcases like those in a normal museum, nor any labels to explain the many items of equipment." It should be added, though, that this museum and others with a similar philosophy of exhibition offer excellent guidebooks that include illustrations of architecture, furnishings, and objects along with a glossary of terms. This affords the viewer the opportunity to approach the museum experience according to the level of interest brought by the visitor. In the final analysis, the experience is a self-directed one—it provides comparison and inquiry but does not attempt to interpret the experience totally for the visitor.

The Old Town Museum in Aarhus, Denmark, has carried this approach one step further by recreating *"Den Gamle By"* (The Old Town Museum) in an expansive park area in the heart of the city. Comprised of fifty-four buildings, a fountain in the town square and two greenhouses, the museum proudly proclaims "it costs nothing to wander around the streets of 'The Old Town' and the open-air town museum is open twenty-four hours a day."[15] Created primarily through the early efforts of Peter Holm and conditioned over the last seventy years, this museum embodies "the splendid illusion of a small, 'tucked away' little market town which the hollow in which it is situated at present emphasizes so wonderfully."[16] Still it is part of the town proper and is a living vital part of life in Aarhus. Citizens of Aarhus must literally walk through The Old Town Museum to reach other city areas. Only when one enters the buildings of The Old Town Museum does one encounter period objects and some brief explanatory labels.

2) Cultural Aesthetic Model

Beyond the experiential approach that is offered by most folk museums in Europe, one also encounters museum exhibits of both folk and popular arts that stress aesthetic values. In the late 1960s, the *Nordiska Museet* in Stockholm mounted an exhibition entitled Nordic Folk Art drawing from their collections of folk art from Sweden, Norway, Denmark, Finland, Iceland and Esthonia. Based on the desire to "exhibit materials and techniques of high quality"[17] strength of design principles, mastery of techniques, command of color use, and varied vocabulary of visual images—the exhibition conveyed the sophisticated level of competence of many examples of folk artistry that indeed rival academically trained artists. (see Fig.

8) At the time this exhibition tendency was new and helped legitimize folk art appreciation by the fine arts community (although this was not really necessary as history has shown that folk art has been widely collected and appreciated by artists and scholars alike). This approach has in recent years been minimized in favor of exhibits that stress traditional values of folk groups which are fundamentally conservative and not artistically innovative.

3) The Folkloristic Model

Robert Wildhaber, a leading scholar on Swiss folk art, has written in a special exhibition catalog of Swiss folk art that a folk art has nothing to do with "art" in the accepted sense of the word. He continued in this fashion, "To state the case in a somewhat exaggerated fashion: A work of art is a unique creation by an individual. Its only purpose is to express ideas and emotions in visual form, and thereby (hopefully) arouse equivalent ideas and emotions in the viewer. Folk art does not have to meet aesthetic standards; being a part of folklore it has to be judged by criteria that pertain to this branch of knowledge. Folklore deals with the traditional behavior of a group. By 'group' we mean either an ethnic unit, inhabitants of a geographically self-contained region, members of the same craft or professions (see Fig. 9), associations of people linked by age or other characteristics they hold in common.... An exhibition of folk art understood in this context should reflect the traditional and typical objects typical of the group."[18] The conceptualization has been the prevalent attitude toward exhibitions of folk arts in European folk museums. And this very approach enables exhibitions to compare the popular arts of the day with the traditional folk arts of the folk community.[19]

No matter which of these models is used to form an exhibition, usually the approach is taken within an historical or chronological framework tied to a particular region. Few attempts have been made to either examine objects in a wide-ranging cross-cultural fashion or to juxtapose early objects with contemporary pieces. Those museums that have attempted innovative approaches to exhibits of materials have been those that are now developing the necessary collections in contemporary and popular traditions.

The Folk Museum and the Popular Artifact

The often quoted metaphor offered by Ray B. Browne in relating folk art to popular art has value here, "Perhaps the best metaphorical figure for all art is that of the flattened ellipsis, or lens. In the center, largest in bulk and easiest seen through is popular art. On either end of the lens are high and folk art.... All four (including mass art) derive in many ways and to many degrees from one another, and the lines of demarcation between any two are indistinct and fluid."[20] This image admits the interplay of factors that shape each type of cultural artifact. Museums will have to contend with the blur of distinctions between these categories of artifact with the onset of modern industrialized society that has already taken a dramatic toll on folk cultural expression. The theoretical constructs of the popular culture scholar have been built around concern for cultural patterns of transmissions, dissemination of the artist's message, and dissection of the nature of the artist himself. The distinction of dissemination as critical in separating folk and popular materials has been summarized by Abraham Kaplan this way, "those elements that are distributed through the mass media are 'mass' culture, and those which are or were at one time disseminated by oral or non-oral methods—on levels 'lower' than mass media—are called folk."[21] Russel Nye has noted that "Popular art is folk art aimed at a wider audience, in a somewhat more self-conscious attempt to fill that audience's expectations, an art more aware of the needs for selling the product, more consciously adjusted to the median taste. It is an art trying to perfect itself, not yet mature."[22] The growing awareness of the interplay of artifacts is signalled by the growing use of the ethnographic term "material culture" to include folk, popular and fine art/artifacts. Museums in Europe that have been deeply rooted in the investigation and exhibition of folk culture have begun to journey into the world of popular culture because of the realization that the distinctions between folk and popular culture are becoming "indistinct and fluid" in the twentieth century. (see Fig. 11)

While it would be premature to conclude that the collection of popular artifacts by folk museums in Europe is a widespread trend, the pattern is being established by the major national museums in Sweden, Norway, Finland, Germany, Austria, France and Switzerland. Collections of popular artifacts can enable a folk museum that already has extensive holdings of folk artifacts to expand its treatment of the life of their populace all within the mission of a cultural history museum. Popular cultural artifacts can be collected inexpensively and procured easily through donations as these materials rarely command the market value of antiques, as most folk art artifacts do today. With a systematic acquisitions policy, the folk museum can cultivate a veritable storehouse of artifacts that can enable future generations to understand the emerging national and local cultural patterns in this century.

Notes

[1]M. Henri Focillon, "Introduction to Art Populaire," in Robert F. Trents, *Hearts and Crowns* (New Haven: New Haven Colony Historical Society, 1977), p. 16.

[2]*Ibid.*, pp. 16-17.

[3]See John L. Fisher, "Art Styles as Cultural Cognitive Maps," in *Anthropology and Art, Readings in Cross-Cultural Aesthetics*, ed. by Charlotte M. Otten (Garden City, New York: The Natural History Press, 1971), pp. 141-162.

[4]Holger Rasmussen, "The Origin and Development of the Danish Folk Museum" (Copenhagen: Museum Off-Print Nationalmuseeet, 1966), p. 10.

116   Popular Culture in Museums and Libraries

[5]*Ibid.*

[6]*Ibid.*

[7]Haaken Shetelig, *Norske Museer Historie* (Oslo), p. 191.

[8]See Richard W.E. Perrin, *Outdoor Museums* (Milwaukee: Milwaukee Public Museum, 1975), pp. 5-27 and Ian Finlay, *Priceless Heritage: The Future of Museums* (London: Faber & Faber, 1977), pp. 160-168.

[9]Fartein Valen-Sendstat, *The Sandvig Collections Guidebook,* trans. James D. Edmondston (Lillehamer, Norway, 1977),p. 10.

[10]Erling Welle-Strand, *Guidebook to the Museums of Norway* (Oslo: The Royal Ministry of Foreign Affairs, 1974), p. 4.

[11]"Introduction," *The Austrian Open-Air Museum at Stubing,* English brochure, p. 1.

[12]Franz Colleselli, *Companion Guide Through the Museum of Tyrolean Folk Art* (Innsbruck: Museum of Tyrolean Art, 1977),p. 3.

[13]Holger Rasmussen, *Extractum ex Ethnologia Europaea,* Reprint, Vol. IV (1970), p. 74. See also J.W. Higgs, *Folk Life Collections and Classifications*, Handbook for Museum Curators (London: Museums Assocs., 1963), pp. 39-50.

[14]*Ibid.,* p. 76.

[15]Bo Bramsen, *The History of The Old Town Museum in Aarhus* (Aarhus, 1971), p. 207.

[16]*Ibid.*

[17]Eva-Lis Bjurnman, *Nordic Folk Art* (Stockholm: Nordiska Museet, 1966).

[18]Robert Wildhaber, *Swiss Folk Art* (published jointly by the German Arts Council and Pro-Helvetia Foundation, 1968), p. 9.

[19]See J. Geraint Jenkins, "The Use of Artifacts and Folk Art in the Folk Museum," in *Folklore and Folklife: An Introduction,* ed. by Richard M. Dorson (Chicago and London: Univ. of Chicago Press, 1972), pp. 497-516.

[20]Ray B. Browne, "Introduction," in *Melville's Israel Potter: A Pilgrimage and Progress,* by Arnold Rampersad (Bowling Green, Ohio: Bowling Green Popular Press, 1969), pp. iv-v.

[21]Abraham Kaplan, "Notes Toward a Definition," in *Popular Culture and Curricula,* ed. by Ray B. Browne and Ronald J. Ambrosetti (Bowling Green, Ohio: Bowling Green University Popular Press, 1972), pp. 5-6.

[22]Russel B. Nye, *The Unembarrassed Muse: The Popular Arts in America* (New York: The Dial Press, 1970), p. 3.

Fig. 1 "Ofenbauerin" at the Austrian Museum fur Volkskunde, Vienna. Standing in a period room setting this ceramic stove depicts a life-size female figure which presents an imposing focal point for the room. This stove combines functional and cultural values, as folk art forms frequently do. (Photo courtesy of the Austrian Museum fur Volkskunde)

Fig. 2 "Joululinto" at the National Museum of Finland, Helsinki. This carved bird with young has a ceremonial quality as it was hung over the Christmas dinner table to represent the Holy Ghost. The carving technique relies on the use of a soft wood which can be split and bent to create a fan-like effect. Today variations of this form are still produced by local craftspeople for sale in "hemslojd" (regional craft) shops in Scandinavia. (Photo courtesy of National Museum of Finland)

Fig. 3 Interior of a dwelling house at the Glomdalsmuseet in Elverum, Norway. The influence of the early models for folk museums has helped shape the approach to the relatively new Glomdalsmuseet. Here one experiences Bernard Olsen's goal, transported "far away in time and space from the crowded modern exhibition." The painted panels in this room depict Jacob's dream. (Photo courtesy of Glomdalsmuseet)

Fig. 4 The Museum fur Deutsche Volkskunde, Berlin. This new modern museum has an active exhibition program that is well financed by the West German government. Extensive collections have all been developed since the second World War to replace the losses incurred at that time. (Photo courtesy of the Museum fur Deutsche Volkskunde)

Fig. 5 Interior of the Museum of Tyrolean Folk Art at Innsbruck, Austria. Here traditional folk art materials have been assembled in an old town building to underscore the contributions of Tyrolean folk artisanry to Austria's cultural heritage. (Photo courtesy of The Museum of Tyrolean Folk Art)

Fig. 6 Nils Olsson's Dalacarnas Workshop at Nusnas, Sweden. Once a folk form bound closely to traditional conservative community values, the "Dala horse" has since become the popular Swedish tourist item. Mass production and wide distribution, through even the finest department stores, has transformed this original folk form into a popular artifact.

Fig. 7 The Forge from Orbaeck, Denmark, at the Frilandsmuseet, Lyngby, Denmark. Within the Frilandsmuseet stands this forge building that enables the visitor a self-directed experience with the way the blacksmith lived and worked. This idyllic scene is typical of the settings provided at the Frilandsmuseet for reassembled buildings. (Photo: Marsha MacDowell)

Fig. 8 Costume exhibition area at the Museum fur Deutsche Volkskunde, Berlin. The stress of this exhibition technique has been on aesthetic values as the folk objects are placed in a gallery-like area that enables the viewer to assess the aesthetic merits of the exhibited objects. (Photo courtesy of the Museum für Deutsche Volkskunde)

Fig. 9 Fishing gear from Lubeck (ca. 1920) at the Landemuseums, Schleswig, West Germany. This exhibition exemplified the approach taken by folklorists to show the way that fishing nets were used through the years in the Schleswig-Holstein region. Such an undertaking with fishing collections is unique due to the scarcity of fishing collections and the amount of space necessary for adequate interpretation. (Photo courtesy of Landemuseums, Schleswig)

Fig. 10 Peasant furniture from Ostrobothnia, Finland, at the National Museum of Finland. Here furnishings are grouped according to object types (styles) from distinctive geographic regions and time periods in Finland. (Photo courtesy of National Museum of Finland)

Fig. 11 "Scherenschnitt" by Louis Sangy (ca. 1900) of Rougemont at the Schweizerisches Museum fur Volkskund, Basel. This paper cut-out scene is typical of a folk art form that has continued to be produced and today one finds popularized versions for sale as decorative accents. (Photo courtesy of the Schweizerisches Museum für Volkskunde)

"Museums, whether they like to admit it or not, are also in the entertainment business."

Edward A. Green, "Cleverly Rearranged Cabinets of Curios"

IX

Popular culture in a natural history museum? Definitely yes, says Edward A. Green in the following article. All museums are in the entertainment business, to mention one aspect of twentieth century popular culture, but like most natural history museums, the Milwaukee Public Museum incorporates ethnology into its scope of exhibition. In this fourth-ranked natural history museum of the United States, Green has been particularly interested in how people expressed their cultures in houses, shops and markets. While some of Green's dioramas and reconstructions represent traditional "primitive" cultures, others capture everyday aspects of twentieth-century life in Guatemala, India, Japan and "Old Milwaukee," where viewers can experience the beginnings of contemporary commercial culture. In addition to providing a profuse portfolio of photographs of some exhibits at Milwaukee, Green places the museum's function into historical, educational and philosophical perspective, and touches upon the problems of selection and adaptation in a museum whose subject is all the world.

Edward Anthony Green, art director at the Milwaukee Public Museum, served in the United States Coast Guard, World War II (1942-1946) in the American Theater of operations, the European-African Middle Eastern and Asiatic Pacific campaigns and is currently active in the Coast Guard Auxiliary. He holds a Master of Fine Arts degree from the University of Wisconsin-Milwaukee and has taught art at several colleges. Green has traveled extensively to most European countries, North Africa, Bermuda, Caribbean Islands, Panama, Caroline Islands, the Philippines, Japan and Korea, and as an active architectural designer he has assisted many museums in their exhibit planning programs, designed private homes in the midwest and a Baptist Missionary Church in Bamenda, British Cameroons. His paintings and prints have won awards in all the state's major art shows and numerous national exhibitions, and he has received a Ford Grant for Urban Neighborhood Design, a Viking Fund for museum seminars and study and a University grant for European museum study. Ed collects tinplate toy trains and he is a first baseman on the Museum Mummies, twice city champions in the Milwaukee Cultural Slow Pitch Softball League, with a 1978 batting average of .729.

Edward Anthony Green

Cleverly Rearranged Cabinets of Curios

"If only one measure of a society could be taken, most telling would be that which showed how it educated its people."

WE ARE LIVING in an increasingly complex world—the simple amount of information available can be overwhelming and a child encountering this fantastic plethora is faced with the chore of sifting and winnowing to create an orderly and understandable sequence. In earlier times for instance, maps were crude and inaccurate, ships moved slowly and erratically but explorers could tolerate both. Their modern space-traveling counterparts journey at vastly increased speeds. For them any lack of precision of navigational deviance, no matter how slight, means death. Planning and criteria designed for the simplified mechanics of earlier centuries no longer are useful, their place having been taken by complex machines and computerized calculations. A task imposed on all generations now is to seek out the fixed points of this involved world for such guidance as they can provide. Guidance that hopefully can begin to lead us out of the morass of waste, destruction, decay, the total annihilation of species, and the unthinking consumption of our natural resources that has gone beyond "alarming" and reached "desperate." This then, is the specific responsibility to which we have matured: to discover if the thinking, foreseeing, constructing animals that we are can preserve life on this planet and survive with grace.

Pitfalls abound at every hand and the learning mind is detoured in a variety of directions, some vastly attractive—one is hard pressed to escape their siren lure. We are grossly over-entertained and more available leisure time might as well be called unproductive time, for often it is filled with images and ideas that at best have little substance in themselves and at worst are downright misleading. Books, magazines, radio, television, movies, the stage all attempt to capture our interest and often the most easily accessible is the direction followed—many times, unfortunately, it is the least desirable route.

Museums, whether they like to admit it or not, are also in the entertainment business. That is, they compete for visitors with all other media and their successes are a direct result of their ability to attract. Their worth, then, follows as to how well this attracted audience grasps the message. It is the designer's task not merely to

125

attract the audience but to combine artifacts, statements, light, color, textures, sound and motion into a communicative whole.

An early encounter, as a design student, with the late Charles Eames, profoundly impressed me. He said, "Design is not the making of objects, but the making of ways to see. Objects alone cannot teach us enough about seeing—it is their juxtaposition in a meaningful whole that really communicates, rather the Gestalt of the total." The Eames house and working environment, like our own home, is filled with children's toys, paintings, trains, sculpture, baskets, dolls, plants, weeds, flowers, fruit, pewter, clocks, decoys, rugs, oil lamps, weather vanes, old signs, books, magazines, pottery, Indian, African and Eskimo art, pillows, weavings and so on and on. To a first-time visitor it is somewhat like being inside a Joseph Cornell box—and it very effectively tells that visitor what manner of people we are—it quickly communicates and answers questions. The viewers, children and adult, are given a chance to exercise their curiosity and experience the pleasure of discovery as they move through this kaleidoscopic melange of "around the world" gathered objects. But not all homes can express such stimulating wealth of human experience.

Growing up in a city, children are given fewer chances to explore, choose and create on their own. Much of the modern architecture is monotonous and boring, cars have made walking almost obsolete, students are bussed to school and we are all confirmed to the regimented beaten paths of our daily existence. But the chance encounter with the unexpected, the surprise around the corner can be provided by a good museum with its wealth of fascinating objects. Museums should be pleasurable or, to state it more directly, museums should be fun. If the people who create museum exhibits have fun in doing so, probably the visitor will enjoy their personal discovery and a stimulation and enrichment of mind, too. One can come away from a museum visit having absorbed a great deal of information without feeling fatigued or confused in spite of having been exposed to a large and varied collection. A visually complex exhibit that is well designed can subtly guide the viewer to inevitable associations and conclusions. Buoyed by these small successes the learning process can be a sought-after activity, and, with more knowledge, one's personal world can become more meaningful and complete.

The reader by now might be asking, "Why the strange title to this treatise?" "Cleverly Rearranged Cabinets of Curios" once captioned a newspaper review of the Milwaukee Public Museum's "People of the South Seas" hall, written by Frank Getlein, then art critic for the Milwaukee *Journal*. Beyond its obvious humorous intent lies a more searching, prodding implication. Knowing Getlein's style, his nimble twisting of words caused me to reflect on the success of my exhibition design—was it just *clever*, a rearrangement of specimens—was it successful at all? Fortunately, this occurred early in my museum career and I began to look at all exhibition presentations in a more thorough manner.

An often asked question of museum people is "At what age or educational level do you direct your exhibits?" This is a difficult question for a museum such as the Milwaukee Public Museum because a general museum audience is made up of a fairly representative population cross-section. University museums, or children's museums, or those that can anticipate a specific audience may deliberately gear their message and probably most do just that. Similarly museums containing the Elgin marbles, Rosetta Stone, the *Night Watch, Mona Lisa, Venus de Milo* (or a two headed calf for that matter) have a certain preconditioned audience that is usually satisfied with the object itself and often make no attempt to probe its relationship to time, place or relative importance. A general museum (be it natural history, physical science, historical or art), that is not blessed with spectacular artifacts must attempt to communicate in a more complete manner.

Museums as we know them began with the founding of the Ashmolean Museum in Oxford followed by the British Museum in London. Certainly, there were private collections long before these public repositories were created. Early man probably picked up a variety of interesting stones and some, more thoughtful than their primitive colleagues, doubtless wondered about these differences. Private collectors then, in their desire to share personal treasure formed the public museums. Sir Hans Sloane (1660-1753) spent his long lifetime collecting as his will states "books, drawings, manuscripts, prints, medals, coins, antiquities, seals, precious stones, mathematical instruments and pictures." Sloan's collection was purchased by the English Parliament at a fraction of its value, and installed in Montagu House which stood on the site of the present British Museum in Bloomsbury. The British Museum, as we know it today, was designed by Sir Robert Smirke, built in stages between 1823 and 1852 and still forms some of the modern buildings. The impetus of this foundation doubtless inspired a goodly number of collections to move into public exhibition and to assume a more permanent status.

The Milwaukee Public Museum started in 1882 and grew by a similar accretive process. But it has always been considered a bellwether in exhibition techniques with the renowned Carl Akeley creating the first diorama (Muskrat House 1890, still on exhibit) and continuing on through a succession of imaginative people who prepared the way for the innovators of our present staff.

Directly, or unconsciously sometimes, I search for better ideas and materials to tell our story which is exceedingly complex for a museum that attempts to "cover the world." This ambitious approach is fraught with difficulties as any attempt to condense so vast a statement into a mere 160,000 square feet of exhibition space is bound to present what probably is an impossible challenge. To condense that much, some human common denominators must be found.

One approach we have used with some success appears in our comparative house types. Having traveled extensively in Europe, Canada and the United States observing hundreds of museums and their audiences I noted the undeniable popularity of open air museums. Originating with such places as Skansen in Sweden (1891) with other excellent examples as Lyngby, Denmark—Bygdoy, Norway—Graz, Austria—Arnhem, The Netherlands—Bokryk, Belgium and their United States counterparts at Williamsburg, Sturbridge and Greenfield Villages and now underway, Old World Wisconsin at Eagle, these museums pack a lot of information into their buildings. Placing everyday objects, furniture and costumes in a complete home environment relates to other people in other times and climes, helping viewers to understand the inhabitants on a people-to-people relationship. This was brought home to me by an incident involving our son, Jeremy, then a kindergartner. His teacher asked if I could conduct a tour of the museum for her class that would take about an hour and a half. Casting about for an idea that would communicate with these youngsters I asked how many of them lived in houses. About 90% of waving hands indicated that percentage did indeed live in a house. Noting some non-rising hands, I asked where they lived. "In an apartment," responded one bright lad, showing that his tender years did not prevent him from making what might be considered a rather subtle distinction for a youngster. Realizing I now had a handle on the problem I responded by explaining we would all vicariously visit the earliest apartment dwellers at Mesa Verde as well as more recent Hopi Pueblo tenants. This seemed to make sense to my youthful audience and I proceeded to "Pied Piper" them through the museum halls. Five-year-olds' imaginations fairly bubbled over, questions and comments flowing freely. For me it was a totally satisfying experience and apparently the kids enjoyed it too. I was especially gratified to receive a letter from one child's parent who wrote, "Our Kevin came home chattering in what was to us, a strange vernacular. We were so intrigued, a visit to the museum as a family became a must. Kevin proudly retraced the route of your tour and gave special attention to the Hopi Pueblo. Believe me, we learned a good deal from our child so obviously the museum is doing a good job in its educational program."

The early success of our Streets of Old Milwaukee, with its turn-of-a-century shops, offices, houses and nickolodeon encouraged us to create more house types featuring people of the world. This minimally labeled presentation provides a pleasant change of pace plus a fine opportunity to play Peeping Tom through the windows of the homes of a variety of other people. I will not attempt a complete catalog here because the accompanying photos can introduce a capsule tour of significant house types. Much better than case exhibits with their more extensive labeling and better, too, than two-dimensional presentations, the slightly scaled down (because of a nineteen foot maximum ceiling height) habitations communicate very directly. Consider the 1890s barber shop with its neat rows of personalized shaving mugs and brushes, the shampoo sink, razors, scissors, spittooon, and yes, the *Police Gazette*—immediately identifiable as a man's world. Youngsters who have never been in even a modern barber shop can, by association, tick off the names and, in most cases,the functions of many items they see. It is a matter of giving a viewer that fixed point of reference, assuming some prior knowledge and taking off from there.

Milwaukee Public Museum-goers can contrast the designed serenity of a Japanese home and garden with the nearby gaudy gold and red activity of a Chinese dwelling and Joss House, the icy coiled symmetry of an Eskimo igloo with the airy stilt houses of the Philippines, or experience the bustle and variety of a Guatemalan or old Delhi marketplace, the marvelous portability of a Blackfoot Indian tipi or the solid practicability of an adobe pueblo.

Another veteran service department at the Milwaukee Museum, Education, has developed superb programs expanding the houses of the world theme by establishing and stocking convenient storage closets containing a multitude of associated items that allow a "hands on" philosophy of direct usage. Thus a butter churn, brick mould or a flail can become a living demonstration, and once experienced, a part of that child's working knowledge. As we are all God's children, uniquely different yet with many similarities, communication and understanding can erase fears and misunderstandings that often lead to difficult to overcome barriers.

Museums are wonderful educational facilities, at once great explorable attics and at the same time friendly communicators. A pleasant first visit can result in continued interest for the viewer and desire for more and varied experiences, enabling him to develop his abilities, his individual judgment and his sense of moral and social responsibilities.

"Cleverly Rearranged Cabinets of Curios" indeed! To paraphrase Will Rogers: "I have seldom met a museum I didn't like." Some are marvelously musty, dusty collections, some are lovely indoor/outdoor assemblages that are in themselves art works. Louisiana, at Humlebaek, near Copenhagen comes immediately to mind. Others again are splendid organizations of fascinating materials with the transportation museum at Lucerne a perfect example. The few that I would find fault with are those that are "over designed." In other words, the exhibit designer's efforts are too much in evidence.

A few simple questions could be asked: does the museum really answer the needs of the viewer, or is it calculated to fulfill the desires of the museum professionals for creative activity and self expression? Is its message understandable? Does it allow for the exercise of the viewers' own imagination? Are the statements truthful and accurate?

I will beg the reader's patience to allow me to close with a personal anecdote which pretty well sums up my own philosophies.

Having concluded a talk in which I had apparently infected the audience with much of my own enthusiasm a listener jumped up with the comment, "You must really love museum work." To which I replied, "Don't tell my director but I would take a stiff pay cut and still completely enjoy my vocation." My wife, also in the audience, initially dumfounded me by replying, "That's not true," but then concluded with, "Ed would work at most any other job and then spend more hours volunteering his services to the museum at *no* pay!" To which I will have to say, "I most emphatically agree."

Portfolio
Comparative House Type Exhibits at the Milwaukee Public Museum

The comparative house type exhibits of the Milwaukee Public Museum are highly concentrated educational experiences at the same time that they are entertaining to the casual visitor. Viewing the everyday lives of remote cultures and relating these to the human common denominators of houses and yards helps contemporary visitors to recognize worth in their own homes, and to find unity in a complex world. Unlike case exhibits, which approach the problem of cultural complexity by means of separation and analysis, the house type exhibits deal with complexity by integration in human terms. The actual number of individual cultural artifacts included in each exhibit is astounding, showing their practicality for solving the ever-present problem of exhibition space in an indoor general museum. Notice that in almost all instances, the exhibits typify the *life of the people* rather than the exceptionally wealthy or sophisticated elite.

Although the *Streets of Old Milwaukee* exhibit is not strictly "twentieth-century popular culture," representing the last decade of the nineteenth century, the specific houses and the artifacts within have been selected for comparison with contemporary Milwaukee and everyday life of the present moment. Several of the businesses represented are very active at the present time. In addition, it will be noted that themes are selected to intersect with other cultures, such as the optometrist in modern Old Delhi, the food preparation in the Hopi Pueblo and colonial America, the clothing and fabrics throughout.

Other aspects of contemporary popular culture that have been built into the exhibits are comments upon prejudicial stereotypes and modern social issues. The Old Delhi exhibit has a "lady doctor" signboard, the Hopi exhibit shows a male doing "woman's work," the African and Spanish-Colonial exhibits counter the negative stereotypes of "primitivism" that have been so injurious to American blacks and Spanish-surname minorities. Ecological, proxemic, religious and familial commentaries are implied in every exhibit, and, consistent with the overall mission of a natural history museum, plants and animals are situated to relate to nature dioramas elsewhere in the museum.

Finally, in regard to the "entertainment business" of a museum, Edward Green has placed humorous surprises in many of the exhibits which delight both children and adults. Green was the designer of the majority of these exhibits.

All photos courtesy The Milwaukee Public Museum.

Fig. 1 The first museum diorama/muskrat house 1890/by Carl Akeley

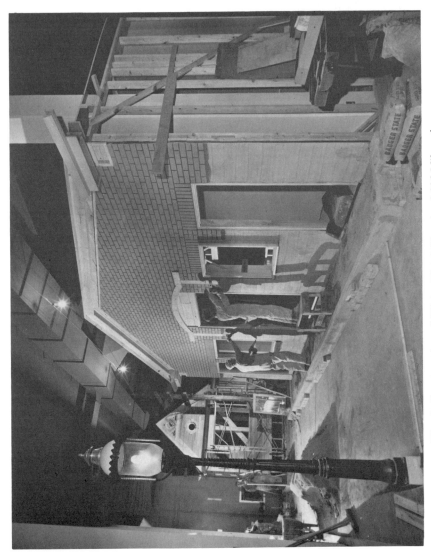

Fig. 2 Construction of Pfister Hotel/Streets of Old Milwaukee

Fig. 3 Grand Avenue/Streets of Old Milwaukee/Chapman's Millinery, Pastime Nickelodeon, Schlitz Saloon

Fig. 4 Original Mader's Comfort/Mader's is now one of Milwaukee's best known restaurants

Fig. 5 Chapman's Millinery/Edith Quade, Director of Education in period costume

Fig. 6 Biddle Street/Apotheke (Apothecary) Early Milwaukee German Signage

Fig. 7 View from balcony/Eschweiler House, Optometry Shop, real Wellsbach gas street lights.

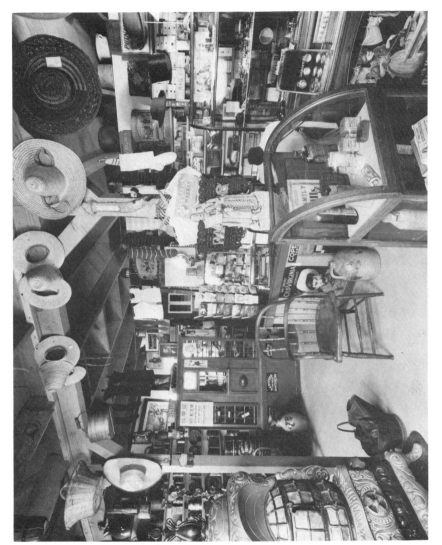

Fig. 8 Interior of Kuhm's General Store/over 3500 items from Herbert Kuhm collection

Fig. 9 Japanese house and garden/the author's favorite design project

Fig. 10 Massive defense walled Chinese house

Fig. 11 Snow igloo interior Netsilik eskimo/Boothia Isthmus/beautifully functional and well designed—seal skins hanging from toggles imbedded in snow walls and roof. Interior temperature can be 50 while exterior temperatures are 30-40 F.

Fig. 12 Phillipine stilt house/Bagobo Tribe/Mindanao/designed by Jim Kelly

Fig. 13 Papuan men's house/New Guinea/skulls of slain enemies decorate entrance designed by Jim Kelly.

Fig. 14 Hopi Pueblo/Arizona/Made of Adobe—Sun dried bricks

Fig. 15 Hopi Interior/Females Cooking—Male weaving

Fig. 16 Kiva of the antelope society/Hopi Indians/Arizona

Fig. 17 Blackfoot Indian Tipi/Northern Montana

Fig. 18 Wealthy house interior/sedentary people of North Africa

Fig. 19 Caribbean courtyard/Mexico, Panama, The Antilles. This employs case exhibits without destroying the effect of housetypes/designed by Lee Tishler

Fig. 20 Spanish colonial interior/Ecuador. Visitors will recognize the antecedents to popular religions artifacts and furniture styles of today/designed by Lee Tishler.

Fig. 21 Early construction/European village opened 1979/France, Swiss Clock Tower, Germany. This exhibit represents the vernacular architecture of Milwaukee's major ethnic groups.

Fig. 22 Market Place/Old Delhi features a snake charmer, Barfi (Candy) brass, tin, silver, bangles, pottery, cobbler, bike and cloth shops/designed by Lee Tishler

Fig. 23 Child in costume using colonial fireplace utensils

Fig. 24 "Hands On" Exhibit using butter churn

Fig. 25 Twins enjoy old hand pump on horse trough in old Milwaukee exhibit

"At the Movie World location are the 1919 Pierce-Arrow Phaeton custom-built for Fatty Arbuckle, a 1949 Daimler Coupe Convertible built for Queen Elizabeth and a 1950 Cadillac Fleetwood that was bullet-proofed for the gangster Mickey Cohen."

Maurice Duke, "Motor Vehicle Museums"

X

One aspect of the energy crisis that will define the twentieth century is the very probable decline of the gasoline-engine personal vehicle. We may find that the centenary of the Duryea marks a final end to the Age of the Automobile, and our descendants will have to visit museums to savor that most democratizing, equalizing, entertaining and expressive institution of twentieth-century America, *the car*. Fortunately, automobile museums abound, and Maurice Duke has gathered here a descriptive listing of most of the major collections in the United States. The historic auto is here both in the character of earliest models and in cars of presidents, kings and generals. And the popular auto is here, as tin-lizzies, good ol' Chevies and hot rods, and as the vehicles from *Bonnie and Clyde* and *Batman*. In addition, this mass-produced popular artifact is shown to have remarkable regional dimensions during its first half-century.

Maurice Duke is a Professor of English and Director of Graduate Studies at Virginia Commonwealth University in Richmond. He has edited or contributed to nearly a dozen books in American literature and is the author of more than twenty articles on that subject. A founding and continuing editor of *Resources for American Literary Study,* he is also coeditor and weekly columnist for the Richmond *Times-Dispatch* Book Page, the literary section of Virginia's largest circulating newspaper. Professor Duke has published popular and scholarly articles on automobile history and automobile racing. He is a licensed amateur sports car racer and competes several times yearly on East Coast tracks. Readers who can supply information on other motor vehicle museums are invited to write to Dr. Duke.

Maurice Duke

Motor Vehicle Museums

THE COLLECTING, RESTORATION and display of automobiles from the past is a new phenomenon in American popular culture. As recently as the 1950s, teenagers were still taking cutting torches to what would not be considered priceless antique cars and converting them into the proverbial "hot rods," a personalized machine that can still be found in the countless rod and custom shows continually conducted throughout the country. By the late '50s and early '60s, however, a new attitude toward the automobiles of the past began to pervade American life. Men who had grown up in the early decades of the century began to view old autos with a nostalgic and romantic eye, and, in an attempt to turn back the calendar to an earlier age, they began buying the automobiles popular in their youth with an eye to using them as leisure vehicles.

At first the restoration and preservation of old automobiles were centered on the pragmatic attitude that they could be cleaned up a bit, fitted with rings and valves and given a coat of paint and put back to use. Soon, however, the notion arose that the cars should be restored to pristine condition, with every bolt, wire and rivet just as it was when the car came from the factory. From this idea grew the antique car clubs, swap-meets and collecting in general that permeates a large segment of the specialty automobile world of today. It is not unusual, for example, to find antique autos selling in the $100,000 range on occasion, and $25,000 collector's cars are commonplace.

With this kind of collecting activity now so popular in America, it follows that the owners of specialty and antique vehicles have been faced with the problems of how to store them. As might be expected, there is no single way, some priceless gems being stored in suburban garages, others in the most modern and sophisticated of museum conditions.

The information that follows is arranged alphabetically by state and includes all data that could be collected by using existing lists of automobile museums, local chambers of commerce, and leads given by individual collectors about others who were their acquaintances. It should be noted, however, that automobile museums pop up and disappear almost overnight as small quantities of cars change hands, or as expected revenue from a newly begun museum fails to materialize. It is highly unlikely, therefore, that the present study is complete. The author would appreciate receiving further information on other collections at the English Department, Virginia Commonwealth University, Richmond, VA 23284. The following list also contains information about some specialty machines, such as military vehicles, trucks and motorcycles.

Alabama

Although construction has not yet begun, anyone interested in the automobile should be aware of the planned International Motor Sports Hall of Fame at the Alabama Motor Speedway at Talladega (P.O. Box 777, Talladega, 35160). Scheduled to begin construction in 1980, the center will have an educational focus and a presentation format centering on the history of motor sports and general automobile design, construction, and safety. Various racing cars from the past are scheduled to be on display to visitors, including those formerly displayed at the Museum of Speed at Daytona Beach, Florida.

Arkansas

The Museum of Automobiles (Petit Jean Mountain, Morrilton, 72110) is an organization that displays automobiles on loan from collectors throughout the United States and abroad. The museum currently displays fifty-two vehicles, ranging from 1908 to 1967 models. About one-third of the display is changed annually. The display area is 22,500 square feet.

California

The Briggs Cunningham Automotive Museum (250 E. Baker St, Costa Mesa, 92626) consists of numerous automobiles which contributed many technical "firsts," were outstanding performers, or set new aesthetic values. Ranging from 1902 to the present, the cars found here span from the primitive to the exotic.

Housed in a specially built 30,000 square foot exhibition hall, the vehicles can be viewed from all angles, including interiors and engines. Almost all the vehicles are kept in running condition, being given "exercise periods" and preventive maintenance, as opposed to the usual practice of putting them in preservatives.

Operation, maintenance, and overhaul is conducted by a group of experts from the museum's shop.

To enhance further this display, one can also find many engines and components on display. Some of these are in cutaway form and operable by the flick of a switch.

Movie World (6920 Orangethorp Ave., Buena Park, 90620) houses a collection that was started twenty-five years ago and consists of approximately five hundred automobiles and one hundred motorcycles.

The collection contains historic movies cars such as the Hannibal 8 and Leslie Special from the movie *The Great Race* and the 1931 Ford Roadster that was used in the movie *Bonnie and Clyde.*

Autos owned by famous people are also part of this collection. At the Movie World location are the 1919 Pierce Arrow Phaeton custom-built for comedian Fatty Arbuckle, a 1949 Daimler Coupe Convertible built for Queen Elizabeth and a 1950 Cadillac Fleetwood that was bullet-proofed for the gangster, Mickey Cohen. Special collectable autos also at the Movie World location are a 1933 Pierce Arrow, Serial #1, built for the Chicago World's Fair, a 1929 Rolls-Royce custom redesigned in 1936 for the Countess de Frasco by Darin of Beverly Hills (it still holds the title of most elegant Rolls-Royce ever built), and many more.

Automobiles and motorcycles are displayed in sets, along with other movie memorabilia.

This collection has been built by purchases at auctions, purchases of several small private collections, acquisition of all of 20th-Century Fox auto collection, part of M.G.M. Studios, and Warner Brothers Studios collections.

The Los Angeles County Museum of Natural History (900 Exposition Boulevard, Los Angeles, 90007) has a collection of automobiles that range in time from 1900 to 1963. Its strength, however, lies in the pre 1920 era. In 1970 this museum began an automobile restoration program. An average of one car is restored each year, at which time it is placed on display.

Colorado

The Colorado Car Museum (1803 N. Cascade Ave., Colorado Springs, 80907) centers primarily on the early days of motoring and on luxury cars associated with historical personages. Vintage cars are displayed among scenes recreating the past along with period music and costumed mannequins. Examples of the luxury cars on display include President Kennedy's 1963 Lincoln Four-door convertible made for him by the Lincoln-Mercury division of the Ford Motor Co.; the 1950 White House Lincoln limousine for President Harry S. Truman and also in the White House fleet during President Dwight Eisenhower's administration; the armored 12-cylinder Lincoln limousine which was the White House limousine for President Franklin D. Roosevelt; the Phantom II Rolls-Royce limousine custom built for Portugal's last king, Manuel II; the Daimler limousine given by the British Royal Air Force as a wedding gift to Queen Elizabeth and Prince Phillip; and the sporty Lancia built for Mussolini's flamboyant son-in-law, Count Ciano.

The Forney Transportation Museum (1416 Platte Street, Denver, 80202) contains over 250 historic items, including automobiles, carriages, motorcycles, and steam engines. The automobiles date from the 'teens, '20s, and '30s, the two motorcycles from the '20s. Early passenger buses, trucks, trolleys, and tractors are also on display.

Dougherty Antique Collection (U.S. 287, Longmont, 80501)

Fig. 1 Auto Racing Hall of Fame in the new speedway museum, Speedway, Indiana. (Photograph courtesy Indianapolis Motor Speedway).

Fig. 2 Popular as an early police motorcycle, this model was also widely used by the military in World War I. (Note the tank-mounted hand shift lever).

Fig. 3 Top: An exhibit of antique fire fighting equipment flanks the Henry Ford Museum automobile collection, which includes a 1956 Ford Thunderbird with its door open for inspection.
Bottom: Bicycles and aircraft share attention in the Transportation Collection of Henry Ford Museum. A 1909 Schacht automobile is on exhibit in front of—among other items—the Oriten ten-man bicycle, the 1926 Fokker F. VIII Trimotor which was the first aircraft to fly over the North Pole and the smaller 1946 Piper J-3 Cub, which is suspended in a flight attitude. (Photographs courtesy Henry Ford Museum).

traces the development of the automobile during its first twenty-five years. Electric and steam cars are included along with the familiar gasoline-powered vehicles. The collection also features trucks, a 1915 Stanley Mountain Wagon, an 1967 Concord Overland Stagecoach, gas tractors, and steam traction engines. Items are displayed in a 20,000 square foot precast concrete building.

The Veteran Car Museum (2030 S. Cherokee, Denver, 80223) houses some two dozen antique and classic automobiles covering nearly seventy years of the history of motor cars. The collection ranges from what is believed to be the oldest operating gasoline car in the state of Colorado through a number of classic American makes, one or two French marques, several British luxury vehicles—which in their day were the pride of the continent—all the way to a custom built Rolls-Royce costing over 20,000 dollars when new.

District of Columbia

Vehicle Hall of the Smithsonian Institution (Washington, 20560) in the Museum of History and Technology presents vehicles which are propelled by three different means: horsepower, motorpower, and manpower. Emphasis is upon the development of these types in the United States. Although the collection is relatively small, it contains a number of significant vehicles.

The central area of the hall contains automobiles and the few motorcycles held in the collection. Notable in this section are the numerous pioneer motor vehicles which represent the first efforts of American inventors; the 1869 Roper steam velocipede, the 1880 Long steam tricycle, the 1894 Haynes automobile, and the 1894 Balzer. Early production cars of Autocar, Olds, Winton, Riker, White and Franklin are also found in this area. Other interesting automobiles of this early era are the racing cars of Alexander Winton, Bullet No. 2 having been driven by the famed Barney Oldfield, and the 1903 Winton which was the first car to be driven from coast to coast. Most of these automobiles are powered by gasoline engines, but there are examples of steam and electric powered cars in the collection.

Commerical motor transport is represented in the two northern corners of the hall. In one corner is a 15-passenger White bus of 1917, with a body by J.G. Brill, while in the other corner is a 1930 Mack truck, Model AC, familiarly known as a Mack Bulldog. Close to the truck is found the first fire fighting equipment, both of horse and man-drawn types.

Not all of the vehicles in the Smithsonian Institution collection are exhibited in the Vehicle Hall. Because of space limitations, approximately half of the collection must remain in the reference collection. A rotation program is in effect, so that all restored vehicles are exhibited to the public over a period of years.

Florida

Bellm's Cars and Music of Yesterday (5500 North Tamiami Trail, Sarasota, 33580) displays 170 antique, classic, and race cars. Included among them are a Rickenbacker, Dorris, Moon, and Mercer. Indianapolis race cars, a three-wheeled Messerschmitt and other small cars of the 'teens, '20s and '30s are also highlights of this collection, which is organized as a tourist attraction.

Florida's Silver Springs (P.O. Box 370, Silver Springs, 32688) is another of that state's tourist attractions, whose Early American Museum section contains a collection of antique cars. The collection, which spans the history of motor car production, is on display in a specially constructed wing of the facility. It contains, among other automobiles, a 1904 Baker Stanhope electric, a unique Gaylord Sportsman, and a Rumpler, one of only two that were built.

Georgia

Stone Mountain Park (P.O. Box 788, Stone Mountain, 30086) is a 3,200 acre park, part of which is devoted to the Antique Auto and Music Museum. Several cars from the teens and '20s are on display among period settings.

Illinois

The Chicago Historical Antique Automobile Museum (3200 Skokie Valley Rd., Highland Park, 60035) has one of the most modern automotive display buildings in the country.

Visitors tour the complex in comfort as an even room temperature is maintained all year long. The entire facility is carpeted, and special musical background with narration accompanies each important vehicle display.

A unique feature of the new museum is "The Gallery," a museum within a museum. As visitors enter any one of five tall arched glass entryways, they are in the gallery. The gallery runs the entire width of the building, 300 feet, and contains a complete collection of automobilia, art and artifacts, rare parts collections, painting, photos, hundreds of model collector cars, and car displays.

A full range of rare antique and classic cars is represented in the museum collection, covering most important cars from Auburn to Zim. Unusual one-of custom cars are well represented, with some of the most famous cars ever built to tour the show circuit. The highlight of the museum collection includes its famous Hollywood Movie-TV "Cars of the Stars" collection, featuring the Batmobile with the Batcycle, Green Hornet Car, Bonnie & Clyde Death Car, Dillinger Car, Evel Knievel stunt motorcycle and Jump Car, 24 Karat Gold Continental, formerly owned by Elvis Presley and restyled by Barris of Hollywood, Munster Drag-U-La, Stutz Bearcat used to make the Bearcats TV series and the Banacek TV Mystery Car from the series of the same name. Cars of Kings and Presidents include President Lyndon B. Johnson's personal limousine.

The Musum has approximately 100 cars that are on show on a

rotating basis, with a maximum of 75 on display at any given time.

Chicago's Museum of Science and Industry (57th St. and Lake Shore Drive, Chicago, 60637) has some twenty vehicles on display. The vehicles are presented in several halls and a racing room in which Craig Breedlove's "Spirit of America" and "Spirit of America Sonic-1," both of which broke land speed records may be seen.

The cars to be seen at Time Was Village Museum (1325 Burlington St., Mendota, 61342) span the years from 1902 to 1963. Housing a total of 41 cars, the museum has its vehicles on display in a separate building devoted entirely to automobiling. Among the items included are car accessories, license plates, early lights, horns, and self-starters.

Indiana

The Auburn-Cord-Duesenberg Museum (Auburn, 46706) contains three showrooms of automobiles from the 1930s: the Ford, Essex and Chevrolet from the common man, the Auburn, Cord and Duesenberg for the cut above the rest, and finally the Rolls-Royce, Cadillac and Mercedes-Benz. The forgotten Auburn-built McIntyre, Kiblinger, and Imp are also here, as are the obscure Winton, Locomobile, and Rauch-Lang. More than 80 automobiles are on display.

The Elwood Haynes Museum (1915 S. Webster St., Kokomo,) was developed as a memorial to the life and accomplishments to one of America's automobile pioneers. In addition to memorabilia connected with the Haynes family, the museum displays two 1923 Haynes autos and one 1923 Apperson, built by the Apperson brothers, Elmer and Edgar, who were associated with Haynes early in his automotive career.

The Indianapolis Motor Speedway's Hall of Fame, (Speedway, 46224) is one of the outstanding structures of its kind in the United States with 96,960 square feet of floor space.

Dozens of race cars are on display in the east wing; and most of the west wing is devoted to a representative collection of classic and antique passenger cars.

Among the race cars on display are eighteen that have accounted for twenty-two Indianapolis victories. The four cars which have won twice are the Boyle Maserati (Wilbur Shaw, 1939-40), the Blue Crown Spark Plug Special (Mauri Rose, 1947-48), the Fuel Injection Special (Bill Vukovich, 1953-54), and the Belond Special (Sam Hanks in 1957 and Jimmy Bryan in 1958).

Other winning cars in the Speedway collection are Ray Harroun's 1911 Marmon Wasp, Joe Dawson's 1912 National, Rene Thomas' 1914 Delage, the Duesenberg which Jimmy Murphy drove to victory in the 1921 French Grand Prix before winning the 1922 Indianapolis race in the same car with a Miller engine, Louis Meyer's 1928 Miller special, Fred Frame's 1932 Miller-Hartz Special, George Robson's 1946 Thorne Engineering Special, Lee Wallard's 1951 Belanger Special, Bob Sweikert's 1955 John Zink Special, A.J.

Foyt's 1961 Bowes Seal Fast Special, Rodger Ward's 1963 Leader Car 500 Roadster, Parnelli Jones' 1963 Agajanian Willard Battery Special, Foyt's 1964 Sheraton-Thompson Special and Bobby Unser's 1968 Rislone Special.

The building in which these cars are displayed is 270 feet long and 220 wide. A transparent dome provides as much natural light as possible.

The J. William Goodwin Museum (South Main at Walnut Street, Frankfort, 46041) has a number of rare vehicles on display, all in operating condition, including a 1932 Duesenberg, 1937 Cord, 1936 Auburn, 1918 Stutz Bulldog, 1905 Gatts, 1904 Haynes-Apperson, 1927 Bugatti, 1900 Frisbie—the only unit ever built—1915 Briscoe—with one headlamp mounted in the center of the radiator—1934 Duesenberg Coupe Convertible with rumble seat, 1914 Stutz Bearcat, 1940 LaSalle handcarved hearse, 1915 Rauch-Lang electric lady's car, and a 1934 Duesenberg chassis with a town-sedan body built to Goodwin's specifications.

Included in the collection is also the first racer to be painted green, a color long considered by race car drivers to bring bad luck. It ran at the Indianapolis 500 in 1946, and was driven by Jimmy Jackson.

In addition to being an antique, each car in this collection is distinguished by some unusual design feature. In 1905, for example, A.P. Gatts built five cars with rear-end cranks, a departure from the conventional front-end cranking systems used by almost all automobiles before the self-starter was adopted. The Gatts two-seater in the Goodwin collection is the only one of the five still in existence, verified as such by a signed statement presented by Gatts to Goodwin.

The 1906 Cadillac has a one-cylinder 10 h.p. engine under the seat. It is cranked from the side. Because Haynes-Apperson was in business for little more than a year, Goodwin's 1904 model is one of few that are still around. Haynes, in 1893-94, made what is said to be the first American "horseless carriage," now in the Smithsonian Institution.

Kansas

Two World War II military vehicles—one a Cadillac staff car—and a 1914 Rauch Lang electric car, are displayed at the Dwight D. Eisenhower Library in Abeline, Kan. 67410 while the Kansas State Historical Society (Tenth and Jackson St., Topeka, 66612) exhibits a Great Smith—a car manufactured by the Great Smith Automobile Company in Topeka in 1908—and a Thomas.

A private Kansas automobile museum, not open to the public, is Wheels of the World Auto Musem (Grandview Plaza, Junction City).

This stable, the Lacer collection, includes mostly original cars put into storage fifteen to thirty years ago, some of which have less than ten thousand miles on them. Lacer has owned over a thousand cars of 130 different makes. The collection now includes sixty-five makes of classic, antique, foreign, special interest, vintage sports, custom, and unusual cars. For contrast, a 1928 Rolls-Royce Phantom I Limousine stands next to a custom-built ultra-streamlined roadster.

Some of the outstanding cars include a 1939 French Delahaye convertible by Henri Chapron, a 1937 BMW two-passenger convertible, a 1950 Allard four-passenger tourer, a 1931 Reo Royale Victoria coupe, a 1941 Hupmobile, a 1921 Dodge, a Riley convertible, a Cord, and an Airflow; also Mercedes, Cadillacs, and members of the MG family. The collection also contains toys, brochures, sales literature, and many other items pertaining to automobiles.

Kentucky

The Patton Museum of Cavalry and Armor (P.O. Box 208, Ft. Knox, 40121) was established to preserve historical materials relating to cavalry and armor and to make these properties available for public exhibit and research. The museum is administered by the U.S. Army Armor Center, Fort Knox, Kentucky, and is one of the largest in the U.S. Army Museum System.

In 1975, the second phase of the building was opened. This doubled the space for exhibits and provided room for the Emert L. "Red" David Memorial Library. The library contains reference materials relating to cavalry and armor, armored vehicles and equipment and other select military subjects.

Museum exhibits and displays depict the early history of Fort Knox and the development of cavalry and armor weapons, equipment and uniforms from the Revolutionary War to the present.

Other historically significant vehicles and equipment are in the outdoor exhibit area in Keyes Park, where the museum is located, and throughout the main garrison area of Fort Knox.

Louisiana

The Fort Polk Military Museum (P.O. Drawer R, Fort Polk, 71459) has over thirty U.S. Army wheeled and track-laying vehicles dating from 1940 to the present. Included are tanks, jeeps, cargo and shop trucks, ambulances, reconnaissance vehicles, high-speed tractors, amphibious vehicles, fire trucks, personnel carriers (wheeled, half-tracked), and self-propelled artillery.

Within its research collection the museum has approximately 1,800 photographs of different types of military vehicles. This collection includes vehicles dating back to 1898.

Massachusetts

The Museum of Transportation (316 Congress St., Boston, 02110) has in the last seven years transformed itself from an antique auto museum into an interactive programming and exhibitions institution. Its programs deal with the social history of transportation and include services to school, community and special needs groups.

The museum, in its collection of motor vehicles, has a heavy emphasis on the 1900 to 1920 period. It has also a small collection of high-performance vehicles from the '50s and '60s. The highlight of that collection is the museum's 315 Ferrari team car which was raced in the European and American Grand Prix circuit. It also has two Stanguellini Formula cars.

The museum's Anderson Collection is composed of fourteen early American and European motor cars. With one exception, they are in original condition, which makes them important as collection objects in that good original vehicles are considerably more valuable than restored motor cars. These cars include 1899 and 1901 Wintons, a 1905 C.G.V. touring car, a 1903 Gardner-Serpollet steam car, two early electric vehicles—a 1905 Electra—mobile and a 1908 Bailey.

Heritage Plantation of Sandwich (P.O. Box 566, Grove and Pine Sts., Sandwich, 02563) is a museum of Americana built on a 76-acre estate on Cape Cod. Its automobile collection is a representative cross section of American autos from the first gasoline carriage through the classic cars that were manufactured into the mid-1930s. The earliest car in the collection is a Stevens-Duryea. Other types include a "buckboard" made in Waltham, Massachusetts, a Sears "highwheeler," and an Oldsmobile Autocrat racing car. There are also two early sports cars, a Mercer and a Stutz' Bearcat, a steamer and an electric.

As for classic cars, the collection contains over a dozen recognized by the Classic Car Club of America; an Auburn, two Cadillacs (one has sixteen cylinders), a Cord, Duesenberg, Franklin, Kissel, LaSalle, Lincoln, three Packards, and an American-made Rolls-Royce.

The collection is in mint condition and all the cars run. Because there are more cars in the collection than the thirty-five that can be displayed at one time, there are occasional changes in the display area.

Michigan

The Alfred P. Sloan Jr. Museum (1221 East Kearsley St., Flint, 48503) centers on eighty-nine vehicles, the strongest part of the collection being Buicks and Chevrolets, while the Gilmore Car Museum (5272 Sheffield Rd., Hickory Corners, 49060) which was established in 1963, has some ninety vehicles on display. Shown in four restored barns, the collection features electric cars, steamers and other turn-of-the-century vehicles.

The Henry Ford Museum (Dearborn, 48121) exhibits one of the most comprehensive collections of automotive vehicles in the world.

The collection traces the development of motor vehicles since before the turn of the century. Historical highlights of the collection include an 1865 Roper steam carriage, one of the oldest existing fully operative cars in the United States.

America's first automobile offered for public sale, an 1896 Duryea motor wagon, the only survivor of thirteen sold that year, and Henry Ford's first vehicle, the 1896 quadricycle, are collection highlights. Others are the 1903 Model T, Ford's first mass-produced car; the Selden Auto Buggy, built in 1905 as a court test of Selden's 1877 patent, and a 1903 Cadillac, built in the first full year of the company.

The variations in design and advances in development are apparent throughout the collection, as evidenced by such cars as a 1904 Model L Packard (the Museum exhibits the only surviving model of the 198 originally produced), 1931 Bugatti Royale (one of eight of these models designed to be the largest and most luxurious cars ever built), 1931 Duesenberg cabriolet (America's premier classic), the innovative 1948 Tucker and a 1956 Ford Thunderbird.

Many vehicles in the Museum's collection have strong connections with history and famous individuals. President Taft's Baker Electric is in the collection, as are F.D.R.'s 1939 "Sunshine Special" Lincoln and the Presidential Lincoln used by Presidents Truman and Eisenhower. The Transportation Collection also spotlights personal cars of J.P. Morgan, Walter P. Chrysler, Charles A. Lindbergh, Thomas A. Edison. It also exhibits the 1940 Chrysler Crown Imperial that served as New York City's parade car for many years.

Racing cars are represented by such models as the 1902 Ford "999," driven by Barney Oldfield, and a 1955 Mercedes-Benz 300 SLR, which was driven to a world championship by Sterling Moss. It is the only Benz racer of its type on exhibit outside the Mercedes-Benz museum in Germany.

Commercial vehicles also share attention in the exhibit. An 1898 Riker Electric truck and a 1906 Rapid bus are two of the many earlier vehicles on exhibit.

The Henry Ford Museum Transportation Collection also includes exhibits of automotive parts and accessories. These include the first three-color, four-way electric traffic light, the first visible gasoline station and collections of head, side and tail lamps, speedometers and horns.

The collection's 1903 Aster and 1904 Indian are representative of some of the first motorcycles used in America. A 1909 motorcycle built by Harley-Davidson, the only American motorcycle manufacturer in business today, is typical of the early machines.

The Hendee Manufacturing Company of Springfield, Massachusetts, America's first manufacturer of motorcycles, is represented in the collection by a 1911 Indian. A 1910 Greyhound, a 1915 Eveready Scooter and Charles Lindbergh's 1919 Excelsior are other motorcycles to be found here.

The Poll Museum (353 E. Sixth St., Holland, 49423) has thirty cars on display, ranging from 1902 onward. This museum, which features other items as well, has antique, classic, and steam cars.

Included among them are a 1921 Pierce Arrow Roadster, a 1931 Rolls Royce Convertible Coupe, a 1948 Tucker, a 1906 White Steamer, and a 1906 Mercedes Touring car.

The National Museum of Transport (3015 Barrett Station Rd., St. Louis, Missouri 63122) centers on the history of the technology and design of transportation and communication. Visitors may see not only automobiles, but also locomotives, railway cars, streetcars, buses, trucks, horse-drawn vehicles, aircraft, as well as pipeline and communication devices. The fifteen cars and some thirty trucks and trailers are displayed lineally.

Montana

The Towe Antique Ford Collection (P.O. Box 748, Deer Lodge, 59722), advertised as being the most complete antique Ford collection on display, is located in Deer Lodge. There are about one hundred fully restored or good, original Fords representing the first thirty-nine years of the Ford Motor Company and at least one car for every year and model manufactured from 1903 to 1942 in the collection. At present, the collection consists of over 150 Fords and Lincolns, and continues to grow. The entire collection is owned by Edward Towe of Circle, Montana, and is displayed by the Powell County Museum and Arts Foundation.

Nebraska

Several Nebraska museums which house automobiles among a number of other artifacts, are available to the cultural historian and the vacationer alike.

Chevyland U.S.A. (Rt. 1, Box 159A, Elm Creek, 68836) as its name implies exhibits a collection of Chevrolets, while the Hastings Museum (Hastings) includes automobiles in its transportation section. Harold Warp Pioneer Village (Minden, 68959) displays in rows more than 250 automobiles, as well as 35 motorcycles from the past. The Plainsman Museum (210 Sixteenth St., Aurora, 68818) also displays antique cars in a linear fashion. And Sawyer's Sandhills Museum (Valentine) has a 1913 Imperial, a 1914 Jeffery, a 1916 Patterson, a 1910 Flanders and a 1924 Flint. Stuhr Museum of the Prairie Pioneer (Rt. 2, Box 24, Grand Island, 68801) displays thirty-five antique automobiles, along with a 200 piece exhibit of farming machinery.

Nevada

The world's largest automobile museum, Harrah's Automobile Collection, is located in Reno (Box 10, Reno, 89504). Open to the public year round, this giant collection contains a gallery of 1,100 restored or preserved vehicles. Not only is Harrah's the major collection in the country, but it is also one of the great auction houses and collection points for automobile collectors throughout the world.

New Jersey
   The New Jersey Antique Auto Museum (RD 1, Box 178-G, Wall, 07719) has over a hundred antique cars in this collection, some on display, some for sale.

North Carolina
   The Daniel Boone Settlement and Recreation Park (Hillsborough, 27278) holds several antique cars, among them a 1902 Cadillac which is billed as the oldest of that marque in existence. And the Estes-Winn Antique Automobile Museum (P.O. Box 6854, Asheville, 28806) displays cars dating back to 1905 in a separate building. The Transportation of the Greensboro Historical Museum (130 Summit Ave., Greensboro, 27401) displays a 1904 Reo, a 1906 Cadillac and two Model T. Fords.

Ohio
   The Allen County Historical Society (620 W. Market St., Lima,45801) holds six vehicles, the most important of which are a 1923 Milburn Light Electric,a 1909 Locomobile Sports Roadster and a 1906(?) Indian motorcycle. Also in this collection is a 1918 Gramm-Bernstein Liberty Truck.
   The Frederick C. Crawford Auto-Aviation Museum of the Western Reserve Historical Society (10825 E. Boulevard, Cleveland, 44106) has approximately 200 vehicles on display. Many of the cars in this museum, which maintains its own restoration staff, are displayed against period backgrounds. Vehicles from the last decade of the nineteenth century to the present are included in the collection. Programs of the museum are designed to help one understand and appreciate the discovery of the automobile and its present role in our lives.
   The Scio Pottery Company Auto Collection (Scio, 43988) houses over fifty motor vehicles from antique, classic motorcycles to race cars.
   Cars consist of Model A Fords, Chevrolets, Packards, Kaiser-Darrins, Thunderbirds, Corvettes, Rolls-Royce, Indy and Midget Racers.
   Featured in this display is the 1952 winner of the Indianapolis 500, the Agajanian Special 98 driven by Tony Ruttman, and car 97, the Belanger Special, driven by Duane Carter and Tony Bettenhausen.

Oklahoma
   An excellent collection of automobiles is on display at Antiques, Inc. (P.O. Box 1887, Muskogee, 74401). Owned by James C. Leake, who has one of the world's largest private collections of Rolls-Royces and Bentleys, the cars number sixty in all. Among the rarest of the vehicles, which also include motorcyles, are a 1901 Panhard et Levassor, a 1901 Locomobile Stanhope, a 1912 Unic, a 1924 Lanchester, a 1937 Hispano Suiza, and a magnificent 1911 Rolls-

Royce Silver Ghost, built for the Maharajah of Mysore of India.

Pennsylvania
The majority of the vehicles displayed in the Broyertown Museum of Historic Vehicles (P.O. Box 30, Broyertown, 19512) were built in the shops and early assembly lines of Berks County vehicle builders in Broyertown, Fleetwood, Hamburg, Kutztown and Reading, all centers of considerable vehicle production from the mid-1800s through the early 1920s. Historic Early Americana is well expressed in the vehicles; the Colonial Era, 1700 to early 1800s; the Horse Power Age, 1850 to 1870; the Horseless Carriage Age; the Brass Age of Automobiles; the Antique Period; Electric Vehicles and Commercial Motor Trucks. Also on display are fire apparatus engines, pumpers and hose carts dating from 1790 through 1937. In addition there are bicycles and motorcycles.

A superb collection of Harley-Davidson motorcyles is most professionally displayed in the Rodney C. Gott Harley-Davidson Motorcycle Museum (1425 Eden Rd., York, 17402).

The more than twenty-five motorcycles on display are rotated periodically so that the entire collection of almost one hundred machines is on display over a period of years.

The collection was compiled by Harley-Davidson through the selection of at least one motorcycle from each year's production, starting in 1903, and placing it on display. The collection continues to be augmented each year by selecting new and innovative motorcyles for the museum inventory.

Although the majority of the motorcylces are production models, there are a few custom-built and racing machines.

The museum is arranged in sections: an historical section, in which a typical machine for each decade of the company's history is displayed; a military and police section; a technological section; a section in which the evolution of the V-twin engine is traced; and a racing section. Adjacent to but not part of the museum is a motorcycle showroom in which each current model is displayed.

Paul H. Stern's Antique Car Museum (121 S. Main St., Manheim, 17545) displays a personal collection of mint restorations of antiques, classics (including a large number of Dual Cowl Phaetons), special interest and futuristic cars. This collection is said to feature the largest group of restored Chrysler antiques in existence. Also, fourteen cars of this collection have been judged as National First Prize winners by the Antique Automobile Club of America.

The Hall of Technology and Industry of the William Penn Memorial Museum (Box 1026, Harrisburg, 17201) has a number of vehicles exhibited on low pedestals with lightweight barriers around them. Among them are a 1902 Gardner Serpollet steam landaulet, a 1903 Mitchell Roadster, a 1903 Pierce Stanhope, a 1904 Franklin rear entrance touring car, a 1905 Autocar roadster, a 1906 De Dion Phaeton, a 1908 Sears roadster, a 1909 Rolls-Royce landaulet, a 1909 Stevens Duryea touring car, a 1910 General Vehicle Company electric truck, a 1912 Delauney Belleville town car, a 1913 Kearns roadster, a 1913 Electric Truck formerly owned by the Curtis Publishing Company, and a 1920 Harley-Davidson motorcycle, Sport model.

Swigart Museum (Huntington) is one of the oldest automobile museums in existence, featuring a rotating display of about forty vehicles, biographical sketches of their owners, and all sorts of automobile memorabilia. In addition, it publishes its own newsletter, the *Museum Park Gazette*, which centers on all facets of the automobile and how it relates to the popular culture experience in America.

Rhode Island

The Newport Automobile Museum (1 Casino Terrace at Bellvue Ave., Newport, 02840) is billed as featuring the largest collection of antique and classic cars in New England. The cars are displayed in an atmosphere of early motoring, with period murals used as backdrops.

South Carolina

The Joe Weatherly Stock Car Museum at Darlington International Raceway (Drawer 500, Darlington, 32532) is located in the heart of the nation's stock car racing country. In addition to the largest collection of the great stock cars of the past, this museum, named for one of the pioneer stock car drivers, contains a full range of racing memorabilia. A special technological feature is the display of myriad illegal racing parts confiscated from various racing teams over the years.

South Dakota

The Horseless Carriage Museum (Highway 16, Rapid City, 57706) advertises itself as displaying over one hundred vehicles, while the Pioneer Auto Museum (Highway 16 and 83, Murdo, 57559) has collected vehicles from over thirty states. The museum's ten-acre display area holds thirty buildings used to exhibit the cars. The museum also has several vintage motorcycles and myriad artifacts centering on prairie life in the early 1900s.

Tennessee

The Smoky Mountain Car Museum (Pigeon Forge, 37863) has on display some thirty automobiles including gas, electric and steam vehicles. The museum also has a number of different makes, including Duesenberg, Cord, Pierce Arrow and Cadillac. Among the special interest cars are singer Hank William, Jr.'s Silver Dollar Car, James Bond's (Secret Agent 007), Aston Martin, Stringbean's (a late performer of the television series *Hee Haw*) Cadillac, Buford Pusser's (star of the motion picture *Walking Tall*) car, and Al Capone's bullet-proof 1928 Cadillac; while the Dixie Gun Works

(Union City, 38261) devotes twelve thousand square feet to antique autos, motorcycles and assorted car parts.

Texas

The San Antonio Museum of Transportation (3801 Broadway, San Antonio, 78209) displays some fifty automobiles, among other transportation items. Some of the noteworthy automobiles in the collection include a 1933 Duesenberg, a 1906 Columbia, a 1933 Auburn Boat-tail Speedster, a 1926 Rolls-Royce Roadster, and a 1899 Locomobile Steamer. Display techniques used here are unusual for a transportation museum in that interest is not on quantity but rather visibility. Any vehicle in the collection can be photographed from at least three sides in its present location. Loan vehicles are ordinarily displayed for no more than nine months, so that variety is guaranteed.

The Pate Museum of Transportation (P.O. Box 711, Ft. Worth, 76101) is becoming known throughout the Southwest as a comprehensive collection of materials centering on myriad forms of vehicles, including automobiles, aircraft, buses and railroad exhibits. Containing just under fifty cars, including classic, antique, and special interest ones, the museum also has a 1,500 volume transportation library.

Virginia

The Historic Car and Carriage Caravan (Luran, 22835) exhibits sixty-three automotive specimens ranging from a rare 1892 Benz to a 1946 Daimler. Almost all the cars in this collection were built before 1930, most in the 'teens. The display features numerous accessories used in the early days of automotive transportation, and mannequins dressed in period clothes are stationed throughout the display.

Rohr's Antique Car Museum (P.O.Box 71, Manassas, 22110) exhibits a one-of-a-kind 1933 Rohr. Other cars in this private collection range from 1904 to 1933. Included also is a 1915 Harley-Davidson motorcycle.

The U.S. Army Transportation Center (Dept. of the Army, Ft. Eustis, 23604) has a Motor Vehicle Collection that includes twenty vehicles, most of which are trucks ranging in size from one-quarter ton to sixteen tons. The majority date from World War II, but there are also vehicles from the periods of the Korean Conflict and the Vietnam War. The first motorcycle in the collection is a recently-acquired Suzuki, used in Army tests in 1972.

Most of these trucks are on static display in the outside display park. An indoor exhibit on the "Red Ball Express" contains a two-and-a-half ton 6 x 6 truck and a one-quarter 4 x 4 "Jeep" in life-size diorama.

"...librarians should get on with the business of collecting popular culture now and simultaneously work out solutions to the problems associated with these unusual collections."

Barbara B. Moran, "Popular Culture and its Challenge to the Academic Library"

XI

Readers who are new to the popular culture field of study will find Barbara Moran's article particularly helpful. She provides a brief history of the movement, identifying key persons, institutions and journals as well as a generally accepted definition of the study area. This article is also an excellent introduction to the issues of the following articles, most particularly for Wayne Wiegand's detailed discussion of the causes and cures of elitism in the academic library, Maurice Crane's comments on copyright issues and Bill Schurk's experiences in collecting. Three more issues that are identified here have been touched upon in earlier articles about museums: the problems of professional training for popular culture, the need for interinstitutional networking, and the question of defining the limits of specialized collections. Moran's article is a valuable account of the "state of the art" of popular culture in today's academic library.

Barbara Moran holds degrees from Mount Holyoke College and Emory University. Before beginning doctoral study she was Head of the Library at Park School, Buffalo, New York. At the present time she is a student in a cooperative Ph.D. program in higher education and library science at the State University of New York at Buffalo.

Barbara B. Moran

Popular Culture and Its Challenge
To The Academic Library

POPULAR CULTURE IS BEING TAUGHT as a subject area in at least a thousand colleges and universities, and academic libraries are now faced with the question of how they can most effectively support that study. This question is complicated by the fact that the material studied in popular culture courses is unlike that traditionally studied in universities, and, for the most part, is material that librarians have traditionally considered unworthy of collecting. But since the mission of the academic library has always been to acquire the materials necessary to meet the educational and research needs of the university, academic librarians must become familiar with the field of popular culture and begin to develop collections in this area even if this collection development forces a change in the usual qualitative standards of acquisition used by academic libraries.

Although popular culture itself has existed for a long time, popular culture as a field of study in higher education is a relatively recent development confined mostly to the last decade. In 1967 Ray Browne arrived at Bowling Green State University in Ohio to become a professor of English. He established there the Department of Popular Culture, the Center for the Study of Popular Culture, and the Popular Press.[1] In 1969 the Popular Culture Association, the professional organization of scholars interested in the field, was formed. The PCA issued the following statement about its purpose:

The Popular Culture Association was founded to study thoroughly and seriously those productions both artistic and commercial designed for mass consumption. The founders were convinced that this vast body of material encompassed in print, film, television, comics, advertising and graphics reflects the values, convictions and patterns of thought and feeling generally dispersed through and approved by American society.[2]

This statement provides a succinct rationale for the study of popular culture, for the scholars interested in the field believe that a given society's values and beliefs are more accurately reflected in its popular artifacts than in its elite culture.

A look at the papers presented at the sixth annual PCA convention provides a fair idea of how popular culture is actually studied as well as an idea of the kinds of materials that are needed by scholars in the field. Some of the titles of the papers at that convention were: *Fate and Free Will in Contemporary Sports Novels; Jaws: A Jungian Interpretation; The Captain America Complex; Everyone Must Get Stoned: The Case for Rock Music; Flintstones as a Detrimental Cultural Myth; Gospel Music and Nashville; Kung Fu or the Resolution of the Dialectic; Morphology of the Halftime Show; Sensuality and Soap: The World of the Daytime Serial;* and *The Spy Story as Modern Tragedy.*[3]

In spite of, or because of, the fact that the material studied in popular culture is unlike that traditionally studied in higher education, interest in popular culture is becoming more and more widespread both in terms of the number of people studying it and in the diversity of their backgrounds. For example, Gordon Stevenson estimates that the number of scholars and teachers with a serious interest in the field could be conservatively numbered at 2,500.[4] Of particular interest to the librarian is the fact that most popular culture scholars have a home discipline outside popular culture. As a matter of fact, Bowling Green is the only university with a Department of Popular Culture. A look at the contributors to the *Journal of Popular Culture* provides an estimate of what proportion of popular culture scholars are from which disciplines. The discipline contributing the most authors to the journal throughout its first five years was English with 40.6%, the second largest number was from history with 15.3%, religion and/or philosophy was third with 13.9%, various interdisciplinary studies contributed 11.7% and sociology contributed 7.1%. Each of the other disciplines contributed less than 2.5%[5]

The journals in the field have proliferated along with the scholars. Not only is there the original *Journal of Popular Culture* but the Bowling Green Center for the Study of Popular Culture publishes the *Journal of Popular Film* and *Popular Music and Society.* In 1978 the Center decided to issue a new journal—*The Journal of American Culture*— because so many manuscripts were being submitted to JPC that the flood could not be handled. In 1977 two other universities began publication of journals in the field: *The Popular Culture Scholar* and *Popular Culture.*[6] In 1980 the Center began two new journals: *Clues: A Journal of Detection,* edited by Pat Browne, and *The Journal of Cultural Geography,* edited by Alvar W. Carlson. In addition an immense number of articles about popular culture appear in other journals, and the Popular Press at Bowling Green publishes about ten books in the subject every year.

It is difficult to ascertain exactly how many students are enrolled in courses in popular culture but classes in the subject are being taught in at least a thousand colleges and universities in all parts of the country. Popular culture has become an integral part of the curriculum in higher education.

Currently there are no data on the number of libraries that have begun to systematically develop collections in popular culture but most estimates are that the number is disappointingly small. The major reason for this lack of response to a new field of study seems to be that popular culture brings an entirely new element to the academic library and most librarians have not accepted popular culture materials as appropriate for inclusion in the academic library. As Wayne Wiegand points out, librarians have always been aesthetically conservative and "in our zeal to transmit our cultural heritage to future generations through high quality library collections, academic librarians follow an aesthetic conservatism in collection development procedures. We scan reviews to distinguish the best literature and then we buy."[7] Wiegand argues that traditional acquisition policies tend to narrow the scope of library collections to professionally accepted literature; in other words, libraries have confined their collection-building to the traditionally defined microscopic view of culture.

Wiegand thinks librarians must undergo an attitudinal change. He does not think they should drastically reverse the guiding principles and practices of current collection building activities because they are doing an adequate job of supporting the high culture interests of the educational clientele. Yet this approach does not go far enough—librarians must broaden their scope to exhibit a macrocultural perspective in building their collections and begin to serve those interested in popular culture also.[8] Once librarians accept popular culture as a valid area for research and study they will begin to shape their collection-building activities accordingly.

When academic librarians become aware that the faculty and students are using popular culture material in their studies, they will then have a rationale to begin acquiring such material. Gordon Stevenson contrasts the positions of the public and the academic library in buying popular culture material. Public libraries that decided to collect popular culture would have to make policy decisions which would affect the very substance of their services. Academic libraries are relieved of making policy decisions of this type by the faculty because academic libraries will acquire what they need to carry out the educational and research policies of the universities of which their libraries are a part and without which they would not exist. He asserts that for the most part it is safe to say that if popular culture studies flourish and if the ranks of the PCA grow, academic librarians will respond to these challenges and develop collections to support the study of popular culture.[9]

So in the future more academic libraries will begin to collect popular culture, and, in fact, some extensive collections of popular culture already exist. Libraries that are just beginning to collect in the field might want to study some of these already existing collections in looking for a model for their own development. The Center for the Study of Popular Culture's Library and Audio Center at Bowling Green University have probably the best developed library of popular culture with a collection of over 500,000 print items and an absolutely unequalled collection of records of popular music.

The large collection of hard-cover books includes mysteries, war, romance and adventure stories, juvenile series, old textbooks, hymnals, high school and college yearbooks. None of these types of material are generally included in a university library. The collection also includes a large number of books originally published as paperbacks. The periodical collections include many "newstand" magazines such as *True Confessions, Lunaticle, Police Gazette* and *Male* which are seldom saved by any libraries. The collection also includes comic books and underground newspapers. In additions to books and periodicals, the Popular Culture Library also collects movie, political and other posters, photographs, baseball cards, pennants, theater programs and political memorabilia.

The Audio Library contains many old records—popular music of every vintage and type including rock, gospel, blues, jazz, country and western, soul and folk. The library has over 600 hours of old radio shows such as *The Shadow* and *The Green Hornet* and another major tape collection of interviews with vaudeville performers, popular musicians and writers. Some of the library's prize recordings are early Ku Klux Klan discs.[10]

Another well developed collection of material in this specialized field can be found at Michigan State University Library's Russel B. Nye Popular Culture Collection which includes over 25,000 pieces of popular culture. The principle categories into which the collection is presently organized are: 1) comic art—includes the comic book and newspaper comic strip; 2) popular fiction—includes dime novels, story magazines, pulps, juvenile series boks, detective mystery fiction, science fiction, western fiction, and women's fiction; 3) popular information materials—includes almanacs, etiquette books, books of advice on life and love, elocution manuals, old school textbooks; and 4) material in print relating to the popular performing arts.[11]

Other libraries with large collections of popular culture are, of course, the unmatched collection of the Library of Congress, the University of Minnesota, The Center for Research Libraries, the New York Public and the Smithsonian Institution.

When other academic librarians decide to begin to collect popular culture where will they find the material needed to start such a collection? First, it is necessary to distinguish between the primary and secondary sources in the field.

The primary sources are books, films, television shows, and whatever artifacts are used to record and transfer popular culture information. Another group of primary sources is the documents concerning the creators of popular culture including materials as diverse as letters, diaries, annual reports of manufacturers and advertisements—in short the whole range of sources usually associated with historical and literary research. Secondary sources include the articles, studies, research reports, etc., which analyze, criticize, or comment on popular culture in any of its aspects.[12]

Primary and secondary sources that are current or recently

produced are fairly easy to acquire. Obviously though the older primary materials are often more difficult to obtain. Gordon Stevenson writes that the most important collections of popular culture are still in the hands of private collectors. They harvested popular culture when no libraries or museums were interested. Stevenson suggested that libraries should make overtures to these private collectors and try to convince them to donate their collections to libraries in return for assurance of their safe-keeping.[13]

Another source of the primary sources in popular culture is Salvation Army Stores, Goodwill Stores, estate sales, garage sales, even garbage picking. Bill Schurk, the librarian at the Bowling Green library, has written vividly about his treasure hunts from these sources to build his library collection.[14]

If it is impossible for libraries to get originals, reprint houses are going into the popular culture field. Xerox has a microfiche series that includes such periodicals as *Shadow* and *Success*. Arno Press has a historical reprint series of books of popular culture printed between 1800 and 1925.

If libraries are going to enter this new area of collecting, and I assume that they will, who will train these new-fashioned bibliographers? At least two library schools are already offering courses in popular culture and there may be more.

Gordon Stevenson has been teaching a course at the School of Library and Information Science at SUNY/Albany since 1972. This elective course, LIB 617, Popular Culture in the Library, has the following catalog description: "The nature and social function of the contemporary popular culture as disseminated by the mass media; the relationship between the popular culture and the library. Bibliographic sources, selection and acquisition problems."[15]

Stevenson uses for a textbook *The Unembarrassed Muse*, an historical study of popular culture in America by Russel B. Nye. After introductory lectures devoted to defining the field and the purpose of the course, Stevenson tries to demonstrate how values and beliefs are manifested in popular culture. Each example of popular culture subsequently examined is considered from the point of view of these values. Students read gothic novels, western novels, science fiction and crime novels and analyze each using reference points drawn from the literature about popular culture.

Stevenson concludes that the issue of popular versus elite culture cannot be avoided but a "discussion of salient points in this long controversy provides effective issues around which to summarize the course and consider the role of the library and the librarian to current mass culture."[16]

Fay Blake, a professor at the School of Library and Information Studies at Berkeley, teaches a course in Popular Culture and the Public Library but her course would also be applicable to academic librarians. She tries to get students to read, listen and look widely at the products of popular culture and to analyze the social implications of their application to the library.[17]

The American Library Association is becoming interested in popular culture also. For the first time ever, in January 1979, at ALA Midwinter in Washington, the Popular Culture Discussion Group met. Participants discussed popular culture and how libraries should respond to this new collecting challenge.

So academic librarianship is beginning to consider adopting a broader perspective in collection development but this movement is still in its beginning stages and there are major issues yet to be dealt with. For example, it is important to completely identify the existing locations of popular culture collections. As Jack Clarke wrote, "a guide to the research collections in popular culture is needed soon if we are to avoid unnecessary duplication and undue frustration by our unsatisfied patrons."[18] A beginning guide to locating library resources has been published. Michael T. Marsden published a National Finding List of Popular Culture Holdings and Special Collections in the Popular Culture Association's *Newsletter* in March, 1977. This is a far from complete list though covering 23 pages and librarians have been urged to register their holdings with Marsden at the Center for the Study of Popular Culture to try to make the list more comprehensive. After existing collections are identified, decisions should be made about collection development.

Should all academic libraries collect popular culture materials or should regionally centered depositories be designated?

Should certain libraries specialize in one type of popular culture as opposed to attempting to accumulate all types?

Since the rise of interest in popular culture has occurred during a decade when academic libraries have experienced cutbacks in funds available for acquisition, and since no single library would be willing or able to collect more than a fraction of the popular culture output, inter-institutional cooperation in acquisitions seems to make the most sense. What network systems should be set up to deal with popular culture items?

How should an interlibrary loan system operate to link scholars to popular culture? This is a difficult question because of the fragile nature of many items which were cheaply made and not intended to last. For instance, neither the Bowling Green Library nor the Nye Collection will send out on interlibrary loan any actual books or materials although photocopies are made for such use.

Closely related to this problem is the question of how these ephemeral materials can be preserved. Should libraries begin systematically microfilming such articles?

Another problem relating to interlibrary loan is the question of copyright law. Although much of the older printed material is in the public domain, the problem is especially tricky when dealing with the reproduction of copyrighted records or tapes.

Since both museums and libraries are collecting popular culture what is the proper collecting sphere of each? For instance, some of the items at the Popular Culture Library in Bowling Green are museum-pieces and the Smithsonian is collecting printed material. Should limits of collecting for each be clearly delineated?

How should libraries classify and catalog print and non-print popular culture items? Do special classification systems need to be constructed? Gordon Stevenson argues in favor of that point. He feels that as the discipline begins to shape up into different subfields and gets some sort of overall profile a modern classification system will be needed. "If there is one area where research by librarians could contribute to popular culture research this is it: the construction of a classification scheme to display the secondary literature in such a way as to show the structure of the field, its frequently discrete subdivisions, the relationship of its various parts and its relationship to other disciplines."[19] Stevenson advocates the construction of some sort of non-alphabetical system which would make use of facet analysis techniques and which would be used to provide a hard-copy classified printout and at the same time be structured to permit on-line interactive searching in automated systems. A system should be developed that could serve as a general national system, but that would also permit librarians to provide an automatic SDI (Selective Dissemination of Information) service to their patrons.

Another issue to be considered is where popular culture material should be kept in the library—in one central specialized collection, as at Bowling Green and Michigan State, or scattered throughout the collection? There are arguments in favor of both arrangements. It must be kept in mind that most universities do not have popular culture departments and that the study is now widely diffused through different and unrelated disciplines, though, as Michael Marsden demonstrated in his PCAN article there are throughout the country numerous special collections of varying kinds of materials.

Finally, research needs to be done on how teachers of popular culture are now using the library and what type of material they would like to see the library acquire to support their teaching and research needs.

It will take academic librarians considerable time to deal with these questions adequately. However, since popular culture is already entrenched as an area of study, librarians should get on with the business of collecting popular culture now and concurrently work out solutions to the problems associated with these unusual collections.

Notes

[1]Gordon Stevenson, "The Wayward Scholar: Resources and Research in Popular Culture," *Library Trends*, 25 (April, 1977), 783.

[2]Ibid., p. 784.

[3]Ibid., pp. 790-91.

[4]Ibid., p. 783.

[5]Survey by Bruce Lohof cited by Stevenson in "The Wayward Scholar," p. 793.

[6]Gordon Stevenson, "Popular Culture and the Academic Librarian," in *Popular Culture and the Library: Proceedings of Symposium II*, ed. Wayne Wiegand (Lexington, Ky.: Univ. of Kentucky College of Library Science, 1978), p. 29.

[7]Wayne Wiegand, "Popular Culture: A New Frontier for Academic Libraries," *Journal of Academic Librarianship*, 5 (Sept., 1979), 200.

[8]Wiegand, p. 204.

[9]Stevenson, "Popular Culture and the Academic Librarian," p. 33.

[10]"Comic Books and Rock 'n' Roll: The Artifacts of Our Society," *At Bowling Green* 8 (Feb., 1978), 6-7.

[11]Michigan State University Libraries, *The Russel B. Nye Popular Culture Collection: A Descriptive Guide* ([East Lansing]: Michigan State University Libraries, 1978), n. p.

[12]Stevenson, "The Wayward Scholar," p. 808.

[13]Ibid., p. 806.

[14]William L. Schurk, "The Popular Culture Library at Bowling Green State University," in *Popular Culture and the Library*, pp. 55-57.

[15]Gordon Stevenson, "Popular Culture Studies and Library Education," *Journal of Education for Librarianship*, 15 (Spring, 1975), 235.

[16]Stevenson, "Popular Culture Studies," p. 247.

[17]Letter received from Fay Blake, 23 Oct., 1978.

[18]Jack A. Clarke, "Popular Culture in Libraries," *College and Research Libraries*, 34 (May, 1973), 217.

[19]Stevenson, "Popular Culture and the Academic Librarian," p. 44.

[20]Michael Marsden, *Popular Culture Association Newsletter* VI:1 (March, 1977), pp. 5-29.

"A glance at library literature demonstrates that librarians talk and write mostly to each other.... Little in library literature reflects a wholistic outlook, or seeks to examine the validity of basic assumptions tenaciously clung to for decades."

Wayne A. Wiegand, "The Academic Library's Responsibility to the Resource Needs of the Popular Culture Community."

XII

Incorporating popular literature into an academic library goes against deeply entrenched traditions of principles of book selection, just as incorporating popular culture courses into a college or university offends many curricular traditions. With the further understanding that popular culture includes such non-book resources as comic magazines, posters and handbills, phonograph records, film and videotapes, the strain upon academic library policies and practices seems to require nothing short of a revolution in the most basic assumptions that underlie the responsible operation of an academic library. But in this article, Wayne Wiegand argues that no such revolution is required, although the traditional prejudices of students entering the library professions and of the library schools that train them may need some major readjustments. The principles, nonetheless, are there, in such august statements as the American Library Association's Library Bill of Rights and the Standards for College Libraries of the Association of College and Research Libraries. From these premises, Wiegand develops a strategy for change.

Wayne A. Wiegand is Assistant Professor of Library Science at the University of Kentucky. His articles on popular culture and libraries have appeared in *The Journal of Academic Librarianship* and *The Best of Library Literature—1979.* He is editor of *Proceedings of the Popular Culture Symposium, College of Library Science, University of Kentucky, October 28, 1977* (ERIC ED 158711), served as Program Chairman for "popular Culture and Libraries" on June 30, 1980 by the Young Adult Services Division of the American Library Association in New York City, and is guest editor of a forthcoming issue of *The Drexel Library Quarterly* devoted to popular culture.

Wayne A. Wiegand

The Academic Library's Responsibility to the Resource Needs of the Popular Culture Community

ARE ACADEMIC LIBRARIANS obligated to meet the curricular and research information needs of popular culture specialists? Ten years ago the answer was an understandable "no!" The movement to study popular culture was just beginning to emerge from more broadly-based American studies programs. The Popular Culture Association and the *Journal of Popular Culture* were fresh and untested by time. Russel Nye had not yet published *The Unembarrassed Muse*; Bill Schurk had not yet organized the Audio Center at Bowling Green State University; and *Popular Culture Abstracts* and the Bowling Green Popular Press were still in Ray B. Browne's "idea bank."

Things are different now. A decade of existence witnessed the transformation and growth of the popular culture studies movement from its embryonic stages to the threshold of intellectual maturity. Academia is beginning to show signs of accepting popular culture studies as culturally valuable, pedagogically viable conduits to advancing knowledge and augmenting societal self-awareness. It is time for academic librarians to fall in line.

The academic library community does have an obligation to meet the curricular and research needs of popular culture specialists, but it is unrealistic to think many academic librarians will readily assume leadership positions in fostering change. Indeed, most are currently indifferent (if not hostile) to the resource needs of popular culture teachers and scholars. Academic libraries are largely preoccupied with the competition for funds from the parent institution just to maintain collections in this inflationary age. As a result, academic librarians tend to hide behind a traditionally narrow and historically safe view of what the legitimate information needs of the academic community are. Russel Nye's recent comment that "the library upstairs couldn't care less" what happened to old detective novels and Harlequin books he was pulling from the Michigan State University Library stacks[1] to put into a new popular culture collection probably represents the normal experience of scholars seeking academic library support of their new courses and non-traditional research interests. But this state of affairs need not remain static. Popular culture specialists should insist that academic libraries begin to assemble and catalog popular culture materials in order to support their courses and research activities. They must point out that the records of man's cultural heritage have changed drastically over the last fifty years. Television, radio, film and sound recordings of various formats have greatly expanded the types of recorded information packages beyond the print medium. The task of modifying the academic library's traditional collection policies to include the acquisition of popular culture materials will require hard work tempered with patience and persistence. But uphill battles are nothing new to popular culture specialists. They already have ten years of experience.

This essay seeks to aid the process by 1) addressing the reasons for the academic librarian's current indifference to collecting non-traditional written and audio library resources; 2) suggesting several ways in which popular culture proponents might enhance their chances for success when approaching academic librarians about starting a popular culture collection and 3) outlining the academic library's capabilities and responsibilities toward meeting the needs of the popular culture research and teaching community. The modern academic library, like most components of institutions of higher education, has both strengths and weaknesses. The challenge for popular culture specialists is to expand the academic library's narrow definition of the information needs of the academic community, to demonstrate how a popular culture collection can answer some of the academic library's weaknesses, and then to harness the strengths of the academic library to insure that in the future popular culture materials are more systematically collected, better controlled bibliographically, and more efficiently circulated.

I

Academic librarians are not born but made through an educational process which is both formal and informal. Twenty-five years ago the Association of American Library Schools' Committee on Recruiting Personnel polled 415 library science students who indicated their intention to enter the field of academic librarianship. When asked why they chose the academic library, a substantial majority indicated that they "liked books, literature, and reading."[2] At the beginning of each semester I request my new students at the University of Kentucky's College of Library Science to fill out a basic information card. One question asks—"Why have you chosen the library profession above others?" Almost invariably, the answer is a variation of "...because I love books." How many of these answers are preconditioned by what the student thinks the instructor (or pollster) wants to hear is difficult to determine. Still one cannot escape the conclusion that "books" have some magic attraction which arouses a protective loyalty even before the aspiring professional becomes comfortable in the library science classroom.

Library science education does little to expand horizons. One critic of modern library science education claims that the average library science faculty teaches "non-research, experience-based, non-cumulative (although possibly additive), subjectively selected and relatively out-of-date literature."[3] Accordingly, the curricula of most library science departments across the nation continue to reflect "book-based" modes of thinking. Nonprint media and non-traditional text and serial resources are discussed only in specialized courses taught by individuals who are recruited because of their "unique" experiences and education in these areas. Basic "core" courses—usually variations of courses in cataloging, classification, and reference (all of which have changed very little over the past fifty years)—treat nonprint media (and especially nonprint mass media) as an errant stepchild. Although library science educators acknowledge that appropriate curricular homes must be found for this offspring of a new age, deciding precisely *where* continues to pose dilemmas.

When library science students graduate from professional training programs they usually assume positions in libraries where lines of organizational structure parallel the course divisions in library school curricula. The neophyte librarian finds nonprint media pigeonholed into functionally specialized departments within the library at best, or at worst, separated from the library altogether (as on most university campuses). Thus, preconceptions brought to a chosen field which were steadily nurtured by library science curricula and faculty are ultimately confirmed by library practice. And since all this takes place in an institutional milieu where limited resources and competing demands are affected by power plays to increase one's institutional visibility, academic librarians gravitate toward a conservatism which proponents of the collection of popular culture materials will find hard to crack.

The professional communications patterns of librarianship also tend to reinforce this conservative outlook. A glance at library literature demonstrates that librarians talk and write mostly to each other, and they concentrate much of their attention on methods to increase the operational efficiency of existing internal library operations. Little in library literature reflects a holistic outlook, or seeks to examine the validity of basic assumptions tenaciously clung to for decades. To cite one example, many university librarians still look to the size of book collections of the member institutions of the Association of Research Libraries as an adequate measure of an academic library's usefulness. Only recently have library science scholars examined techniques, tested and developed in the private sector, and subsequently called attention to "out-comes," "results," and "output" as perhaps more realistic measurement devices for a collection's utility.

For all of these reasons, then, teachers and scholars who want academic librarians to initiate popular culture collections in order to service student and research needs are meeting indifference—and in some cases resistance—which parallels the negative responses they encounter from their conservative, culturally elitist academic colleagues.

II

How can popular culture proponents alter this indifference? Several constructive steps are possible, but popular culture scholars and teachers should first become acquainted with the climate which governs the acquisitions process in the academic library. From that position, proponents of change can identify the best strategy to approach the conservative library situation. Surprisingly, the foundation for cooperative action between non-traditional scholars and academic librarians already exists in standards and guidelines previously approved by the library profession. Only the popular culture community's ignorance of these guidelines and standards combined with the academic library community's traditional interpretation of their dictates limit their utility.

The first set of guidelines with which the popular culture community should be concerned is the Library Bill of Rights, originally passed by the Council of the American Library Association in 1939 and reaffirmed by that same body every year since. The Library Bill of Rights makes explicit "a responsibility of library service" that "books, and other library materials, should be chosen for values of interest, information and enlightenment of all people in the community."[4] Traditionally, academic librarians have concentrated on "books," and have chosen a high culture definition of "values" when meeting the academic community's information needs. Popular culture proponents must direct the attention of librarians to their stated responsibility to choose "other library materials" when they identify the "values" of collecting popular culture materials.

A second significant set of guidelines falls into the category of professionally approved "standards." In 1959, the Association of College and Research Libraries (ACRL) passed the "Standards for College Libraries" which have been revised periodically ever since. The introduction to the latest revision, passed by the ACRL Board of Directors in July, 1975, states that the role of the academic library "has ever been to provide access to the human records needed by members of the higher education community for the successful pursuit of academic programs."[5] Again, academic librarians have elected to define "human records" narrowly. The popular culture community must work to generate a broader definition.

Even more recently, a committee of the Association of Research Libraries drafted a sister set of guidelines called "Standards for University Libraries." Standard A. 1. states: "In order to support the instructional, research, and public service programs of the university, the services offered by a university library shall be such as *to facilitate use of recorded information in all formats by all of the library's clientele* [italics mine]." Section B. 2. should be of special interest to proponents of popular culture collections: "A university library's collections *shall contain all of the varied forms of recorded information* [italics mine]."[6]

Academic librarians also look to published collection guides for help in their collection-building activities—a third source of conservative influence on the climate governing the acquisitions process. Currently no single comprehensive guide exists which takes a holistic view of "all of the varied forms of recorded information." The closest reference source the academic library community has at this writing is *Books for College Libraries,*[7] a guide which seeks to identify a basic core collection of 40,000 titles. Now in its second edition, *BCL* purports to address the book needs of typical four-year liberal arts undergraduate curriculum. Yet by its very existence *BCL* also tends to reinforce the traditional interpretation of an academic library's primary goal—to collect *books* which support the institutional curriculum.

The Library Bill of Rights, the different sets of "standards," and the collection guides all combine with the academic librarian's conservative outlook towards his craft to reinforce a narrow perspective on the acquisitions process in the academic library. Yet enough stated openings exist—especially those occasioned by a broad interpretation of the Library Bill of Rights and the "standards"—which should permit popular culture proponents to exert persistent pressure founded on a sound educational base. Few will argue seriously that popular culture materials do not fall into the category of "recorded information."

Academic librarians also respond to internal institutional pressures in developing academic library collections. The curriculum, of course, exerts the greatest influence. Collection development librarians closely scrutinize the courses offered by each department on campus and attempt to estimate the resource demands which these courses will make on the academic library. Librarians usually give special attention to departments which are expanding their curricula. They are particularly alert to the needs of graduate courses, undergraduate honors programs, or a series of structured seminars. All of these kinds of courses make heavy demands on library facilities because of their built-in research requirements. Traditionally, however, these courses are forums in which print resources are the primary devices for communicating information, and academic librarians are naturally predisposed to service these areas *first* because of their background, training and practical experience. Indeed, they often look to the research demands and reading requirements of these kinds of courses to demonstrate the utility and high service potential of the academic library. But popular culture proponents can also benefit from this line of logic. They should be able to point out to the academic library community that popular culture materials—all "forms of recorded information"—will be heavily utilized by students in popular culture classes. They should have at hand statistics to demonstrate the potential use by populations, departments and courses which the academic library should service. They should also argue that by collecting popular culture materials to meet these non-traditional information needs, the academic library will be increasing its utility to the total academic community.

Another, though surprisingly less potent, internal influence is the explicit educational aim and philosophy of the parent institution. In developing academic library collections, librarians must ask whether the institution devotes its energies to a single educational purpose or whether its self-assigned task is more general. Academic librarians recognize that the library is only one arm of the institution, pledged like each other component part to fulfill the institution's long-range educational goals. Here is another place the traditionally narrow definition of "recorded information" is highly vulnerable. If popular culture courses are introduced into the curriculum, it behooves the academic library to collect materials to service these courses' concomitant information needs.

A third internal institutional influence in collection development is the faculty. Twenty-five years ago, many faculty members actively participated in collection development. They browsed through the stacks, identified specific gaps in the collection, and made recommendations to the academic librarian for purchase of new materials. Their recommendations were usually heeded, although academic librarians usually checked that library collections weren't becoming skewed to appease the most aggressive and vociferous faculty members. Today the situation is different. For whatever reason (lack of time, interest, etc.), many faculty members have relinquished the responsibility to participate in the collection-building process. In part, they are guilty of some of the same sins as academic librarians—too close an identification with their classroom activities at the expense of a general concern with their students' total learning environment. What the faculty has not perceived, however, is that in the course of withdrawing from the collection development process they have left a void which could only be filled by the academic librarian armed with his conservative training and practical experience, his limited collection guides, his narrow definition of "recorded information" and affected by competing demands for the academic library's limited funds. By relinquishing the responsibility to participate in the collection-building process, faculty members abandon partial control of an important device designed to service their students' (and in the university community, their own research), information needs.

A fourth internal institutional influence on collection development, and one that is assuming increasing importance in recent years, is the formally developed and frequently Board-of-Trustee approved collection development policy. These policies are usually designed to identify the academic library's primary collecting responsibilities. Normally, they include six components:

(1) a statement of philosophy which identifies the selection procedures and criteria; (2) a listing of the various institutional parties responsible for materials selection; (3) an outline of the standards which govern selection and evaluation; (4) a definition of the procedures used to apply these criteria; (5) a statement demonstrating how the academic library's service philosophy fits the standards for selection and evaluation; and (6) guidelines for considering materials about which complaints have been received. Unfortunately, collection development policies tend to reflect and reinforce the print biases of academic librarians and their culturally elitist allies on the faculty. Most attention is directed toward the acquisition of books and professional and/or scholarly journals, with nonprint and/or mass media usually meriting separate consideration in addended sections. On occasion "Special Collections" are addressed in another section, but these usually speak to existing special collections rather than outlining the criteria for commencing new ones.[8] In the future, popular culture proponents may find previously-approved collection development policies the largest single obstacle to adjusting the academic librarian's inherent print-biased and culturally elitist approach to his craft, especially if these collection development policies have received formal administration and/or Board approval. With this fact in mind, popular culture teachers and scholars who discover that collection development polices are currently being designed on their campuses, would be well advised to participate actively in the process to insure the inclusion of a broad definition of "varied forms of recorded information."

Other influences affect the selection of library materials to a lesser degree. Many academic libraries still participate in approval plans which are implemented through wholesale book distributors. Librarians draw up "need profiles" of their libraries which they file with contracted distributors. The latter then send "on approval" those books whose subject content appears to match the library's stated needs. While academic librarians retain the right to return all books, most do not exercise this option unless the annual budget has been either expended or encumbered. Returning books is time-consuming and costly, so the natural inclination is to catalog them into the collection. Marginal cases decided early in the fiscal year are thus allowed to eat into the library's total collection budget, and the collection of "lower priority" materials suffers as a result. The academic librarian's priorities, of course, comprise a form of pre-selection which usually works to the disadvantage of popular culture specialists.

Academic library collection development has an inertia of its own which is aided and abetted by the academic librarian's preconceived predilections, conservative training and book-oriented practical experience. Add to this the tacit (if not conscious) support of an academically conservative, culturally elitist faculty on most campuses, and one can readily see the reasons why popular culture proponents receive little support from academic librarians in building collections of popular culture materials.

What can popular culture proponents do to counter this indifference? Some specific suggestions have already been made, but these are only part of a broader approach which requires two major steps. A first step obliges popular culture proponents to add their voices to the many who are pointing out to public and academic libraries across the nation that more and more information is being transmitted to the American populace through mass media, both print and nonprint. These voices are not asking the academic library to forsake its traditional tasks, for they readily acknowledge that for over a century both students and scholars have benefited from the use of academic library collections. They also recognize that knowledge has been significantly advanced because of the systematic collection and organization of print materials which is being aided by increasingly sophisticated library methodology. Although they do not ask academic librarians to abandon their traditional tasks, they are fully justified in requesting that the academic library community expand its perspective to include newer dimensions of a technological age. The popular culture community must specifically identify its information needs to academic librarians, demonstrate that it is a viable component of the academic community which is worthy of attention in the library's collection-building activities, and then join in the fight for an adequate share of the library's funds by advancing its demands. Popular culture proponents must show that no longer can academic librarians continue to rely on collecting print media and still expect to meet the goal of fulfilling academia's curricular and research information needs.

A second step should be easier. Like most other members of institutional bureaucracies, academic librarians have entered the age of accountability. They are increasingly being forced by their parent institutions to justify the funds they request for the academic library. Library literature abounds with suggestions on how to meet this accountability challenge, and on how to devise methods for evaluating both the quality and quantity of library use. Traditional methods are strikingly primitive. Most academic librarians still cling to circulation figures, size of collection, number of reference questions asked, etc., as adequate measures of an academic library's worth. These measures, while certainly helpful, have one major shortcoming. They look at performance through the academic librarian's eyes, and quietly gloss over a more direct approach which many academic librarians subconsciously would prefer to ignore—determining academic library performance by specifically defining *user* needs. By demanding improved measures of academic library performance, accountability will definitely and inevitably test tradition. The quality of academic library collections will increasingly be determined by patron needs, and patrons will find academic libraries useful only when the sources of information they need are there, or when the library maintains finding-aids to locate these sources quickly and efficiently.

The pressure for adequate performance measures exposes an academic library weakness which popular culture proponents should be quick to exploit, for the promise of increased use provides the most potent argument in academic library circles which any popular culture proponent can advance in advocating that academic libraries should collect popular culture materials.

III

How can the academic library community help the popular culture community? First, academic librarians should introduce the topic of collecting popular culture materials and examine its validity as an area for future study and research within the confines of their own professional associations. Only there can the profession's collective intelligence be marshalled to deal with some of the unique problems inherent in acquiring, processing, cataloging, storing, and circulating popular culture materials. Only there can the bibliographic control of popular culture materials be adjusted to fit the existing bibliographical systems and structures, both of which are rapidly being linked and controlled via computerized networks.

Second, the academic library community must also identify current pockets of popular culture materials and set up a national strategy for the efficient collection of the materials in the future. Working within the entire library and museum communities, academic librarians should establish a series of collection and distribution centers strategically located throughout the nation which can systematically collect and distribute popular culture materials via interlibrary loan. For those materials which cannot be transported from library to library for reasons of security or preservation, the regional centers should provide convenient access to visiting students and scholars. Some foundation for such a regional system already exists: (1) the Library of Congress collects many types of popular culture materials simply by fiat of copyright law; and (2) the Popular Culture Library at Bowling Green State University acts as a de facto national center because of its wide-ranging collection activities. But additional centers need to be established in other parts of the country, perhaps by harnessing the cooperation already being exercised by scores of library consortia, and through numerous existing urban, regional and state networks.

Third, the cataloging and classification of popular culture materials must somehow be adapted to the existing bibliographic network structure to facilitate information retrieval. The popular culture and the library communities must work together to formulate a common language for access by subject, key words, codes, titles, etc., to all types of bibliographic entities in order to accommodate easy retrieval. It will be imperative to develop easy-to-use thesauri or dictionaries to assist individual librarians and patrons at all levels of expertise. In addition, machine-readable cataloging data will also need to include an identification of the location of the popular culture materials.

The academic library and popular culture communities need each other. The academic library community has an obligation to service the curricular and research needs of all members of the academic community. The popular culture community has an obligation to identify clearly, concisely and persistently what its own specific information needs are. The academic library community needs to collect popular culture materials to provide further support to its claim of being a viable, necessary arm of higher education and to augment its questionable performance rate. The popular culture community needs the academic library to provide organization and bibliographic control for the materials it seeks to study. If a goal of both communities is to advance knowledge and augment societal self-awareness, then both must respond to a challenge for cooperation if either wishes to accelerate the pace.

Notes

[1]"Question and Answer Session," in Wayne A. Wiegand (ed.), *Current Issues Symposium II: Popular Culture and the Library* (Lexington, Ky.: Office of Continuing Education, College of Library Science, University of Kentucky, 1977), p. 62.

[2]Association of American Library Schools, Committee on Recruiting Personnel, "Why Library School Students Chose the Library Profession," (n.p., 1953), p. 20 (mimeographed), as found quoted in Perry Morrison, *The Career of the Academic Librarian: A Study of the Social Origins, Educational Attainments, Vocational Experience, and Personality Characteristics of a a Group of American Academic Librarians* (Chicago: American Library Association, 1969), p.10.

[3]L. Houser and Alvin M. Schrader, *The Search for a Scientific Profession: Library Science Education in the U.S. and Canada* (Metuchen, N.J.: The Scarecrow Press, Inc., 1978), p. 146-147.

[4]"Library Bill of Rights," as found in *ALA Handbook of Organization, 1977-1978* (Chicago: American Library Association, 1978), p.101.

[5]"Standards for College Libraries," *College & Research Libraries News*, 36 (October, 1975), p. 277.

[6]"Draft: Standards for University Libraries," *College & Research Libraries News*, 39 (April, 1978), p. 90, 92.

[7]*Books for College Libraries: A Core Collection of 40,000 Titles*, 2nd ed. (Chicago: American Library Association, 1975), 6v.

[8]See some sample development policies in Calvin J. Boyer and Nancy L. Eaton (eds.), *Book Selection Policies From College, Public, and School Libraries* (Austin, Texas: Armadillo Press, 1973).

"...the coin-operated cassette vendor is our non-verbal indication that we're willing to share what we have with the world."

Maurice A. Crane, "Speaking of the National Voice Library...."

XIII

Many of the great collections of twentieth-century popular materials have been built upon the hobbies of non-professionals, just as many older cultural collections were founded by antiquarians, amateur explorers and *idee fixe* booklovers. The G. Robert Vincent Voice Library of Michigan State University is one of these. Maurice A. Crane, the librarian of this notable collection, tells of its history in a lively vernacular style that harmonizes well with an oral history collection, and along the way discusses the many practical, technical, legal and philosophic issues that develop as a private archive "goes public."

Maurice A. Crane, who holds a Ph. D. in American literature, has taught at University of Illinois, the University of London, Ryukyu Daigaku and Michigan State University. An accomplished jazz musican and recording artist, he is founder of "The Geriatric Six-Plus-One," he has written scholarly and popular articles, a book of verse, as well as close to a dozen film soundtracks, and he is also a regular newspaper reviewer of symphony concerts. Crane also appears frequently on radio and TV, teaches a humanities course on comedy, and works fulltime as the one-person staff of the Voice Library. This article is drawn from papers that he presented at a Popular Culture Association national convention and at the National Archives in Washington, D.C.

Maurice A. Crane

THE NATIONAL VOICE LIBRARY is the name which G. Robert Vincent gave to his private collection of recordings, cylinders and tapes of famous speakers. If the moniker seems a bit grandiose, let me explain that Bob Vincent was the chief sound engineer at the Neremberg Trials and at the opening of the U.N. in San Francisco, a longtime employee and associate of Thomas Edison, and for years ran his own recording studio in Radio City, servicing all the networks and numerous motion picture companies. One can read his profile in *The New Yorker* and in the New York *Times* Sunday magazine. He was often mentioned in Eleanor Roosevelt's column, "My Day," and was a dinner guest of Eleanor and Franklin during the time when they seemed to have leased the Pennsylvania Avenue address *in perpetuo*. He appeared on the *Today* show, and his shop, which is now my shop, was once a way station on the endless road of Charles Kuralt.

Bob was also a packrat, the kind of collector who saves depression glass during the depression, when everyone else is throwing it out. More precisely, the kind of man who saved Ed Murrow when he was as common a throwaway as Walter Cronkite. And he knew everybody. When I first went to work with him doing a series for Mutual radio called "Spin Back the Years," I was overwhelmed by the framed 8 by 11 glossies covering his office wall. "The Best to My Dear Friend, Bob Vincent," or some similar message from Trygvie Lie and Jan Christian Smuts and Carlos Romulo, Duke Ellington, Arturo Toscanini, Otis Skinner, Frederick March. I felt as if I were looking into one of Thomas Wolfe's refrigerators.

Bob was in semi-retirement in California with his wife Vi and his son Ken, a "boy" of my age, when Dick Chapin, head of the MSU library convinced him to come to Michigan State and spend the rest of his life on the university payroll, codifying, cataloging, and arranging his collection into a uniform storage-and-retrieval system. Bob says he never understood that a lifetime job at a university ended at age seventy. Dick says he never suspected that Bob was immortal. Bob Vincent is spry, witty, agile, and young looking, but it is hard to lie about your age when you were an officer in World War I and when your library contains a recording of the voice of Teddy Roosevelt which you yourself made in 1912.

Bob was about 75 years old when he retired kicking and

screaming and five years older than he should have been. He moved the National Voice Library (in the form of dubs of all the tapes he thought worthwhile) into the basement of his home and continued to operate as a lecturer and consultant from there. Dr. Chapin wondered aloud if the Voice Library should fold, continue as a non-growing archive, or turn into something else. It had become part of the library merely because a librarian had discovered it. Its function and purpose were unclear; its future was cloudy.

There was a hiatus of six months between Vincent's June retirement and my taking over on January 1, 1974, during which time most of the world seemed to get along perfectly well without it. The people who suffered most during those particular months appeared to be those political appointees on the federal level who were constantly being embarrassed by Senator Sam Ervin's committee. How well I know. The complete Senate Watergate hearings are the first and last really expensive purchase I made.

How do you proceed when you take over a one-man hobby operation for which there is no crying need? We made a lot of changes during the first week. Bob felt the title National Voice Library belonged to him, and I had to give the university's collection a name which he could not find fault with. I found it: the G. Robert Vincent Voice Library. The card catalog, which had been under double lock, went out into the hall, where anyone could use it without permission. Next, we melded copies of all the Voice Library cards with the general card catalog so that a person looking up Hitler, for instance, could see not only books and articles, but all of Hitler's speeches, all dated, and all the speeches and reminiscences by others in which Hitler figured prominently as subject matter. Dr. Chapin took the next logical step and got the G.K. Hall Company of Boston to publish a Dictionary Catalog of our holdings. What we did was to "go public."

Our holdings are listed along with books and articles in the general catalog, and our card catalog has been published by G.K. Hall as an aid to scholars and teachers across the country. And as a clearinghouse for M.S.U. classroom aids I think we're legally safe: I hope so, because it is *possible* to lecture on Joseph McCarthy without using tapes to show his voice and unique inquisitorial style, I guess, just as it is *possible* to teach Rembrandt without using a slide projector, but what professor would choose to do it?

"Going public" has also brought up many unanswered questions about copyright. What are the benefits to be derived from exclusive ownership of a voice? Suppose people *would* come from all over the country to put on earphones in East Lansing to hear Ty Cobb announce his joy at never having to play baseball again; what real benefit would accrue to MSU? Could it ever justify depriving the the Cobb Museum of Cobb's voice? When you measure the diminished availability of materials not on the open market against the pride of exclusive possession the net loss is overwhelming.

There has persisted in Michigan for all of my life a folk tale about the man who invented a wonderful gas-saving carburetor and whose invention was purchased by Ford or Chrysler or General Motors, which, owning the patent, quite legally locked the invention in a dungeon somewhere. In this story, these malefactors of great wealth are well within the law; they are merely sinners against the human race. They have made the supply of a needed commodity artificially rare and therefore artifically valuable.

Now, suppose someone comes along and creates and copyrights an entire package which includes the Ty Cobb which Bob Vincent alone had preserved. Does our library become deprived of the right to send free of charge to other people the same materials which this entrepreneur received *gratis* just because he has copyrighted *his* package for sale? Who would benefit from this? The Cobb estate? The history-of-baseball buff? Am I to stop sending out voices which are not available on the open market at any price against the chance that some commercial adventurer with a good attorney has somewhere risen up in conflict with our educational institution?

Am I to live with the comparable fear that my federal government has taken to itself the exclusive right to certain "found" materials, and has placed the replication of those materials outside my legal rights? I do not think it is simony; in fact I can understand very well beginning to sell things which have traditionally been free, if long-deprived artists or authors are to benefit. What we must beware is preventing students from hearing materials or charging them for a privilege which had been free in the past in the name of an abstract principle.

It is easy to get angry, as a very patient Someone did, at a Kosher law that makes it illegal to swallow gnats (although at an oasis it is impossible to avoid doing do) and legal to barbecue camels, although no one would want to do so. When a law flies in the face of human nature, one looks for ways of avoiding trouble by obeying its letter while disobeying its spirit, waiting for the day when wiser heads will prevail and when, in Cicero's phrase, "human nature will ratify Law."

But to leave copyright for a moment. We had other problems as we started. Bob Vincent was a recording engineer. My Ph. D. is in American literature. Between us we knew nothing about librarianship. This did not put us at an enormous disadvantage since nobody knew much—at least no one had set any precedents— on filing our kind of voice materials. As a matter of fact, Bob appalled librarians by not doing what they call "attributions." Since he knew which of the tapes he had recorded live, which he had taken off the air, which he had bought, and which he had recorded from his own and his friends' records, and since he alone had the keys to the card catalog and access to the tapes, "attributions" did not seem to be a serious problem. They are now.

Tapes present many problems which librarians could not help us with. Interviews, and even most speeches, do not have useful titles. I tried following the Vatican precedent of using the first two words as a title (as in *Quadrigessimo Anno* and *Rerum Novarum*) but I found that sixty percent of my material was called "Ladies And." Speeches and performances and interviews don't have titles but they do have dates and our filing system is a combination of Alphabetical and Chronological orders. We file by the speaker's name (like an author card), then *within* any speaker we go into chronological order by the day of utterance, followed by subject cards, i.e., people talking *about* the speaker in subalphabetical order according to *their* names. Then we go on to the next speaker in alphabetical order.

We had another problem. Libraries can duplicate their holding of individual book entries. But when we say we have three Eugene Debses and seventeen Nicolai Lenins, we have to make sure that each new gift is in fact the fourth Debs or the eighteenth Lenin and not a duplicate of something on the shelf. We cannot shelve it like a book, as librarians do, alongside all the other copies of *Moby Dick* or *Gatsby*. Actually, the hard and fast no-duplicate policy also had to be modifed when we discovered that anthologies of voices such as the *Lowell Thomas Remembers* series on educational TV were as important sociologically for their context as for the individual speeches they contained. But by and large our anxiety not to catalog duplicates has made us one of the few libraries in the world where the librarian must go through each new acquisition himself.

We don't have indices and we don't have contents pages and there's no sure way to flip through a tape even for those who are accustomed to listening to double-quick soprano—looking for a particular ten-second quote.

So the card catalog becomes a work of art as precise as the Petrarchan sonnet. There are no wasted words. It informs the reader of the speaker, the main topic, other subtopics hit upon, the day, the place of the delivery, the source, the length. Five minutes after he reads the card the patron should be listening to any one of our twenty thousand voices. If he needs the talk for classroom presentation or research and it is not under restrictive copyright, it should be on the high speed copier within five minutes.

To indicate our willingness to make copies, we placed in a prominent position a specially altered candy-vending machine, which sells sixty-minute 3-M cassettes for 85¢. A buff who needs higher quality reproduction or an impoverished academic who reuses his K-Mart cassettes until they self-destruct can bring his own, of course. But the coin-operated cassette vendor is our non-verbal indication that we're willing to share what we have with the world.

Although more than two thirds of the collection is stuff that I have taped myself or gotten in trade from other voice collectors, I came into this business from twenty-five years in the university classroom, and I do not share some librarians' and archivists' anal retentive notions of exclusivity. We had the only known voice of Ty Cobb when I arrived. In the first week on the job I sent a dub to the

Ty Cobb museum in Georgia. Any time a college professor learns something new and exciting and pertinent he runs into the classroom and gives it away to twenty-five kids. Power may not belong to the people but information *does.* Robert Hutchins said during the Hitler years that you don't really have to burn the books; all you have to do is leave them on the shelves unread for a generation or two. I find the concept of the world's largest collection of exclusive, unshared, and unlistened-to-tapes to be hilarious. I know it's also tragic, but I find such an archive to be wildly comical.

The people in the business with whom I exchange dubs like bubble gum cards—the guys I find most compatible are the man from the American Political Items Collectors who trades me Hardings I didn't have for Bryans he didn't have, the Civil War buff in New England who sent me two 90-year-old ex-privates, one Blue, one Grey, recalling the Battle of Gettysburg 75 years after the fact, because I had sent him a couple of Generals talking into Mr. Edison's machine 30 years after the War; and George Garabedian out in Burbank—so pleased that I had sent him without charge (as always) a couple of Amelia Earharts hours after he'd asked for them, that he sent me some 120 of his albums of thirties and forties radio and has continued to be a telephone and trading pal ever since. Incidentally, after I taped all the Garabedian materials, I sent them in Russ Nye's car to J. Fred MacDonald, who runs the Institute for Popular Culture Studies at Northeastern Illinois University and who is a principal benefactor as well as a principal beneficiary of our voice library, and I know that he'll pass them along to someone else, because that's the way this fraternity works.

It's a start, but by God! it's not enough. I get calls and letters pretty regularly from confused people who say something like "I know this sound nuts but the nice man at the National Archives or the nice man at the Library of Congress said he didn't have what I wanted but that I could probably get it from East Lansing, Michigan." Some day I'm going to start taping the different ways Easterners say "East Lansing Michigan!!" I'm especially happy to serve these people and I do it as fast as I can, because I know that Les Waffen and Gerry Gibson and Ron Leavitt's reputation as voice touts are at stake. When I can't find the item I look through Gary Shumway's Oral History Directory, which I know to be very incomplete, since I'm not even in it, and then through a handful of catalogs we have lying around. Librarians are the most dedicated people in the world and in a couple of years I have caught one of their diseases: I just don't like to leave a request unanswered. I think that "We don't have it" is no more acceptable an answer than "We can't cure your fatal disease, Ma'am, and we're too busy now to find you the name of someone who can."

There has to be a way that we can get hold of each other's catalogs. I don't want anybody having to buy my catalogs for forty-five bucks, and G.K. Hall doesn't want anybody buying it for any less, and we're all going to have to wait a long time before it comes out as a movie. What we'd better do, and soon, before there become so many of us that back-cataloging will be prohibitive, is develop a unified system of cataloging voice entries on IBM cards, establish an information bank somewhere, and put terminals into every participating voice collection, so that part of our automatic cataloging process for our own libraries will be feeding the national computerized union catalog.

Then when someone comes to us and says, "Do you have the January 3, 1956 Fulton Lewis interview with Senator Joseph McCarthy?", no matter who or where we are we can say "Yes," meaning either "It's right here in our holding" or "I'll punch it up, find the nearest library that has it, and get them to send it to us over the phone in a few minutes, so you can get on with your research."

This is going to be a very expensive undertaking in both money and time and we are going to have to find and shake a number of money trees to get it started. But the eventual savings and value will be fantastic. Right now, because we have a Professor of Labor and Industrial Relations who is eager to do it, Michigan State's Voice Library is beginning to duplicate much of the valuable oral history of American labor already available down at the Walter P. Reuther archives at Wayne State University in Detroit. It's on Phil Mason's shelves and now it's on my shelves because right now that is the only way to make it immediately available in both Detroit and Lansing.

Like anything in any library some of the stuff we collect will never be used, and we don't know *which* stuff it is. We are going to run out of space and help and money and time to do specialized research because the cataloging and circulation desk aspect of the library will overwhelm us. Further, the important special research we *do* will be known of and available only locally, causing—and this is a great waste in the academy generally—someone else to go over the same or similar ground not knowing that it has already been plowed and harvested.

Lord knows where copyright law is going to take us on this. I used to worry about it a great deal, until I figured that if I was going to be Bert Lahr as the Cowardly Librarian I would wind up with an acquisitions department and a time capsule, collecting exciting, interesting, valuable voices and sinking them in cement. So what we do is send out tapes free of charge for educational purposes and ask our patrons, who range from Paramount Pictures and the BBC to little girls practice-teaching American history in Livonia, to send a charitable donation to an organization called Friends of the Library, which is not related to us, from whom we have not and will not receive a cent, and whose bookkeeping we are not privy to. Its general purpose is to bring 13th century French manuscripts to Ingham County Michigan, where they belong. They get the money, the donor gets an easy conscience and a tax break, and I keep my amateur standing. I think that's a crazy Rube Goldberg way to operate a railroad, but, as my son the attorney says, it keeps me out of jail.

It's not enough. We are going to have to plump for national rulings, something stronger than gentlemanly guidelines. Surely we'll be able to copy a Presidential address. But what about the opposition's reply on an equal-time broadcast? And what about one member of the opposition replying on his own on a magazine format talk show? And what about political broadcasts which masquerade as talk shows? Is somebody going to draw the line for us? Not against us? *For* us.

Are there enough of us to warrant working on a single legally airtight deposit form for our collections? Are there enough of us to constitute the nucleus of a consortium operating on an agreed set of rules, allowing materials to pass among us "privately" like money through the branches of a great medieval banking family?

No one has the right to disobey a law because he doesn't like it or doesn't understand it. Full obedience to bad laws, experimental laws, underdeveloped laws is the only condition that motivates us to work for their alteration. I think that the umbrella of the fair use clause of Section 107, allowing copies to be made for criticism, comment, news reporting, teaching, scholarship and research without infringing on the copyright is going to keep most of the raindrops from falling on our heads while we live with the law, discover what works, what doesn't, and what perhaps never will. No one wants an unreasonable law, an unnatural law, an unenforceable law. The first copyright act, Dick Chapin tells me, was under Queen Anne in 1710 and was entitled in part "An Act for the Encouragement of Learning by Vesting the Copies of Printing in the Authors." That's a fair enough criterion for me. If the current act appears in any of its parts to *discourage* learning, we owe it to our congressman to make him more aware of that shortcoming. He doesn't want to discourage learning any more than we do.

"Perhaps the most difficult requests I've encountered in the past ten years have come from non-academic Audio Center patrons—a person seeking a recording of the Turkish National Anthem, a woman trying to create an audio background for her daughter's tap-dance routine, and an elderly couple looking for a tune they danced to when they were young (even though they can remember only one word—'dream'—from the title)."

William L. Schurk and B.Lee Cooper, "William L. Schurk: Audio Center Director—A Close Encounter with a Librarian of a Different Kind"

XIV

All of us habitually assign values to cultural artifacts, and this is generally a good thing. Life without standards for selecting the good, the beautiful and the useful would be life without meaning. But within the professions that serve libraries, museums and the academies, the tendency to fix value-judgments must be tempered by foresight and by a very broad view of "culture," because we are trying to collect and conserve for a future whose interests and values we cannot presume to be the same as ours. In popular culture, a non-judgmental attitude may be even more important because personal and community tastes and preferences about popular items are strongly held and vehemently expressed. The cultivation of such a neutral attitude is only one of the topics of this lively discussion between William Schurk and B.Lee Cooper. Other topics include acquisition policies and techniques, bootleg recording operations, support for and utilization of the Audio Center's collection, and projections of the future for the Audio Center at Bowling Green State University.

William L. Schurk's background and experience are incorporated in the interview; B.Lee Cooper, who designed, recorded, transcribed and edited the interview, is more fully described in the introduction to the article following this one.

B. Lee Cooper
&
William L. Schurk

William L. Schurk: Audio Center Director— A Close Encounter with a Librarian of a Different Kind

After reading several fascinating newspaper reports[1] about the record and tape collections housed in the Bowling Green State University Library, I finally had the good fortune to meet William L. Schurk—Bowling Green's colorful, hyperactive Audio Center Director last fall during a "Popular Culture Symposium" conducted at the University of Kentucky.[2] This close encounter prompted me to tape a series of interviews with this interesting individual. Spending several days with an unconventional, creative, encyclopedic library administrator helps one to understand the kind of enthusiasm which sparked the building of the nation's largest popular music collection. The following interview is the result of six hours of discussion with Mr. Schurk concerning the operation of Bowling Green's Audio Center.

*   *   *   *

Cooper: I'm gratified that you've agreed to share some of your experiences at the Audio Center with me. Can you begin by outlining the history of the Center's creation?

Schurk: I'll be happy to share my perspectives on the Audio Center's growth. In July 1967 I joined the University's library staff. After devoting a year to assembling a collection of recording industry trade journals (*Billboard, Record World* and *Cash Box*) and discographic tools (*Gramophone, The Schwann Long Playing Record Guide, American Record Guide* and *Audio Cardolog*) as record selection guides, to developing student service procedures and staffing assignments, and to meeting with on-campus academic department heads, directors of traditional audio-visual library programs from several states, and a variety of folklorists, newsmen and radio broadcasters, the Audio Center finally opened in 1968.[3] As you probably know, the Center controls all record resources on the Bowling Green campus except for those classical recordings housed in the College of Musical Arts and the language tapes being utilized in University Hall Listening Labs by the Foreign Language Department. Among the materials included in our collection are blues, folk, swing, rock, bluegrass, gospel, jazz and country recordings, television and motion picture soundtrack music, prose, poetry and dramatic readings, selected kiddie records, plus tapes of early radio shows and interviews with celebrities. These items of audio information are available on either LP albums, 45 r.p.m. and 78 r.p.m. records, cylinder recordings, or reel-to-reel and cassette tapes. During the past ten ten years the University's audio holdings have grown in market value by nearly $500,000. During the same period our service statistics have skyrocketed from only occasional use of an album or two to 7,765 record and tape users during the 1976-1977 academic year.[4]

C: In my efforts to locate written descriptions about the functions of Bowling Green's Audio Center, I was surprised to find only one published report by you—and that was a transcription of the 1977 speech which you delivered at the University of Kentucky.[5] Why haven't you made greater efforts to issue reports about the Audio Center's unique activities through professional library journals?

S: Honestly, the day-to-day responsibilities of managing Audio Center Operations, of searching for new sources to obtain recorded materials, of cataloging recordings, and of attempting to coordinate inter-library loans and audio resource exchanges leave me very little time for personal publication activities. Nevertheless, I have given a number of oral presentations similar to the one which you heard me deliver in Lexington last October. In July of 1974, for instance, I addressed the Music Library Association at their annual meeting in New York City. I represented the field of popular music on a panel which included scholars and bookmen from several specialized record libraries. Although no transcript of my talk was printed, a bibliography of popular music books and magazines which I had compiled for the presentation was published by the Country Music Foundation (C.M.F.) as part of the small booklet. Bill Ivey, Executive Director of the C.M.F., who was also on the panel representing the Country music record collecting field, edited this pamphlet.[6] I gave a similar talk in Columbus, Ohio in 1971 during the Midwest Regional meeting of the Music Library Association. It was very well received.

A few years ago Dr. Ray Browne, Director of the Center for the Study of Popular Culture, and I published a pamphlet describing the collecting activities of both the Popular Culture Library and the Audio Center.[7] That same pamphlet, unbeknownst to either of us, was later published as an article in an anthology dealing with special library collections.[8] It was printed verbatim—the entire pamphlet—without my knowledge or permission.

I have planned to write an Audio Center essay for some time now, but I just haven't gotten around to it. The Association for

Recorded Sound Collections publishes a journal which would certainly be an appropriate forum for me to describe our Center. I'd also like to write articles about the Center's activities for the *Wilson Library Bulletin* and *Library Journal*. Of course, I intend to continue to encourage other writers to investigate, analyze and acquaint scholars and the general public with our audio resources.

C: Are there other academic libraries which have attempted to preserve, catalog and circulate recorded music resources?

S: There are several record collections which are extremely significant in specialized musical fields. Three of the most famous academic library illustrations are the Rutgers University Institute for Jazz Studies, Tulane's New Orleans jazz collection, and UCLA's John Edwards Memorial Foundation collection of traditional American blues and folk music. Some non-academic libraries also assemble large ranges of recorded material. The Rogers and Hammerstein Archives of the New York Public Library System might be an example of this type of collection. Of course the Library of Congress also maintains a Music Library.[9] On the other hand, the Country Music Foundation's collection is strictly a privately funded endeavor. There are quite a few other specialized collections, but they're too numerous to mention. Bowling Green has one of the largest audio collections retained by an academic institution primarily because it covers such a wide spectrum of recorded materials.

C: In several newspaper and magazine reports that I've read about your collection-building techniques, you are quoted as saying that you take *everything*. One article printed in *The Nation* stated that among your "hundreds of special wants" were an album by a rock-and-roll Madrigal-styled group called the Jamies, a copy of "It's Love, Love, Love" by Guy Lombardo, any recordings on Sun, Chess, or Vee-Jay labels, a Frank Crummit and Julia Sanderson 78 r.p.m. album set, and any 78 r.p.m. records featuring Ku Klux Klan songs.[10] I realize that you can trade or sell duplicate records, so I can understand some aspects of your eclecticism. But exactly how have you formally defined the acquisition policy for the Audio Center?

S: As I stated before, we do not collect either classical records or foreign language tapes—so the "We'll take everything!" position is obviously an overstatement. Nevertheless, our acquisition policy (see "Appendix A") is broad enough to encompass the goals of an Audio Research Resource Department. The word "everything" really means that I do not qualitatively define records as "good" or "bad" according to some musical or library acquisitions standard. I would rather not put myself into the judgmental position of rejecting a piece of audio material solely on the grounds that it was of inferior quality musically, either technically or artistically, only to discover

Bill Schurk, librarian of the Audio Center at Bowling Green State University, examines popular records with illustrations imbedded in the disk. A small portion of the Audio Center collection is in the background. (Photograph courtesy Bowling Green State University).

later that it was *indeed* a key part of the American recording history. Because of limited funds, however, I am extremely selective about the individual records I *buy*. I try to gear my purchases to the stated classroom or research projects needs of those faculty members and students who request particular items. Also, when I discover reissue packages, which are occasionally of limited pressings, I will attempt to purchase these immediately because they tend to have a very short market life span. In selecting the materials for the Audio Center, I always try to anticipate the needs of our patrons.

Let me elaborate on the Audio Center's service function for a moment. When the Center was first organized during 1967, I spoke personally with faculty representatives from various academic departments and described the types of services which we planned to offer; I also urged them to assist me in selecting recorded materials for inclusion in the Audio Center's collection. I'm not saying they weren't receptive—but most faculty members are still very much bound by the "book" tradition which libraries and graduate schools fostered over many years. Most instructors were initially unwilling to accept non-print resources from other media to supplement their educational endeavors. Since 1970, of course, the doors have opened wider and I have found that more and more people, *especially* Bowling Green's faculty members, are extremely receptive to the idea that recordings can be valuable teaching tools as well as significant primary source materials for research into political and social themes.

C: I have heard that once a popular recording drops from the "Top 40" charts, it is very difficult to acquire. How are you able to secure single records and albums which were popular several years or even decades ago?

S: I shop—or more accurately "scavenge"—anywhere that I can to secure recordings for the Audio Center. Frankly, Top 40, Top 50, and Top 100 records are the easiest ones to get—even *after* they have gone off the chart. My main sources for records have been garage sales, Salvation Army and Goodwill stores, Volunteers of America shops, flea markets, antique stores, and junk shops. These unorthodox outlets are the best sources for either the purchase of single discs at a very special price or of an album at a reduced rate.

Until a couple of months ago most singles at second-hand stores were priced at a dime apiece, sometimes 15¢. I now encounter thrift shops where the price of a single 45 r.p.m. is 25¢. Imagine my dismay. The other weekend, for instance, I went to a Cleveland Salvation Army Store and I selected a stack of 45 r.p.m records which I wanted before noting the inflated prices—25¢ apiece. Of course I began to re-evaluate the whole stack and even tried to secure a price reduction. Finally, I put all of the discs back except one, a scarce recording of a 1955 country tune on the M-G-M label.

In terms of acquisitions, the Audio Center has also been the recipient of a number of large gifts from both private record collectors and other individuals who have accumulated recordings. One of the largest single donations was made by Bill Randle, a former disc jockey from Cleveland. We got thousands of records from him—33s, 45s, 78s—containing valuable early jazz and rhythm-and-blues performances. Another radio personality who was known to his younger listeners from the early 50s as "Kousin Kay," also made a large donation to the Center. Walter Kay had been featured on a children's radio show that programmed songs and moralistic "kiddies' stories" based on the exploits of commercial figures such as Hopalong Cassidy, Roy Rogers, and Bugs Bunny. He had kept copies of those broadcast recordings in his own home in Brecksville. While debating what to do with this collection, he had contacted a number of other libraries, but the directors had responded that they could envision no use for them. Of course, when they were offered to us, I gladly accepted the entire collection. One of my student assistants and I rode with my father in his station wagon to Brecksville and picked up between four and five thousand juvenile recordings, mostly 78s—a lot of them very rare items. It's much easier when a significant gift collection is brought to the campus, though. Mr. Alfred K. Pearson of Gardner, Massachusetts recently donated his entire jazz record collection to us—a thousand discs. Most of these recordings have been cataloged in the Center's collection. In fact, almost every record we got from Mr. Pearson was a rare 78 dating between 1925 and 1945.

Another significant gift was acquired through an arrangement I made with Dr. David Stupple of the Sociology Department at Eastern Michigan University in Ypsilanti. I met him at the Second Annual Popular Culture Association Meeting held in Toledo in 1971. He remarked to me that he'd heard several fine comments about the Center's collection of recordings. Then he asked if we would be interested in acquiring his rhythm-and-blues record collection. I said "Yes" without any hesitation, and he invited me to his home in Ypsilanti. I carefully went through all his records, listening to ten hours of music in the process. We finally called it a night at 1:00 a.m., packed up all his records, and brought them back to Bowling Green to become part of our collection. They included nearly one thousand 45s dating from around 1954 to 1959 and including many very rare, very important recordings on such labels as Chess, Checker, Vee Jay, Atlantic—the key recording companies for rhythm and blues since the early fifties. I think that Dr. Stupple had been president of the "Bill Haley Fan Club" at one time, so his collection also yielded all of Bill Haley's early 45s. All the records included in the Stupple Collection were in "mint" condition.

In addition to donated collections and the junk shop/flea market buying, I also engage in the purchase of recordings from mail order auction lists. These forms are circulated by various types of people, some honest and some not so honest. They may be issued as single sheets or booklets from individual dealers, or they may come as an adjunct unit of a collector's trade magazine such as *Record Exchanger*. For example, I recently subscribed to a magazine called *Goldmine* which was originally in Detroit, Michigan. It's a newspaper that just lists dealers and private individuals who are interested in selling or auctioning off records—single 45s, some 78s, and a number of LPs. The problem with this approach is that the prices are *very high*—at least they tend to be much higher than junk shop charges of 25¢, 50¢ or even 75¢ for an album. Through auction lists you may wind up paying $5 $10 or even $15. for the same 75¢ second-hand store album. The advantage of the auctions is that they tend to sell records which are in better condition than the normal junk store variety. Many times I have gone into a junk shop and found a disc in one place and its LP cover in another. Some fool has separated the two items and thereby ruined the record.

It's also very touchy when you deal with people by mail. You must hope that they are honest, and will honor your bid (if you *are* the highest bidder) and not simply elect to deal with friends who may be aware of the level of each bid which comes in. One must also be wary of the manner in which auction records are graded—as "new," "mint," or "very good."[12] Some people don't even want to consider an album unless it's in pristine condition; that is, the cover can't be split, it must be in its original sleeve, and it should be sealed. Recently, a friend of mine bought a sealed record, brought it to the Audio Center to tempt me, and opened it only to discover that the *wrong* record was inside. A number of unscrupulous dealers have gained access to cellophane wrap machines which can seal a record as cleanly as a record dealer, and no one is the wiser until the cover is exposed. Many times a buyer is miles away from where he purchased the album before he discovers the switch. Most times one is left with no recourse.

C: Do you ever attempt to secure unauthorized or "bootleg" recordings[13] for your collection?

S: Remember that the term "bootleg" covers a variety of audio sins. These items are not simply taped copies of regularly released recordings. Mostly they are illegally released duplications of previously unreleased material, some made during concert performances and others stolen directly from recording company vaults. One general definition of a "bootleg" might be a record which is manufactured without the artist's knowledge or permission. Over the past decade we have acquired a number of bootleg recordings for the Audio Center.

Of course the bootleg gambit is nearly as old as the recording business itself. Live opera performances of the early 1900s were recorded behind the scenes on cylinder recorders. There were also the six-inch Little Wonder records. We have quite a large collection of these. The most famous one I know of is a 1914 recording entitled

"Back to the Carolina You Love" by Al Jolson (Little Wonder 20) worth somewhere between $20 and $26 dollars, depending on the condition. When the *Great White Wonder* album, featuring outtakes from Bob Dylan's recording sessions, hit the market in the early 1970s, it became the hallmark of modern rock-and-roll bootlegging. Of course, being the social historian that I am, I thought that this important item should be added to the audio collection. Not that I ever intend to rip-off anyone, certainly not Bob Dylan or Columbia Records, but I felt that the album was *the* prime example of what was being done in respect to illegal record marketing. After that first two-record bootleg set proved to be a financial success, hundreds of illegal recordings were released.

The quality of most concert-recorded bootleg discs is poor. Obviously, the need for taping secrecy, the type of low-visibility equipment employed (usually small, hand-held recorders), and the amateur skills of the operator contribute to this low-grade production. In addition, when the bootleg disc is printed, the vinyl quality is sometimes so poor that after a few plays the grooves fail to track smoothly. Finally, the bootleg packaging process is often strictly hit-and-miss with jumbled listings of songs and artists— and no information about the date or the location of the recorded event. There are occasional instances, however, when a bootleg disc—particularly one containing songs that have been lifted directly from unreleased studio-recorded master discs—is of the highest technical quality. I have even heard a few concert-recorded bootlegs that sounded clearer than the original record company studio-produced releases.

C: How does the Audio Center staff catalog a record album once it arrives at the library?

S: Our records are shelved according to company label and number. This kind of information permits us to locate recordings easily. We have a number of student assistants who help us in shelving both cataloged and uncataloged recordings. We have manufacturers' catalogs and other tools of the record trade including *The Record World, Cash Box, Billboard* and various collectors' journals which feature special discographies, biographical notations and reference sources which enable us to place recordings in a chronological sequence. The Record Research books published by Joel Whitburn list all "Top 100" songs from the *Billboard* charts since 1940. Songs are listed alphabetically and by recording artists in Whitburn's books, along with the date the record first appeared on the *Billboard* chart, how many weeks it remained on the chart, the highest chart position it reached, and also the record company name and number.[14]

C: Bowling Green State University has become a national focal point for Popular Culture study, research and publication. In at least two instances I would suspect that you have designated assignments in regard to university-produced scholarly publications. In specific terms, what is your relationship with Dr. Ray B. Browne, Director of the Center for the Study of Popular Culture and editor of The *Journal of Popular Culture* and the *Journal of American Culture?*

S: Dr. Browne is in charge of the Bowling Green Department and oversees all publishing ventures of the Bowling Green University Popular Press. He's a fascinating man. He earned his Ph.D. at UCLA in American folklore, literature and history. His dissertation research was conducted on foot in his native Alabama where he carried a tape recorder through the back hills gathering the State's oral history in folk songs and tales. Since I am employed by the University Library, I do not report to Dr. Browne. We are close friends and colleagues, though, and I serve voluntarily as an advisory editor for the *Journal of Popular Culture (JPC)*. In terms of publication activities, I have written numerous record reviews for the *JPC*.

Dr. R. Serge Denisoff is a Professor of Sociology at Bowling Green who is an expert on protest music of the mid-twentieth century. In 1971 he launched a journal called *Popular Music and Society (PMS)* as an offshoot of *JPC* which specializes in the scholarly analysis of contemporary music. On request I contribute record reviews to this fine journal.

C: There must be a great diversity in the levels of audio research which you are called upon to assist. I would suspect that the resource requests of undergraduate students are much easier to meet than those of Bowling Green professors and scholars from other universities. Is that true?

S: Frankly, there is no correlation between the academic standing of the person requesting Audio Center assistance and the complexity of his or her record request. The reasons for this are numerous. Experienced researchers tend to initiate tightly structured, logically-ordered audio resource requests which can easily be located in our stacks or through standard record references. Conversely, a freshman student may make requests that are so vague that an Audio Librarian becomes frustrated while attempting to provide specific answers to questions which defy resolution. "Do you have any songs about war?" is one of the most dreaded overkill questions at the Center. Perhaps the most difficult requests I've encountered in the past ten years have come from non-academic Audio Center patrons—a person seeking a recording of the Turkish National Anthem, a woman trying to create an audio background for her daughter's tap-dance routine, and an elderly couple looking for a tune they danced to when they were young (even though they can only remember one word—"dream"—from the title).

Within the past two years, I can recall filling several unique requests for Bowling Green instructors and their students: a) a program of ice skating music for a Physical Education teacher, b) a variety of album covers from the 1950-1975 period for an Art professor who wanted his students to review the techniques of commercial art, c) soundtracks from selected radio and television news programs and documentaries for two history instructors, d) a series of children's records for four elementary education student teachers, and e) a taped recording of "Sparky's Magic Piano" which was originally performed on a Sonovox—an electronic music device—for a music major.

C: Do you permit Bowling Green students and other researchers to borrow albums or tapes from the Audio Center for designated periods of time?

S: Nothing circulates from our collection—but this is not unusual in research libraries which assemble original resource materials. We gladly tape specifically requested items which are to be used for either scholarly purposes or in classroom presentations. The new copyright laws have given us not only the right but also the responsibility to ask patrons to be concise in their duplication requests. Without this element of selectivity, our academic credibility would dissolve and we might become a subsidiary bootleg outlet.

C: I have read several reports which estimate the value of the Audio Center's collection of recordings at between $250,000 and $500,000. Yet I note that your annual budget allocations to purchase new materials have never exceeded $4,000 during any one of the past ten years.[15] How have you been able to enrich your holdings so dramatically on such a meagre annual allowance?

S: As I mentioned earlier, I purchase most recordings for the Audio Center from sources which tend to sell singles and albums at very low prices. At the rate records are going today, a 12″ LP which sold for $3.98 ten years ago would not cost $7.98. From this perspective you can see why our collection is worth so much money. Just try to buy 65,000 LPs at an average list price of $6.00 each. You have $400,000 right there. And that's *just* list price. Considering the fact that at least half of our 65,000 albums are worth much more, and that brings the value of the Audio Center collection close to a million dollars. And I haven't even included the 65,000 45 r.p.m. records, 30,000 78 r.p.m. discs, or the 700 cylinder recordings in that estimate.

Your comment about the meagre budget for building the Audio Center collection is doubly humorous. I not only have to pinch the University's pennies, but I also have to be willing to spend my own money when a bargain appears. I know that sounds administratively crazy, but I'm actually sitting on a bundle of receipts—somewhere in the neighborhood of $3,500—waiting for University reimbursement. Yet I consider these investments to be worthwhile. I just enjoy getting rare records—whether I spend 10¢ for a mint copy of an RCA Victor label 45 r.p.m. by Little Richard which is worth $50. or pay $12. for a Whippet label album by the Robins (who later became part of the Coasters of "Searchin'," "Charlie Brown," and "Yakety Yak" fame). I must admit that my personal record collection hasn't grown much since I took this job. But with the Audio Center's resources at my disposal, I can hear and enjoy music for eight to ten hours a day.

C: In a recent issue of the *Wilson Library Bulletin*, Gordon Stevenson decried the loss of valuable oral history resources—78 r.p.m. records created by black singers during the twenties, thirties, and forties—because of the failure of librarians to collect, catalog and preserve these items.[16] The work you have been doing at Bowling Green since 1967 would seem to allay his fears. I assume that many humanistic scholars [17] and philanthropic organizations are anxious to assist you in your record collecting and cataloging activities. Have you been able to secure financial assistance from agencies such as the National Endowment for Humanities or the Rockefeller Foundation to assist you in preserving contemporary recordings?

S: I'm not sure that your characterization of either the scholars of philanthropic organizations being "anxious" to help the Audio Center is entirely accurate. Nevertheless, I have received some grant money to assist in acquiring hardware—not records—for the Audio Center. In 1975 I was given a small Faculty Development Grant by the University to purchase a portable cassette tape recorder for instructional experimentation. I also used H.E.W. Title VI monies in 1977 to purchase several large pieces of recording equipment—including two Sony open-reel take decks, four small cassette players and eleven sets of headphones. I also used these grant funds to acquire a Soundcraftsman graphic sound-equalizer which I use to enhance the sound of some of our radio tapes and older 78 r.p.m. recordings.

Representatives from the National Endowment for the Humanities were invited to visit the Audio Center a few years ago so that we could develop an appropriate grant request from that body. Unfortunately, these people weren't interested in fostering "Popular Culture" studies at that time. The only other substantial grant that I can recall receiving was a $25,000 "seed money" allotment in the late 1960s from H.E.W. Title II to build the book and recording collections in both the Audio Center and the Popular Culture Library. Although scholars such as Gordon Stevenson, Wayne Wiegand, R. Serge Denisoff, Russel Nye and Ray Browne continue to argue for greater attention to preserving audio resources, I'm afraid that there isn't a groundswell within library organizations, governmental agencies or private humanistic organizations to fund such activities.

C: Have you encountered any efforts by overly enthusiastic private collectors to secure rare recordings from your collection by either purchase or theft?

S: Several years ago I was forced to change the locks to the Audio Center cataloging and record storage areas after we discovered that several recently acquired discs—including a Capitol recording of "Waitin' in Your Welfare Line," an RCA print entitled "Rindercella," and a Rojac label tune called "Christmas in Vietnam"—had been stolen. I don't want to blame a serious collector for this activity, though. Since that incident we've had no security problem. No one is allowed to enter the stack area without my permission. My staff is paranoid about strangers in the collection area.

There are many private record collectors who *wish* they had our materials, and many of them long to see *everything* we have. I either personally escort them through our collection area, or they don't look at all. We don't let any collectors look through our record holdings by themselves, and I frankly don't have time to hover over a collector's shoulder while he "Oohs" and "Aahs" over our holdings. Sometimes we have had people make offers to purchase our materials; of course, I refuse to trade, or sell, anything unless it turns out that we do have a duplicate of a particular recording.

C: You are clearly in a unique position as the Audio Librarian in charge of the nation's largest popular music collection. I'm interested in your observations on two career-related issues. First, what kind of training—professional and general—has enabled you to head this kind of library operation? My second question isn't intended to be embarrassing, though it may sound that way. There seems to be great potential for the charge that a "cult of personality" dominates the development of Bowling Green's Audio Center. I sense that you are presently indispensable because of your total knowledge of the audio collection and your grasp of innovative resource acquisition techniques. Are you grooming a successor for your post—and working with organizations such as the American Library Association (A.L.A.) to foster in-service administrative training programs for future Audio Center directors?

S: Your questions aren't embarrassing, but I doubt that you'll find my responses very enlightening. My original career goal was to be a mechanical engineer with the General Motors Corporation. That goal simply didn't pan out. My interest and involvement with records and libraries date back to the early 1950s. I have an extremely large private collection of albums, 45s and 78s which I began to build in 1951. During my youth I worked in Cleveland

Public Library as a student. Later I was also employed as a clerk in the C.P.L.'s library for the Blind and as a student assistant in the old Bowling Green State University Library building. When I finished my bachelor's degree in 1966 I took a part-time position in the General Reference department at the Cleveland Public Library and began graduate study in library science at Western Reserve University.

The former Director of Bowling Green's campus library system, Dr. A. Robert Rogers, had offered me the Audio Center position when I was still an undergraduate student. This may sound strange because I was an English major at the time, with only five or six courses in library science. Of course, Dr. Rogers knew of my previous library experience and obviously recognized that the special audio collection systems which was being considered would require someone with flexible training and out-of-the-ordinary administrative interests. Humorously, I play no musical instruments, can't read music, and have only a layman's background in electronics. Still, after receiving my M.S.L.S. from Western Reserve in 1967 I was named Director of the Audio Center. To conclude the answer to your first question, though, I'd say that my qualifications for this position are based upon four elements: a) broad experience in dealing with library patrons of all ages and interests, b) sound academic training in *both* the humanities and library science areas, c) a vast avocational knowledge of contemporary music combined with a strong vocational commitment in assembling, cataloging and assisting researchers in using recorded resources, and d) administrative and personal skills in dealing with academic colleagues and non-university clients.

If I left tomorrow, dozens of librarians—former students of mine, record dealers and collectors, and probably an English major or two—would apply for the vacant directorship. My tiny personnel budget has been a major deterrent to training a cadre of Audio Librarians. Most of my graduate assistants are paid by either the English or Popular Culture Departments; only a few work for me for library science credit.

The point that I must make about your "cult of personality" comment hinges upon a realistic evaluation of what has occurred in the Audio Center during the past decade. I've grown from a wet-behind-the-ears graduate into an experienced administrator. My philosophy of assembling the broadest possible range of audio materials[18] has dominated all phases of the Center's evolution. My "indispensability" rests on my knowledge of where we have come from, where we are, and where we still have to go. No single person could learn what I have in less than five years. I'm still a very young man at thirty-eight, and I hope to devote the remainder of my professional career to improving the Audio Center. My experience, commitment, enthusiasm and knowledge—these *are* irreplaceable.

The major stumbling block for training potential audio center directors (at least among the individuals I've encountered at

Bowling Green during the past decade) is the inability of persons to conceive the remarkable breadth of the recorded music field. How many people do you know that like, understand, and appreciate jazz, country, rhythm-and-blues, gospel, rock and other forms of music as well as motion picture soundtracks, radio shows, hymns and songbooks? Not many, I'll wager. I don't either. Call it "eclecticism" or whatever; it's a personality trait that has aided me in collection building and in dealing with an unbelievable diversity of patrons. If I was biased and dictatorial—and narrow in my acquisition program—*then* I'd plead guilty to your "cult of personality" charge. But I'm not any of these things.

C: You've accomplished so much during the past decade that I want to conclude our discussion with two speculative questions. How do you project the development of Bowling Green's Audio Center by the year ... 2000? And what impact do you envision the increased availability of popular music and other recorded resources will have on teaching and scholarly research over the next quarter of a century?

S: I hope that I'm still around—and directing the Audio Center—in twenty-five years. Most of my visions about collection building, sound delivery systems, cataloging and circulation practices for audio resources, and national recognition for Bowling Green as a scholarly resource are far from being fulfilled. Specifically, I want to rewire the entire Audio Center for stereo sound. I'd also like to improve the control console so that we could handle all types of audio recordings. This would mean some expansion from our present open reels decks (10½ inch maximum), cassette players and standard or transcription turntables. Although some people may speculate that records and tapes might be obsolete by the turn of the century, I don't subscribe to that theory. Anyway, how could a social historian interpret America in the 1960s and 1970s without listening to 45s, albums and cassette tapes?

By 2000 A.D. I pray that I'll have a sufficient staff to process all the recordings that have been acquired since 1967. Now you've really got me dreaming. I'd like to think that several "angels" would provide restricted grants to the Audio Center to purchase private record collections which will become available during the next two decades. Other funding, from the University budget or federal grants, should be devoted to equipment acquisition and staff improvement.

Traditionally writers who have conducted research in non-classical music realms have dealt primarily with jazz and blues. By the year 2000 I trust that scholarly studies and discographic resources will be plentiful in all forms of contemporary music—rock 'n' roll, country, gospel, rhythm and blues, and so on. Similarly, I expect additional development in the field of scholarly journals dealing with various audio subjects ranging from country discographies to radio programs. 1 also see greater international exchanges of ideas and resources. Not many Americans realize how thoroughly the music of the black man has been researched in Great Britain already. And can you imagine what will happen when the Germans begin to systematically organize record lists? Seriously, I know that you have already worked with essays from *Buch Und Bibliographie*. That kind of discographic work is just beginning. More song indexes are needed, too. I'm afraid that there are few library training programs that are currently paying much attention to specialized sound collections. Most Media Service Librarians are more skilled in video than audio today.

C: Thanks for sharing your ideas with me. I'm sure that you'll greet 2000 A.D. as Director of the Audio Center. My dream would be that your Bowling Green collection would be the center of a nationwide network of audio resources for academic research. Good luck to your library work.

Notes

[1]Examples of the newspapers which have featured stores on the Audio Center include: " 'Eavesdropping' New Feature at University's Unusual Audio Studio," *The* (Bowling Green, Ohio) *Daily Sentinel-Tribune* (July 23, 1968), p. 2; "Gypsy, Elvis, 007 Are Now Part of Bowling Green's Curriculum," *The* (Cleveland) *Plain Dealer* (July 4, 1969), n.p.; Norman Mark, "What You'd Throw Away Fills Culture Center, "Batman—Ph.D." *The Chicago Tribune Magazine* (October 26, 1969); pp. 72-78; Bill Marvel, "That Calendar? Grist for Scholars?" *The National Observer*, IX, (July 20, 1970), p. 22; Glenn Waggoner, "Pop Music Lover Plays All Day in Job as BGSU Audio Center Head," *The* (Toledo, Ohio) *Blade* (August 19, 1971), n.p.; John S. Brecher, "Is Clyde McCoy a Piece of History? Maybe So. But Maybe Not," *The Wall Street Journal*, CLXXX (September 12, 1972), pp. 1, 36; Adele U. Schweller, "Popular Culture Center A Leader," *The Dayton (Ohio) Leisure Magazine* (February 20, 1972), pp. 4-5; and Frances Sullivan, "Bowling Green's Pop Culture Attic," *The (Toledo, Ohio) Blade Sunday Magazine* (March 3, 1974), pp. 6-9.

[2]The proceedings of this October 1977 symposium, which was organized by Dr. Wayne A. Wiegand and sponsored by the College of Library Science, are recorded in *Popular Culture and the Library: Current Issues Symposium II* (Lexington: Univ. of Kentucky, 1978), 67 pp.

[3]"Audio Center Opened at University Library," *Bowling Green Alumni Bulletin*, LIV (September-October 1968), p. 6. The most recent University report on the ten-year development of the Audio Center may be found in Bruce Dudley, "Comic Books and Rock 'N' Roll: The Artifacts of Our Society," *At Bowling Green: News For Alumni*, VIII (February 1978), pp. 3-7.

[4]Circulation statistics for the Audio Center are provided by Mr. Schurk in his "Annual Report to the Director of Libraries." The Audio Center Director shared photocopies of these reports from May 30, 1968 through August 15, 1977 with the author.

[5]William L. Schurk, "The Popular Culture Library at Bowling Green State University," in *Popular Culture and the Library: Current Issues Symposium II*, edited by Wayne A. Wiegand (Lexington: Univ. of Kentucky, 1978), pp. 53-59.

[6]William L. Schurk, "Recommended Popular Records for a Non-Classical Record Record Library," in *Selected Recordings and Publications in the Popular Music Field*, edited by William Ivey (Nashville: The Country Music Foundation Press, 1975), pp. 1-9.

[7]William L. Schurk and Ray B. Browne, "The Popular Culture Library and Audio Center— Bowling Green State University" (pamphlet). Bowling Green, Ohio: Center for the Study of Popular Culture, n.d.

[8]Mr. Schurk was unable to locate either the author or title of this anthology.

[9]It should be noted that Bowling Green State University is one of the nine academic libraries which contribute information on an annual catalog basis to the *Music, Books on Music, and Sound Recordings* catalog issued by the Library of Congress. The other institutions which

provide audio data to Washington are: University of Toronto, Stanford University, University of Chicago, University of North Carolina, Oberlin College, Ohio State University, Harvard University, and the University of Illinois.

[10]Roy Bongartz, "Center For Popular Culture," *Nation*, CCXVII (September 17, 1973), pp. 239-242.

[11]Mr. Schurk neglected to mention one of his most publicized record acquisition coups. In September 1973 he purchased the entire stock of a Springfield, Ohio company called "The Record Shop," *The BG News*, LVII (October 9, 1973), p. 3., and Edward Morris, "America's Biggest Jukebox," *The Press*, III (January 1978), pp. 1, 4. He also failed to mention the large number of used 45 r.p.m. juke box records which were annually donated to the Audio Center by The Ohio Vending Company. Finally, although commenting on the gifts from individual radio personalities, he neglected to note that various nearby stations—WMGS and WOHO, for example—regularly channel promotional recordings to the Audio Center. See Edward Morris, "Bowling Green U.'s Keen Audio Center,"*Billboard*, LXXXVII (December 20, 1975), p. 27.

[12]To illustrate Mr. Schurk's warning in a humorous fashion, the "grading system" developed by record dealer Richard A. Bass to describe the condition of his auction discs is reproduced below:

N——New
VG——Very Good, Excellent (like new to very minor surface scratches that are inaudible)
G——Good (minor scratches that are only slightly noticeable if at all)
G——Good (noticeable scratches but music predominates)
F——Fair (extensive scratches—music and scratches fight it out)
P——Poor (very extensive scratches—scratches blot out most of the music, may skip)

See "Auction 17—Blues, R & B, Soul, Rockabilly, R & R, C & W, and Black Vocal Groups 45s, 78s, and LPs" (Postal date May 28, 1978) mailed to B. Lee Cooper by Richard A. Bass, 915 York Street, Oakland, California 94610 USA.

[13]A fine story on the Audio Center's bootleg record resources was published in *The BG News* under the title "Bootleg Cuts Available." Unfortunately the photocopy of this essay which I secured from Mr. Schurk lacks both a publication date and a page number. Among the specific bootleg albums cited by Chris Flowers, the author of the student newspaper article, were: The Beatles' *Kum Back*, Bob Dylan's *Great White Wonder*, and Crosby, Stills, and Nash's *Wooden Nickel* in addition to untitled discs by The Band, Jethro Tull and The Rolling Stones.

[14]Published in Menomonee Falls, Wisconsin, by Richard Research, Inc., Joel C. Whitburn's *Billboard* chart data have become the key scholarly reference for chronicling the rise and fall of popular recordings. The different sets of listings provided by Whitburn include: *Top Pop ("Hot 100") Records, 1955-1972* (1973), *Top Pop Records, 1940-1955* (1973), *Top LP Records, 1945-1972* (1973), *Top Country & Western Records, 1949-1971 (1972)*, *Top Rhythm & Blues ("Soul") Records, 1949-1971* (1972), and *Top Easy Listening Records, 1961-1974* (1975). These basic chronological listings are updated annually with supplementary booklets.

[15]Schurk, "Annual Report to the Director of Libraries" (1968-1977). See note 4 above.

[16]Gordon Stevenson, "Race Records: Victims of Benign Neglect in Libraries," *Wilson Library Bulletin*, L (November 1975), pp. 224-232. Also see two other Stevenson essays: "Popular Culture and the Public Library," in *Advance in Librarianship—VII*, edited by Melvin J. Voight and Michael H. Harris (New York: Academic Press, 1977), pp. 177-229 and "The Wayward Scholar: Resources and Research in Popular Culture," *Library Trends*, XXV (April 1977), pp. 778-818.

[17]The Popular Culture Movement has been criticized by a variety of academicians including Dwight MacDonald, Russell Kirk and William Gass. And beyond the realm of academia, many theologians, politicians, journalists and business men have condemned the study of contemporary film, television, radio and popular music as "faddism." Nonetheless, Popular Culture Studies have received positive attention from a broad spectrum of teachers, writers, lecturers, and research specialists including Carl Bode, Leslie A. Fiedler, Russel B. Nye, Marshall Fishwick, John Cawelti, Fred E.H. Schroeder, Susan Sontag, Roderick Nash, David Noble, Jerome Rodnitzky, Ray B. Browne, David Madden, Arthur Berger, Richard A. Peterson, David Feldman, Paul M. Hirsch, Marshall McLuhan, Gordon Stevenson, and R. Serge Denisoff, among hundreds.

[18]The breadth of Mr. Schurk's definition includes not only records (33 1/3, 45, and 78 r.p.m), tapes, (reel-to-reel and cassette), and cylinders, but also album covers, record jackets and sleeves, reference books and discographies, biographical studies on popular artists, sheet music and lyric magazines, portraits of pop singers, record auction lists and rock concert posters.

"...librarians should be forewarned that several special interest groups would like to influence library acquisition practices in respect to popular records."

B.Lee Cooper, "An Opening Day Collection of Popular Recordings: Searching for Discographic Standards"

XV

Without a doubt the general public thinks of popular culture in terms of pop music, even before it would think of television, bestsellers and Big Macs. This is understandable, because pop music is almost inescapable in today's world. And yet nowhere has there been a practical guide available for a library to get a start in this rapidly changing area. For this, B. Lee Cooper's article is truly a pioneer, being at once a theoretical discussion of popular music of recent decades and its place in the library, a practical rationale for an acquisition policy, and an exemplary discography for getting a library off to a high-quality start on a popular music collection. In his concluding remarks, Cooper identifies some of the *controversial* aspects about his own recommended rationale, policies and discography; anyone who is working with the selection and acquisition of popular materials for a library, a museum or for teaching should read these brief, self-critical questions. They represent a model of intellectual openness in these popular areas where dogmatic partisanship of "true believers" is as dangerous to responsible collecting as are any elitist prejudices or establishment resistance to popular collecting.

B. Lee Cooper is Professor of History and Vice President for Academic Affairs at Newberry College in South Carolina. He has authored a variety of essays which illustrate techniques for utilizing popular music lyrics and science fiction stories as learning resources. Dr. Cooper's articles and record reviews have appeared in *Audiovisual Instruction, The History Teacher, Social Education, The Journal of Negro Education, Rockingchair, The Library-College Experimenter, Media and Methods, The Journal of Popular Culture, Social Studies, The JEMF Quarterly, Music World and Record Digest, The History and Social Science Teacher, The International Journal of Instructional Media, Religious Education,* and *The American Historical Association Newsletter.* He has also presented papers on teaching with popular culture materials at meetings of the American Historical Association, the National Council for the Social Studies, the Great Lakes Regional History Conference, the American Psychological Association, and the Popular Culture Association.

B. Lee Cooper

An Opening Day Collection
of Popular Music Resources:
Searching for Discographic Standards

It is obvious that if academic librarians begin to take popular culture as seriously as (teaching and writing) scholars, there are likely to be 'a number of complex problems of a practical nature which will have to be considered. Because we have been taught to exercise qualitative judgments in building collections, we will need to find new guidelines and strategies to provide alternatives to our traditional selections criteria.

Professor Gordon Stevenson
School of Library and Information Science
State University of New York at Albany

DURING THE PAST decade a variety of scholars—including musical theorists, psychologists, cultural historians, teachers of poetry and literature, sociologists, and linguists—have begun to investigate the meaning and social impact of popular music with great care. And while many people, including librarians, have questioned the educational merits of such an endeavor, this serious study is no quirk. It marks a concerted effort to comprehend the meaning of the immense popularity and influence of contemporary singers, song-writers, and their songs.

Despite the growing number of articles published in scholarly journals, the many presentations delivered at professional meetings, and the numerous courses which have been implemented and taught on campuses throughout the United States, it is notable that informed discussions about the acquisition, classification, and distribution of contemporary music resources have not surfaced in many library journals.[1] In addition, only one brief essay has been published since 1970 which attempts to define the role of a reference librarian in assembling media and print resources and in providing technical assistance to a faculty member teaching a course on popular music.[2] Worse yet, the larger question of collection construction has been almost totally neglected.[3] Most librarians would readily acknowledge that responding to a specific album request from a single professor is an easy task compared to the complex challenge of assembling an entire collection of contemporary recordings appropriate for general use by both students and instructors. Clearly, the library profession needs to establish a set of guidelines for creating a general collection of popular music sources.

Traditional training in library science does not include the critical review and evaluation of the works of popular recording artists. The following pages offer two forms of bibliographic/discographic assistance to librarians who are searching for constructive suggestions about building basic, representative holdings in the area of popular music.

I. Recognizing the Need

Although experts on popular music disagree on many issues, they tend to agree that music of today is notably different from music produced during any other period in history. There are at least three reasons for this. First, commercial distribution and radio broadcasting of popular songs have created a vast listening public which is constantly exposed to new tunes in cars, homes, elevators, department stores, and so on. The popular song is a universally available phenomenon. Second, technological advancements in musical instruments and other sound-producing equipment (tape recorders, speakers, and amplifiers) enable singers to produce such high quality recorded material that, as a recent audio cassette advertisement declares, "You can't tell whether it's Ella Fitzgerald (live) or Memorex." Finally, the quality of song lyrics has increased so dramatically that many English teachers refer to popular song-writers such as Bob Dylan, Joni Mitchell, Paul Simon, and Carole King as "poets."[4] But while the lyrics of some contemporary songs have been richly praised as poetry, the words of other popular tunes have been condemned by politicians, theologians, and journalists as sinister propaganda tools.[5] Because modern singers (unlike their pre-1960 predecessors) tend to deal lyrically with controversial issues, they have frequently created considerable concern about the social influence of popular music. Anti-war chants, religious tunes, women's liberation melodies, and social protest songs have been used to challenge the governmental ideals of the United States. It is this thematic quality of contemporary music which should be of particular interest to most teachers.

The attitudes and images portrayed in modern lyrics demand careful study and reflection because they strike at the heart of the major social and political issues of contemporary life—ecology, women's liberation, political cynicism, militarism, personal freedom, drug abuse, and governmental responsibility.[6] Contemporary songs are invaluable tools for pursuing the twin educational goals of self-knowledge and social analysis. If teachers want their students to examine American society through the lyrical observations of contemporary songwriters such as John Lennon, Curtis Mayfield, Stevie Wonder, Neil Diamond, Paul McCartney, and Peter Townsend, then academic libraries must make appropriate instructional materials available. Teachers who recognize the value of recorded resources will soon spur librarians to develop core collections of popular music albums which can be successfully utilized as learning resources in courses ranging from cultural history to contemporary poetry. Ideally, however, librarians would anticipate this coming need.

But librarians should be forewarned that several special interest groups would like to influence library acquisition practices in respect to popular records. For several years sales directors of commercial recording companies such as RCA, Columbia, and Capitol have observed the growing interest of academicians in non-print instructional resources. They have also noted with great interest the bulk purchasing potential of library budgets. This has led to the institution of a variety of special sales arrangements. To cite just one example, Columbia Records offers a one-year library subscription service which permits a librarian to select seventy (70) records from an annual list of 250 choices. The fee for this record purchasing plan is $250 annually. The Columbia advertising letter notes that this service

> ...offers you the *very latest* CBS, Columbia, Epic and associated label releases, at the same time that they are delivered to regular retail record shops—but you pay only 45% of the suggested list prices: a 55% discount! Leonard Bernstein and the New York Philharmonic; Barbra Streisand; Glenn Gould; E. Power Biggs; Neil Diamond; Eugene Ormandy and the Philadelphia Orchestra; Bob Dylan; Willie Nelson; Walter Carlos; the Isley Brothers; Chicago; Lazar Berman; Paul Simon; Johnny Cash; Rudolf Serkin; Miles David.... These are just a few of the artists whose releases will be sent *directly from the CBS/Columbia pressing plant to your library, postpaid.*[7]

The issue is not the cost-efficiency of the Columbia plan, but *how* Columbia determines *which* recordings *should* be available in a general collection. Although the brochure describing the Columbia Subscription Service states that the company will provide "a permanent classic 'basic repertory' list" to enable librarians "...to build or replenish your classical foundation...," no such list of contemporary music "classics" is mentioned. This leaves the librarian with the impression that recordings by Bob Dylan, Willie Nelson, The Isley Brothers, and Chicago are of equal worth (or, from a negative standpoint, non-worth).

II. Approaching the Issue

The availability of rock discographies—lists of popular albums and single records—is limited. One source of contemporary music analysis is the randomly structured record review sections in publications such as *Stereo Review, High Fidelity,* and *The Rolling Stone.* Since these reviews tend to deal with albums released within three months of the review, they are hardly a suitable guide for creating a broad historical collection. The selected discographies recommended below are drawn primarily from recent texts written about the Rock Era, 1950-1979. Although they do offer greater historical perspective than standard record review, only a few contain entries with full bibliographic notations—complete album title, performing artist(s), recording company, location of production and/or distribution center, and date of release.

Selected Popular Music Discographies

"Youth and Music," in *Values and Youth: Teaching Social Studies in an Age of Crisis—No. 2,* edited by Robert D. Barr (Washington, DC: National Council for the Social Studies, 1971), pp. 99-103.

"Selected Discography: 1953-1971," in *The Story of Rock* (2nd ed.) by Carl Belz (New York: Harper and Row, 1972), pp. 244-273.

"A Discography of Popular Hits, 1955-1971," in *"...And The Hits Just Keep on Comin'"* by Peter E. Berry (Syracuse, New York: Syracuse University Press, 1977), pp. 169-276.

Alan Betrock (comp.), *Girl Groups: An Annotated Discography, 1960-65* (New York: A. Betrock, n.d.), pp. 1-28.

John Blair (comp), *The Illustrated Discography of Surf Music, 1959-1965.* Riverside, California: J. Bee Productions, 1978.

Harry Castleman and Walter J. Podrazik (comps.), *All Together Now: The First Complete Beatles Discography, 1961-1975.* New York: Ballantine Books, Inc., 1975.

Harry Castleman and Walter J. Podrazik (comps.), *The Beatles Again.* Ann Arbor, Michigan: The Pierian Press, 1977.

"Selected Discography of American Protest Songs," in *Great Day Coming: Folk Music and the American Left* by R. Serge Denisoff (Baltimore, Maryland: Penguin Books, Inc., 1971), pp. 190-192.

R. Serge Denisoff (comp.), *Songs of Protest, War, and Peace: A Bibliography and Discography.* Santa Barbara, California: American Bibliographical Center—Clio Press, Inc., 1973.

Joe Edwards (comp.), *Top 10's and Trivia of Rock and Roll and Rhythm and Blues, 1950-1973.* St. Louis, Missouri: Blueberry Hill Publishing Company, 1974. (Supplements for 1974, 1975...also available).

Robert D. Ferlingere (comp.), *A Discography of Rhythm & Blues and Rock 'N' Roll Vocal Groups, 1945 to 1965.* Hayward, California: California Trade School, 1976.

"Discography," in *Blues From the Delta* by William Ferris (Garden City, New York: Doubleday and Company, Inc., 1979), pp. 205-220.

Paul Garbaccini (comp.), *Rock Critics' Choice: The Top 200 Albums.* New York: Quick Fox (Omnibus Press), 1978.

Phyl Garland, "Basic Library of Rhythm-and-Blues," *Stereo Review,* XLII (May 1979), pp. 72-77.

"Discography," in *The Sound of Soul: The History of Black Music* by Phyl Garland (Chicago: Henry Regnery Company, 1969), pp. 199-202.

"Play List," in *The Sound of the City: The Rise of Rock and Roll* by Charlie Gillett (New York: Outerbridge and Dienstfrey, 1970), pp. 343-346.

Fernando L. Gonzalez (comp.), *Disco-File: The Discographical Catalog of American Rock and Roll and Rhythm and Blues, 1902 to 1976* (Second Edition). Flushing, New York: P.O. Box 1812, 1977.

"Selected Discography," in *Feel Like Going Home: Portraits in Blues and Rock 'N' Roll* by Peter Guralnick (New York: Outerbridge and Dienstfrey, 1971), pp. 212-217.

"A Selective Discography" in *Rock: From Elvis Presley to the Rolling Stones* by Mike Jahn (New York: Quadrangle Books, 1973), pp. 295-302.

"A Discography," in *It's Too Late To Stop Now: A Rock and Roll Journal* by John

Landau (San Francisco, California: Straight Arrow Books, 1972) pp. 224-227.

"Discography," in *Soul Music!* by Rochelle Larkin (New York: Lancer Books, 1970), pp. 181-189.

Mike Leadbitter and Neil Slaven (comps.), *Blues Records, 1943-66: A Discography.* New York: Oak Publications, 1968.

"Bibliography—Record Albums Cited," in *Country Music U.S.A.* by Bill C. Malone (Austin, Texas: University of Texas Press, 1968), pp. 367-378.

"Notes and Discographies," in *Mystery Train: Images of American in Rock 'N' Roll Music* by Greil Marcus (New York: E. P. Dutton and Company, Inc., 1975), pp. 209-264.

Jean-Charles Marion, "Essential Recordings: Part 1—A Beginners Basic Library," *Record Exchanger,* IV (1975), pp. 25, 30.

Christopher May, "A Basic List of Rock Records," *BRIO,* XIII (Autumn 1976), pp. 34-38.

Charles Miron (comp.), *Rock Gold: All The Hit Charts From 1955 to 1976.* New York: Drake Publishers, Inc., 1977.

"The Motown Era Discography," in *The Motown Era* (New York: Grosset and Dunlap, Inc., 1971), pp. 5-16.

Joe Murrels (comp.), *The Book of Golden Discs* (rev. edition). London: Barrie and Jenkins, Ltd., 1978.

"Discography," in *The Poetry of Soul* by A. X. Nicholas (New York: Bantam Books, (1971), pp. 93-98.

"Discography," in *Woke Up This Mornin': Poetry of the Blues* by A. X. Nicholas (New York: Bantam Books, 1973), pp. 119-122.

Stephen Nugent and Charlie Gillett (comps.), *Rock Almanac: Top Twenty American and British Singles and Albums of the '50's, '60's, and '70's.* Garden City, New York: Anchor Press/Doubleday, 1976.

Jim O'Connor, "A Rock and Roll Discography," *School Library Journal,* XXII (September 1975), pp. 21-24.

Michael Olds, "From Sergeant Pepper to Captain Fantastic: A Basic Rock Collection," *Hoosier School Libraries,* XVI (December 1976), pp. 17-19.

Jerry Osborne (comp.), *55 Years of Recorded Country/Western Music.* Phoenix, Arizona: O'Sullivan, Woodside and Company, 1976.

Jerry Osborne (comp.), Popular and Rock Records, 1948-1978 (2nd Edition). Phoenix, Arizona: O'Sullivan, Woodside, and Company, 1978.

Jerry Osborne (comp.), *Record Albums, 1948-1978* (2nd Edition). Phoenix, Arizona: O'Sullivan, Woodside and Company, 1978.

Michael R. Pitts and Louis H. Harrison (comps.), *Hollywood on Record: The Film Stars' Discography.* Metuchen, New Jersey: Scarecrow Press, Inc., 1978.

Dan Price, "Bibliography of Bob Dylan: Articles and Books, By and About; Albums and Singles Published; and Unreleased Recordings," *Popular Music and Society,* III (1974), pp. 227-241.

Steve Propes, *Golden Goodies: A Guide to 50's and 60's Popular Rock and Roll Record Collecting.* Radnor, Pennsylvania: Chilton Book Company, 1975.

Steve Propes, *Those Oldies But Goodies: A Guide to 50's Record Collecting.* New York: Collier Books, 1973.

Jim Quirin and Barry Cohen (comps.). *Chartmasters' Rock 100: An Authoritative Ranking of the 100 Most Popular Songs For Each Year, 1956 Through 1975* (2nd ed.). Covington, Louisiana: Chartmasters, 1976.

Ulrich Raschke, "One Hundred Times Pop Music: Concrete Advice For the Construction of a Basic Collection," *Buch and Bibliographie,* XXVII (July-August 1975), pp. 661-682.

"Rock Albums of Interest," in *Pop, Rock, and Soul* by Richard Robinson (New York: (Pyramid Books, 1972), pp. 181-182.

"Albums of Interest," in *The Rock Scene* by Richard Robinson and Andy Swerling
(New York: Pyramid Books, 1971), pp. 162-166.

"Selected Discography," in *Minstrels of the Dawn: The Folk-Protest Singer As
a Cultural Hero* by Jerome L. Rodnitzky (Chicago: Nelson-Hall, Inc., 1976),
pp. 181-184.

H. Kandy Rohde (ed.), *The Gold of Rock and Roll,* 1955-1967. New York:
Arbor House, 1970.

The Rolling Stone Record Review. New York: Pocket Books, 1971.

The Rolling Stone Record Review—Vol. II. New York: Pocket Books, 1974.

"Chicago R & B Hits, 1945-59," in *Chicago Breakdown* by Mike Rowe (New York:
Drake Publishers, Inc., 1975), pp. 217-218.

Ellen Sander and Tom Clark, "A Rock Taxonomy," in *Trips: Rock Life in the Sixties*
by Ellen Sander (New York: Charles Scribner's Sons, 1973), pp. 162-258.

William L. Schurk, "Recommended Popular Records for a non-Classical Record
Library," in *Selected Recordings and Publications in the
Popular Music Field,* edited by William Ivey (Nashville,
Tennessee: The Country Music Foundation Press, 1975), pp. 1-9.

"Discography," in *Honkers and Shouters: The Golden Years of Rhythm and Blues*
by Arnold Shaw (New York: Collier Books, 1978), pp. 529-541.

"Discography," in *The Rockin' 50's: The Decade That Transformed the Pop Music
Scene* by Arnold Shaw (New York: Hawthorn Books, Inc., 1974), pp. 282-288.

"Discography," in *The World of Soul* by Arnold Shaw (New York: Paperback
Library, 1971), pp. 361-368.

John L. Smith (comp.), *Johnny Cash Discography and Recording History, 1955-1968.*
Los Angeles, California: John Edwards Memorial Foundation, Inc., 1969.

Clive Solomon (comp.), *Record Hits: The British Top 50 Charts, 1954-1976.* London:
Omnibus Press, 1977.

Joel Whitburn (comp.), *Pop Annual, 1955-1977.* Menomonee Falls, Wisconsin:
Record Research, Inc., 1978.

Joel Whitburn (comp.), *Top Country and Western Records, 1949-1971.* Menomonee
Falls, Wisconsin: Record Research, Inc., 1972. (Supplements for 1972-73, 1974...
also available).

Joel Whitburn (comp.), *Top Easy Listening Records, 1961-1974.* Menomonee Falls,
Wisconsin: Record Research, Inc., 1975. (Supplements for 1975, 1976...also
available).

Joel Whitburn (comp.), *Top LP Records, 1945-1972.* Menomonee Falls, Wisconsin:
Record Research, Inc., 1973. (Supplements for 1973, 1974...also available).

Joel Whitburn (comp.), *Top Pop Records, 1940-1955.* Menomonee Falls, Wisconsin:
Record Research, 1973.

Joel Whitburn (comp.), *Top Pop Records, 1955-1972.* Menomonee Falls, Wisconsin:
Record Research, Inc., 1973. (Supplements for 1973, 1974...also available).

Joel Whitburn (comp.), *Top Rhythm and Blues Records, 1949-1971.* Menomonee
Falls, Wisconsin: Record Research Inc., 1973. (Supplements for 1972-73, 1974...
also available).

"Discography," in *Electric Children: Roots and Branches of Modern Folkrock*
by Jacques Vassal (New York: Taplinger Publishing Company, 1976), pp. 252-257.

"Discography," in *Pop Music and the School,* edited by Graham Vulliamy and
Ed Lee (Cambridge: Cambridge University Press, 1976), pp. 195-204.

III. Focusing on Specific Albums

The Librarian concerned with record selection might begin
with the question "What is popular music?" The answers to this

query vary so dramatically that some librarians might wonder whether any reasonable (or rational) discographic guidelines for a core collection of contemporary recordings are possible. Among recent definitions of "Popular Music," the following selections are typical:

> ...From a theoretical standpoint rock and roll music is a regular, continuous four-beat rhythm in a twelve-beat or thirty-two beat blues song pattern. The accompaniment usually includes electronically-amplified guitars. Typical performances contain extreme voice range and a standard change of tone.[8]

> Pop music, normally called "rock music" today, cannot be defined by musical scores. Cataloging of its notes and music has been done in retrospect. Playing and listening enjoyment, rhythm, loud beat and variation, immediacy, casual and improvised composition, experimentation and stereotypes, dissonance and displacement, irony and earnest but naive seriousness, sentimentality and bad taste, pathos and brutality, though, coldness, reflection, vibration, pulsation, tenderness, intelligence, abstraction, intoxication, sorrow, forgetfullness, stimulation, trembling, dreams, and life: that is pop music.[9]

> For a time rock 'n' roll had become a life style, but in the early '70's it tended to recede more to the old-time status of pop music as primarily an entertainment form... Almost any type of number—hard rock, soft rock, rock revival, country and western, soul, ballad—had a chance at hit status, and the "Top 40 Charts" in both albums and singles indicated that no one type of music had a monopoly on public attention.[10]

> Popular music is the sum total of those taste units, social groups and musical genres which coalesce along certain taste and preference similarities in a given space and time. These taste publics and genres are affected by a number of factors, predominately age, accessibility, race, class, and education... People select what they like from what they hear. The reasons for this selection are influenced by many factors some of which have little to do with the esthetic quality of a song or instrumental piece.[11]

Carl Belz has suggested the ultimate commentary on this definitional dilemma by noting that "...any listener who wants rock defined *specifically* is probably unable to recognize it."[12]

The final section of this essay suggests an "Opening Day Collection" of 33 1/3 r.p.m. recordings which should adequately serve sociology, English, history, psychology, and political science teachers who wish to involve their students in a critical examination of lyrical commentaries about contemporary American society. While it would be easier to provide complete record lists from major music corporations—Columbia, RCA, Capitol, MCA, etc.—and to claim that academic libraries should acquire *all* of the recordings released by these companies, such an assertion would be professionally disgraceful, if not financially disastrous in an age of shrinking library budgets. The careful selection of appropriate popular music resources by academic librarians is mandatory. But who should initiate such judgments? Ideally, the foremost popular music scholars and teachers experienced in the use of musical resources should offer suggestions to assist acquisitions librarians. Unfortunately, this does not happen frequently, mostly because teachers, scholars, and librarians are not communicating. On the one hand, librarians have been deaf to the value of the non-traditional oral history contained in contemporary lyrics; on the other hand, most popular music scholars have condemned academic bookmen as bibliographic elitists who treasure only the latest printed literary criticism on Steinbeck and Hemingway while ignoring the audio social commentaries of Phil Ochs, Bob Dylan, Les McCann, Joni Mitchell, Janis Ian, Stevie Wonder, and others. Such unproductive relations must cease. Instead, they should be replaced by tough-minded, critical exchanges over *which* records by *which* artists ought to be housed in the library for student and faculty use.

The following recommendation of an "Opening Day Collection" of popular music resources attempts both to fill a gap in library literature and to foster discussion and debate among librarians and their academic patrons. Obviously, a discographer inevitably falls prey to subjectivity in assembling a relatively brief list of recordings which is designed to illustrate the most relevant musical trends and social commentary over the past quarter century. The criteria and organizational structure used to assemble this listing are outlined below:

A. Although the 45 r.p.m. record remains the chief quantative source of identifying "hit" music (even though it is clearly *not* the financial basis for celebrity status when compared to concert performance receipts and album sales income), this discography consists entirely of 33 1/3 r.p.m. recordings. Stated simply, albums offer academic librarians greater cost-efficiency on a song-per-dollar-invested basis.

B. The record anthology, featuring either popular tunes by various artists or the "Greatest Hits" of a group or an individual performer, constitutes this discography's structural backbone.

C. With few exceptions, the recordings listed in this discography are currently available at most retail music stores or can be easily purchased by librarians through wholesale record distribution outlets. Exotic foreign rock import discs, bootleg records, and rare, out-of-print 1950's rhythm and blues albums have purposely been omitted from this discography.

D. The organizational pattern of this discography avoids two traditional arrangements. First, the "alphabetical listing by artist" format was rejected because of the desire to emphasize album-length anthologies. Second, the traditional division of songs or albums into genre categories such as "Jazz," "Rock," "Rhythm and Blues," "Pop," "Folk," "Country and Western," "Soul," and "Bluegrass" was avoided because so many popular artists such as Bob Dylan, Elvis Presley, Carole King, and Paul Simon frequently cross these narrow stylistic barriers. The specific discographic structure utilized in the following pages is outlined below:

I.   ANTHOLOGY ALBUMS—Featuring Songs by Various Artists
           Artists
           A. Chronological Song Order

                B. Random Song Order

                C. Recordings of "Live" Performances

                D. Special Collections

II.   GREATEST HITS ALBUMS—Featuring Individual or or Group Performances

                A. Chronological Song Order

                B. Random Song Order

                C. Recordings of "Live" Performances

                D. Special Collections

III.   STANDARD ALBUMS

                A. Individual Artists

                B. Group Performances

IV.   OTHER TYPES OF ALBUMS

                A. Motion Picture Soundtracks

                B. Novelty and Comedy Recordings

                C. Bootleg Releases

                D. Imported Recordings

                E. Special Collections and Documentary Recordings

An Opening Day Collection of Popular Music Resources for College and University Libraries

I. Anthology Albums—Featuring Songs by Various Artists

    A. Chronological Song Order

        1. *Dick Clark/20 Years of Rock and Roll* (BDS 5133-2). New York: Buddah Records, Inc., 1973.

        —Features Carl Perkins, the Kingsmen, Van Morrison, Curtis Mayfield, and others.

        2. *History of Rhythm and Blues, 1947-1967*—8 Volumes (SD 8161-4/ 8193-4/8208-9). New York: Atlantic Recording Corporation, 1968 (Vol. I-VI) and 1969 (Vol. VII-VIII).

        —Features the Ravens, the Cardinals, Leadbelly, the Orioles, Joe Turner the Chords, Ivory Joe Hunter, the Coasters, the Drifters, Clyde McPhatter, Ben E. King, Barbara Lewis, Wilson Pickett, Aretha Franklin, Otis Redding, and others.

        3. *Rock 'N' Soul: The History of Rock in the Pre-Battle Decade of Rock*— 9 Volumes (ABCX 1955-64). Los Angeles, California: ABC Records, Inc., 1973.

        —Features Willie Mae Thornton, the Cadillacs, Frankie Lymon and the Teenagers, Shirley and Lee, the Dells, Lloyd Price, the Olympics, Little Ceasar and the Romans, Gene Chandler, the Impressions, and others.

        4. *The Roots of Rock 'N Roll* (SJL 2221). New York: Arista Records, Inc., 1977.

        —Features Wild Bill Moore, Johnny Otis, Nappy Brown, Big Maybelle. the Ravens, Clarence Palmer and the Jive Bombers, and others.

        5. *This Is How It All Began: The Roots of Rock 'N' Roll as Recorded From 1945 to 1955 on Specialty Records* — 2 Volumes (SPS 2117/2118). Hollywood, California: Specialty Records, Inc., 1969/1970.

—Features Roy Milton, Don and Dewey, Larry Williams, Lloyd Price, Little Richard, and others

B. Random Song Order

1. *And The Rock Lives On . . .* 3 Volumes (SVL 1020/21/22). Sunnyvale, California: Sunnyvale Records, 1978.

   —Includes Robert and Johnny, The Capris, Billy Bland, The Fiestas, The Royaltones, Lee Allen, Billy Myles, The Turbans, and others.

2. *At The Hop* (AA 1111/12). Los Angeles, California: ABC Records, Inc., 1978.

   —Includes Danny and The Juniors, Three Dog Night, Del Shannon, The Impressions, Lloyd Price, Sonny James, The Royal Teens, Pat Boone, George Hamilton IV, and others.

3. *The Blues*—5 volumes (LPS 4026/27/34/42/51). Chicago: Cadet (Chess) Records, n.d.

   —Includes Little Walter Chuck Berry, Howlin' Wolf, Muddy Waters, Willie Mabon, and others.

4. *The Blues are Black* (P 13211). New York: Columbia Records/CBS, Inc., 1976.

   —Includes Mississippi John Hurt, Blind Lemon Jefferson, Leadbelly, Bessie Smith, Robert Johnson, Billie Holiday, Elmore James, and others.

5. *Cadence Classics*—3 Volumes (BR 4000/4001/4002). Los Angeles, California: Barnaby Records, 1975.

   —Features the Everly Brothers, Link Wray, The Chordettes, Eddie Hodges, Bill Hayes, Johnny Tillotson, and Lenny Welch.

6. *Classic Blues*—2 Volumes (BLC 6062/6062). New York: ABC Records, Inc., 1973.

   —Features Ray Charles, T-Bone Walker, Jimmy Witherspoon, John Lee Hooker, Jimmy Reed, and Otis Spann

7. *Cruisin' The Fifties and Sixties: A History of Rock and Roll Radio*— 13 volumes (INCM 2000-2012). Sunnyvale, California: Increase Records, 1970 (Vol. 1956-62), 1972 (Vol. 1944 and 1963), and 1973 (Vol. 1964-67.

   —Features Janis Ian, Sandy Posey, Barry McGuire, Chuck Berry, Shep and the Limelites, Little Anthony and the Imperials, Big Jay McNeeley Wilbert Harrison, Bobby Day, the Tuneweavers, Bo Diddley, the Charms, and others.

8. *Discotech* #1 (M6 824 S1). Hollywood, California: Motown Record Corporation, 1975.

   —Includes Stevie Wonder, Martha Reeves and The Vandellas, The Temptations, Junior Walker and The Allstars, Marvin Gaye, and others.

9. *Echoes of a Rock Era*—3 Volumes (RE 111/112/113). New York: Roulette Records, Inc., 1971.

   —Features Sonny Til and the Orioles, the Penguins, the Moonglows, Maurice Williams and the Zodiacs, Mary Wells, the Shirelles, and others.

10. *The 50's Greatest Hits* (G 30592). New York: Columbia Records/CBS, Inc., 1972.

    —Features Johnny Mathis, Doris Day, Johnny Ray, the Four Lads, and others.

11. *14 Golden Recordings From the Historic Vaults of Duke/Peacock Records*—2 *Volumes* (ABCX 784/789). New York: ABC Records, Inc., 1973.

    —Features Johnny Ace, Bobby Bland, Roy Head, Ernie K—Doe, Junior

Parker, Willie Mae Thornton, and others

12. *14 Golden Recordings From the Historical Vaults of Vee Jay Records* (ABCX 785). Los Angeles, California: ABC Records, Inc., 1973.
    —Features Dee Clark, Gladys Knight and the Pips, John Lee Hooker, and others.

13. *Alan Freed's "Golden Pics"* (LP 313). New York: End Records, n.d.
    —Includes Little Richard, The Nutmegs, Chuck Berry, The Willows, Little Walter and others.

14. *Alan Freed's Memory Lane* (R 42041). New York: Roulette Records, Inc., n.d.
    —Includes The Moonglows, Jesse Belvin, Little Anthony and The Imperials, Jerry Butler, and others.

15. *Golden Goodies*—19 volumes (R 25207/09-19/38-42/47-48). New York: Roulette Records, Inc., n.d.
    —Includes The Spaniels, Joey Dee, Buddy Knox, Frankie Lymon, The Tune Weavers, The Dubs, Dave "Baby" Cortez, Johnny and The Hurricanes, The G-Clefs, Larry Williams, Jack Scott, The Rays, and others.

16. Great Bluesmen—Recorded Live at the Newport Folk Festivals in Newport, Rhode Island, 1959-1965(   ). New York: Vanguard Recording Society, Inc., 1976.
    —Includes Son House, Skip James, Sonny Terry, Brownie McGhee, Mississippi, Fred McDowell, and others.

17. *Greatest Folksingers of the 'Sixties* (VSD 17/18). New York: Vanguard Recording Society, n.d.
    —Features Ian and Sylvia, Buffy Sainte-Marie, Joan Baez, Odetta, Phil Ochs, John Hammond, Bob Dylan, Judy Collins, Theodore Bikel, Tom Paxton, Pete Seeger, and others.

18. *Heavy Hands* (CS 1048). New York: Columbia Records/CBS, Inc., n.d.
    —Includes Taj Mahal, Freddie King, Johnny Winter, and others.

19. *Heavy Heads* (LPS 1522). Chicago: Chess Records, n.d.
    —Features Bo Diddley, Little Milton, Muddy Waters, and others.

20. *History of British Rock*—2 Volumes (SASH 3704-2/3705-2/3712-2) Los Angeles, California: Sire Records, Inc. (ABC Records, Inc.), 1974, 1975.

21. *Jim Pewter's 10th Anniversary Salute to Rock 'N Roll* (FR 1006). Los Angeles, California: Festival Records, 1976.
    —Includes Dale Hawkins, Chuck Berry, Mickey and Sylvia, The Big Bopper, Bobby Herb, The Diamonds, and others.

22. *Juggernauts of the Early 70's* (DSX 50146). Los Angeles, California: ABC Records, Inc., 1973.
    —Features Jim Croce, Three Dog Night, Smith, Mama Class, and others.

23. *Jukebox Jive* (NU 9020). Minnetonka, Minnesota: K-tel International Inc. 1975.
    —Features Ronnie Hawkins, Paul Anka, Del Shannon, Buddy Knox, Chris Montex, the Clovers, and Sue Thompson.

24. *King-Federal Rockabillys* (King 5016X). Nashville, Tennessee: Gusto Records, 1978.
    —Includes MacCurtis, Charlie Feathers, Ronnie Molleen, Joe Penny, Bob and Lucille, Bill Beach, and Hank Mizell.

25. *Don Kirshner Presents "Rock Power"* (P 12417). New York: CBS Records, 1974.
    —Features the Doobie Brothers, Bachman-Turner Overdrive, Dr. John,

Alice Cooper, and others.
26. *Mindbender* (TU 2440). Minnetonka, Minnesota: K-tel International, Inc., 1976.
  —Features Neil Sedaka, Kiss, LaBelle, Elton John, C. W. McCall, and others.
27. *Motown's Preferred Stock*—3 Volumes (m 6-881/882/883 S1). Hollywood, California: Motown Record Corporation, 1977.
  —Features the Four Tops, Mary Wells, Michael Jackson, Martha Reeves and the Vandellas, Gladys Knight and the Pips, the Spinners, Marvin Gaye and Tammi Terrell, the Marvellettes, the Temptations, Smokey Robinson and the Miracles, Edwin Starr, and Jr. Walker and the All Stars.
28. *Nuggetts: Original Artyfacts From the First Psychedelic Era, 1965-1968* (Sash 3716-2). Los Angeles, California: Sire Records, 1976.
  —Includes The Mojo Men, The Castaways, The Amboy Dukes, The Knickerbockers, The Standells, and others.
29. *Old King Gold*—10 Volumes (KS 16001-10). Nashville, Tennessee: Gusto Records, 1975.
  —Features Hank Ballard and The Midnighters, The Platters, Otis Williams and The Charms, Bill Doggett, Billy Ward and the Dominos, Little Willie John, Freddy King, Wynonie Harris, Earl Bostic, and others.
30. *Original Early Top 40 Hits* (PAS 1013). New York: Paramount Records, 1974.
  —Features Pat Boone, Gale Storm, Tab Hunter, Sanford Clark, and others.
31. *Original Golden Hits of the Great Blues Singers*—3 Volumes (MHG 25002-3/11). Chicago: Mercury Records, n.d.
  —Includes Lightnin' Hopkins, Little Junior Parker, Lowell Fulsom, Howlin' Wolf, Bobby Bland, Willie Mabon, Muddy Waters, and others.
32. *Original Golden Hits of the Great Groups*—3 Volumes (MGH 25000/07/10). Chicago: Mercury Records, n.d.
33. *Original Golden Instrumental Hits* (MGH 25001). Chicago: Mercury Records, n.d.
  —Includes Phil Upchurch, Lee Allen, The Mar-Keys, Ace Cannon, Booker T. and the MG's, The Champs, Les Cooper, and others.
34. *Original Golden Rhythm and Blues Hits* (MGH 25006). Chicago: Mercury Records, n.d.
  —Features Jimmy McCracklin, Don Gardner and Dee Dee Ford, Clarence Henry, Little Walter, and others.
35. *Original Golden Teen Hits*—3 Volumes (MGH 25004-5/09). Chicago: Mercury Records, n.d.
  —Includes Thomas Wayne, The Shirelles, Sammy Turner, Gary U.S. Bonds, Rufus Thomas, Jan Bradley, Johnny Preston, and others.
36. *Original Golden Town and Country Hits* (MGH 25008). Chicago: Mercury Records, n.e.
  —Features Jerry Wallace, Patti Page, Patsy Cline, Rusty Draper, Leroy van Dyke, and others.
37. Lloyd Price, Sam Cooke, Larry Williams, and Little Richard, *"Our Significant Hits..."* (SP 2112). Hollywood, California: Specialty Records, Inc., n.d.
38. *Rock Begins*—2 Volumes (SD 33-314/315). New York: ATCO Records, 1970.

—Features Bobby Darin, Ray Charles, the Coasters, La Vern Baker, Chuck Willis, and others.
39. *Rock Invasion, 1956-1969* (LC 50012). New York: London Records, Inc., 1978.
    —Includes Rod Stewart, Joe Cocker, Lonnie Donegan, Unit Four + 2, The Zombies, the Nashville Teens, and others.
40. *Rock On—The Musical Encyclopedia of Rock N' Roll: The Solid Gold Years* (PG 33390). New York: Columbia Records/CBS, Inc., 1975.
    —Feaures Jimmy Dean, Johnny Horton, Don Cherry, Guy Mitchell, Marty Robbins, Frankie Laine, Johnny Mathis, Bobby Vinton, and others.
41. *Rock and Roll Show* (GT 0002). Nashville, Tennessee: Gusto Records, Inc., 1978.
    —Includes Bill Doggett, Sammy Turner, The Moonglows, Chuck Berry, Billy Wards and The Dominos, Jerry Lee Lewis, and others.
42. *A Salute To Rock N' Roll: 20 Original Hits* (FR 1006A). Sherman Oaks, California: Festival Records, Inc., 1976.
    —Features Jan Bradley, Mickey and Sylvia, Dale Hawkins, Johnnie and the Joe, and others.
43. *Solid Gold Old Town* (SD 9032). New York: Cotillion Records, 1971.
    —Includes The Royaltones, the Fiestas, The Harptones, Billy Bland and others.
44. *Soul Train Hall of Fame* (AVIII 8004). New York: Adam VIII, Ltd., 1973.
    —Features Sam and Dave, The Isley Brothers, Otis Redding, the Edwin Hawkins Singers, James Brown, Clarence Carter, and others.
45. *Soul Train Hits That Made It Happen* (AVIII 8005). New York: Adam VIII, Ltd., 1973).
    —Features Joe Tex, the Cornelius Brothers and Sister Rose, Al Green, Curtis Mayfield, the O'Jays, the Four Tops, and others.
46. *Sounds Spectacular* (TU 2400). Minnetonka, Minnesota: K-tel International, Inc., 1975.
    —Features the Ohio Players, the Edgar Winter Group, Gloria Gaynor, Frankie Valli, B.W. Stevenson, and others.
47. *Phil Spector's Greatest Hits* (2 SP-9104). Los Angeles, California: Warner Brothers Records, Inc.), 1977.
    —Features the Ronettes, the Crystals, the Righteous Brothers, Sonny Charles and the Checkmates Ltd., Ike and Tina Turner and others.
48. *Super Bad* (NU 427). N.E. Minneapolis, Minnesota: K-tel International 1973.
    —Features the Staple Singers, Timmy Thomas, the Chi-Lites, the Main Ingredient, and others.
49. *Super Groups of the 50's* (SPC 3271). Long Island City, New York: Pickwick International, Inc. (Mercury Records), n.d.
    —Features the Diamonds, the Platters, the Crew Cuts, and the Gaylords.
50. *The Super Hits—5 Volumes* (SD 501/8188/8203/8224/8274). New York: Atlantic Recording Corporation, 1967 (Vol. I), 1968 (Vol. II and III), and 1970 (Vol. IV and V).
    —Features Crosby, Stills, Nash and Young, Led Zeppelin, Cream, Vanilla Fudge, Wilson Pickett, the Buffalo Springfield, the Bee Gees, Aretha Franklin, Barbara Lewis, the Young Rascals, Eddie Floyd and others.
51. *Superhits of the Superstars* (TU 2451). Minnetonka, Minnesota: K-tel

International, Inc., 1975.
—Features Sugarloaf, Phoebe Snow, Hot Chocolate, Gwen McCrae, and others.
52. *Surfin' Roots* (FR 1010). Sherman Oaks, California: Festival Records, Inc., 1977.
—Includes the Beach Boys, The Surfaris, The Chantays, Dick Dale and The Del-Tones, and others.
53. *20 Original Winners of 1964* (R 25293). New York: Roulette Records, Inc., n.d.
—Features Marvin Gaye, The Reflections, Jimmy Hughes, and others.
54. *26 Hit Rock Classics* (P 212065). New York: Columbia Records/CBS, Inc., 1974.
—Includes Johnny Nash, Curtis Mayfield, The O'Jays, The Isley Brothers, Lenny Welch, The Chambers Brothers, Aretha Franklin, and others.
55. *The Unforgettable Hits of the '40's and '50's* (R 214291). University City, California: MCA Records, Inc., n.d.
—Features the Andrews Sisters, Bing Crosby, The Mills Brothers, Ray Bolger, and others.
56. *The Very Best of the Oldies*—2 Volumes (UA-LA 335E). Los Angeles, California: United Artists Music and Record Group, Inc., 1975.
57. *You Must Remember These*—2 Volumes (Bell 6078/6079). New York: Bell Records, 1972.
—Features the Mello Kings, the Nutmegs, the Turbans, the Silhouettes, the Delfonics, the Box Tops, Lee Dorsey, and James and Bobby Purify.
58. *Your Hit Parade* (P 12750). New York: HRB Music Company, Inc. (Columbia Records, Inc.), 1975.
C. Recordings of "Live" Performances
  1. *The Birdland All-Stars Live at Carnegie Hall.* New York: Roulette Records, Inc., 1975.
  —Includes Count Basie, Charlie Parker, Bille Holiday, Lester Young, and Sarah Vaughan.
  2. *The Blues...“A Real Summit Meeting”* (BDS 5144-2). New York: Buddah Records, Inc., 1973.
  —Features Willie Mae Thornton, Eddie Vinson, Arthur Crudup, Muddy Waters, and others.
  3. *New Orleans Jazz and Heritage Festival—1976* (SLD 9424). Los Angeles, California: Island Records, Inc., 1976.
  —Includes Professor Longhair, Lee Dorsey, Ernie K. Doe, Robert Parker, Irma Thomas, Allen Toussaint, Earl King, and Lightnin' Hopkins.
  4. *Newport in New York '72: The Soul Sessions—Vol. 6* (CST 9028). New York: Buddah Records, Inc., 1972.
  —Features Billy Eckstine, Curtis Mayfield, B.B. King, Herbie Mann, Les McCann, and Robert A. Flack.
  5. *Stars of the Apollo Theatre* (KG 30788). New York: Columbia Records/ CBS, Inc., 1973.
  —Features Bessie Smith, Big Maybelle, Cab Calloway, Sarah Vaughn, Billie Holiday, and Ella Fitzgerald.
D. Special Collections
  1. Eric Clapton, Jeff Beck, and Jimmy Page, *Guitar Boogie* (LPS 46242). New York: RCA Records, 1971.
  2. *Dance! Dance! Dance!* (CD 2023). New York: Telehouse, Inc., nd.
  —Features Little Eva, Joey Dee and the Starliters, The Orlons, Wilson

Pickett, Hank Ballard and the Midnighters, The Olympics, and others.
3. *Alan Freed's Rock N' Roll Dance Party*—4 Volumes (Wins 1010-13). New York: Wins Records, n.d.
4. Alan Freed, *Rock 'N' Roll Radio—Starring Alan Freed "The King of Rock 'N' Roll"* (MR 1087). Sandy Hook, Connecticut: Radiola Company, 1978.
5. *The Guitar Album* (Polydor Super 2659-027). London: Polydor, Ltd., 1972.
   —Features Jimi Hendrix, Duane Allman, Freddie King, Eric Clapton, Albert King, Peter Townshend, B. B. King, Shuggie Otis, John McLaughlin, Link Wray, and others.
6. *Pop Origins* (LP 1544). Chicago: Chess Records, n.d.
   —Includes Howlin' Wolf, Dale Hawkins, Bo Diddley, Muddy Waters, and others.
7. *Risky Blues* (KS 1133). Nashville, Tennessee: Gusto Records, Inc., 1976.
   —Features Bull "Moose" Jackson, Checkers, Hank Ballard and The Midnighters, and others.
8. *A Tribute to Burt Bachrach: Composer, Arranger, Conductor* (SPS 5100) New York: Scepter Records, Inc., 1972.
   —Features Dionne Warwick, Jackie DeShannon, Chuck Jackson, Jerry Butler, and others.
II. Greatest Hits Albums—Featuring Individual or Group Performances
   A. Chronological Song Arrangements
      1. The Beatles, *The Beatles/1962-1966* (SKBO 3403). New York: Apple Records, Inc., 1973.
      2. The Beatles, *The Beatles/1967-1970* (SKBO 3404). New York: Apple Records, Inc., 1973.
      3. Ray Charles, *The Ray Charles Story—Volume One* (SD 8063). New York: Atlantic Recording Corporation, 1962.
      4. Ray Charles, *The Ray Charles Story—Volume Two* (SD 8064). New York: Atlantic Recording Corporation, 1962.
      5. Eric Clapton, *History of Eric Clapton* (SD2-803). New York: ATCO (Atlantic Records), 1972.
      6. Elvis Presley, *Elvis—The Sun Session*. New York: RCA Records, 1976.
      7. *The Sun Story, Volumes 1-6: The Story of the Legendary Sun Label of Memphis, Tennessee* (9930-901/2/3/4/5/6). Sunnyvale, California: Sunnyvale Records, 1977. (Individual Albums by Johnny Cash, Jerry Lee Lewis, Charlie Rich, Carl Perkins, Roy Orbison, and Carl Mann).
   B. Random Song Order
      1. Bachman-Turner Overdrive, *Best of B.T.O.* (SRM-1-11-1). Chicago: Phonogram, Inc., (Mercury Records), 1976.
      2. Joan Baez, *The First 10 Years* (VSD 6560/61). New York: Vanguard Recording Society, Inc., n.d.
      3. La Vern Baker, *La Vern Baker: Her Greatest Recordings* (SD 33-372. New York: ATCO Records, 1971.
      4. The Band, *Anthology* (SKBO 11856). Hollywood, California: Capital Records, 1978.
      4. Hank Ballard and the Midnighters, *Hank Ballard and The Midnighters* (King 5003X). Nashville, Tennessee: Gusto Records, 1977.
      5. The Beach Boys, *Endless Summer* (SVBB 11307). Hollywood, California: Capitol Records, Inc., 1974.
      6. *The Beatles, Rock 'N' Roll Music* (SKBO 11537). Hollywood, California: Capitol Records, Inc., 1976.
      7. The Bee Gees, *Bee Gees Gold* (RS 1-3006). New York: RSO Records, Inc.,

1976.
8. Chuck Berry, *Chuck Berry's Golden Decade* (CH 1514). New York: Chess/Janus Records, 1972.
9. Chuck Berry, *Chuck Berry's Golden Decade—Volume 2* (CH 60023). New York: Chess/Janus Records, 1972.
10. Bo Diddley, *Bo Diddley's 16 All-Time Greatest Hits* (CK 2989). New York: Chess Records, 1973.
11. James Brown, *Solid Gold: 30 Golden Hits in 21 Golden Years* (2679044). New York: Polydor, Inc., 1978.
12. Captain and Tennille, *The Captain and Tennille's Greatest Hits* (SP 4667). Beverly Hills, California: A & M Records, Inc., 1977.
13. The Carpenters, *The Singles, 1969-1973* (SP 3601). Beverly Hills, California: A & M Records, Inc., 1973.
14. Johnny Cash, *Johnny Cash's Greatest Hits—Volume One* (CS 9478). New York: Columbia Records/CBS, Inc., n.d.
15. Johnny Cash, *The Johnny Cash Collection: His Greatest Hits—Volume II* (KC 30887). New York: Columbia Records/CBS, Inc., n.d.
16. Ray Charles, *Greatest Hits* (ABCS 415). New York: ABC Records, Inc., 1971.
17. Chicago, *Chicago IX: Chicago's Greatest Hits* (PC 33900). New York: Columbia Records/CBS, Inc., 1975.
18. Eric Clapton, *Clapton* (PD 5526). New York: Polydor, Inc., 1973.
19. The Clovers, *The Clovers: Their Greatest Hits* (SD 33-374). New York: ATCO Records, 1971.
20. The Coasters, *The Coasters—Their Greatest Recordings: The Early Years* (SD 33-371). New York: ATCO Records, 1971.
21. Eddie Cochran, *Eddie Cochran: Legendary Masters Series* (UAS 9959). Los Angeles, California: United Artists Records, Inc., 1971.
22. Judy Collins, *Colors of the Day: The Best of Judy Collins* (Elektra 75030). New York: Elektra Records, 1972.
23. Sam Cooke, *The Best of Sam Cooke* (LSP 2625). New York: RCA Records, 1965.
24. Creedence Clearwater Revival, *Creedence Gold* (9418). Berkeley, California: Fantasy Records, 1972.
25. Creedence Clearwater Revival, *More Creedence Gold* (9430). Berkeley, California: Fantasy Records, 1973.
26. Jim Croce, *Bad, Bad LeRoy Brown: Jim Croce's Greatest Character Songs* (JZ 35571). New York: Lifesong Records, Inc., 1978.
27. Jim Croce, *Photographs and Memories: His Greatest Hits* JZ35010) New York: Lifesong Records, Inc., 1974.
28. Deep Purple, *When We Rock, We Rock—And When We Roll, We Roll* (PRK 3223). Burbank, California: Warner Brothers Records, Inc., 1972.
29. John Denver, *John Denver's Greatest Hits* (CPL 1-0374). New York: RCA Records, 1973.
30. John Denver, *John Denver's Greatest Hits—Volume 2* (CPL 1-2194). New York: RCA Records, 1977.
31. Neil Diamond, *His 12 Greatest Hits* (MCA 2106). Universal City California: MCA Records, Inc., 1974.
32. Dion and the Belmonts, *The Dion Years, 1958-1963* (2103-707). Sunnyvale, California: GRT Corporation, 1975.
33. The Doobie Brothers, *Best of the Doobies* (BSK 3112). Burbank California: Warner Brothers Records, Inc., 1976.
34. Fats Domino, *Fats Domino: Legendary Masters Series* (USA 9958). Los

Angeles, California: United Artists Records, Inc., 1971.
35. Donovan, *Donovan's Greatest Hits* (PE 26439). New York: Epic Records/ CBS, Inc., n.d.
36. The Doors, *13* (EKS 7407a). New York: Elektra Records, 1970.
37. The Drifters, *The Drifters Golden Hits* (SD 8153). New York: ATCO Records, n.d.
38. The Drifters, *The Drifters—Their Greatest Recordings: The Early Years* (SD 33-375). New York: ATCO Records, 1971.
39. Bob Dylan, *Bob Dylan's Greatest Hits* (PC 9463). New York: Columbia Records/CBS, Inc., n.d.
40. Bob Dylan, *Bob Dylan's Greatest,* Vol. II (PG 31120). New York: Columbia Records/CBS, Inc., 1971.
41. The Eagles, *Their Greatest Hits, 1971-1975* (Asylum 7E-1052). Los Angeles, California: Elektra/Asylum/Nonesuch Records, 1976.
42. Duane Eddy, *The Vintage Years* (SASH 3707-2). Los Angeles, California: Sire Records, Inc., 1975.
43. The Everly Brothers, *The Golden Hits of the Everly Brothers* (WS 1471). New York: Warner Brothers Records, Inc., 1962.
44. The Fifth Dimension, *Greatest Hits* (SCS 33900). Los Angeles California: Liberty/U.A., Inc., Soul City Records, n.d.
45. The Five Keys, *The Five Keys* (King 5013X). Nashville, Tennessee: Gusto Records, 1978.
46. The Five Royales, *The Five Royales* (King 5014X). Nashville, Tennessee: Gusto Records, 1978.
47. The Flamingos, *Flamingos: Chess Rock 'N' Rhythm Series* (ACRR 702). Englewood, New Jersey: Chess Records, 1976.
48. The Four Seasons, *The Four Seasons Story* (PS 7000). New York: Private Stock Records, Ltd., 1975.
49. Aretha Franklin, *Aretha's Greatest Hits* (SD 8295). New York: Atlantic Recording Corporation, 1971.
50. Aretha Franklin, *Aretha Franklin's Greatest Hits, 1960-1965.* New York: Columbia Records/CBS, Inc., n.d.
51. Marvin Gaye, *Marvin Gaye Anthology* (M9 791 A3). Hollywood, California: Motown Record Corporation, 1974.
52. Grand Funk, *Grand Funk Hits* (ST 11579). Hollywood, California: Capitol Records, 1976.
53. The Guess Who, *The Greatest of the Guess Who* (AFL 1-2253). New York: RCA Records, 1977.
54. Bill Haley and His Comets, *Golden Hits* (MCA 2-4010). Universal City, California: MCA Records, Inc., 1972.
55. Don "Sugarcane" Harris and Dewey Terry, *Don and Dewey* (SP 2131). Hollywood, California: Specialty Records, 1970.
56. Dale Hawkins, *Dale Hawkins: Chess Rock 'N' Rhythm Series* (ACRR 703). Englewood, New Jersey: Chess Records, 1970.
57. Jimi Hendrix, *The Essential Jimi Hendrix* (2RS 2245). Burbank, California: Warner Brothers Records, Inc., 1978.
58. Buddy Holly and the Crickets, *Buddy Holly Lives: 20 Golden Greats* (MCA 3040). Universal City, California: MCA Records, Inc., 1978.
59. Howlin' Wolf, *Chester Burnett Aka Howlin' Wolf* (2 CH—60016). New York: Chess/Janus Records, 1972.
60. The Impressions, *The Impressions, Featuring Jerry Butler and Curtis Mayfield: The Vintage Years* (Sash 3717-2). Los Angeles, California: Sire Records, Inc., 1976.

61. Jay and the Americans, *The Very Best of Jay and the Americans (UA-LA 357). Los Angeles, California: United Artists Records, Inc., 1975.*

62. *The Jefferson Airplane, Flight Log, 1966-1976* (CYL 2-1255). New York: Grunt (RCA) Records, 1977.

63. Elton John, *Elton John's Greatest Hits—Volume II* (MCA 3027). Universal City, California: MCA Records, Inc., 1977.

64. Elton John, *Greatest Hits* (MCA 2128). Universal City, California: MCA Records, Inc., 1974.

65. Janis Joplin, *Janis Joplin's Greatest Hits* (PC 32168). New York: Columbia Records/CBS, Inc., 1973.

66. Carole King, *Her Greatest Hits: Songs of Long Ago* (JE 34967). New York: Ode Records/CBS, Inc., 1978.

67. Kris Kristofferson, *Songs of Kristofferson* (PZ 34687). New York: Monument Records (Columbia Records/CBS, Inc.), 1977.

68. John Lennon, *Shaved Fish* (SW 3421). New York: Apple Records, Inc., 1975.

69. Jerry Lee Lewis, *Jerry Lee Lewis: Original Golden Hits—Volume 1* (Sun 102). Nashville, Tennessee: Sun International Corporation, n.d.

70. Little Richard, *Little Richard's Grooviest 17 Original Hits* SPS 2113). Hollywood, California: Specialty Records, n.d.

71. The Lovin' Spoonful, *The Very Best of the Lovin' Spoonful* (KSBS 2013). New York: Buddah Records, n.d.

72. The Mamas and the Papas, *Farewell To the First Golden Era* (DS 50025). New York: ABC Records, Inc., n.d.

73. Barry Manilow, *Greatest Hits* (A 2I 8601). New York: Arista Records 1978.

74. Johnny Mathis, *All-Time Greatest Hits* (PG 31345). New York: Columbia Records/CBS, Inc., 1972.

75. Curtis Mayfield, *Curtis Mayfield: His Early Years With the Impressions* (ABCX 780-2) Los Angeles, California: ABC Records, Inc., 1973.

76. Clyde McPhatter and The Dominoes, *The Dominoes, Featuring Clyde McPhatter* (King 5006X). Nashville, Tennessee: Gusto Records, 1977.

77. The Moonglows, *Moonglows: Chess Rock 'N' Rhythm Series* (UAS 9960) Los Angeles, California: United Artists Records, Inc., 1971.

78. Ricky Nelson, *Ricky Nelson: Legendary Masters Series* (UAS 9960) Los Angeles, California: United Artists Records, Inc., 1971.

79. Nilsson, *Greatest Hits* (AFL 1-2798). New York: RCA Records, 1978.

80. Phil Ochs, *Chords of Fame* (A & M SP 4599). Beverly Hills, California: A & M Records, Inc., 1977.

81. Roy Orbison, *The All-time Greatest Hits of Roy Orbison* (MP 8600). Nashville, Tennessee: Monument Record Corporation, 1972.

82. Johnny Otis, *The Original Johnny Otis Show* (SJL 2230). New York: Savoy (Arista) Records, 1978.

83. Peter, Paul and Mary, *10 (Ten) Years Together: The Best of Peter Paul and Mary* (WB 2552). Burbank, California: Warner Brothers, Inc., 1970.

84. Wilson Pickett, *Wilson Pickett's Greatest Hits* (SD 2-501). New York: Atlantic Recording Corporation, 1973.

85. The Platters, *Encore of Golden Hits* (SR 60243). New York: Mercury Record Corporation, n.d.

86. Elvis Presley, *Elvis* (DPL 2-0056). New York: RCA Records, 1972.

87. The Ravens, *"The Greatest Group of Them All": Roots of Rock and*

Roll, Volume 3 (SJL 2227). New York: Savoy (Arista) Records, 1978.

88. Lou Rawls, *The Best From Lou Rawls* (SKBB-S11585). New York: Capitol Records, Inc., 1976.

89. Otis Redding, *The Best of Otis Redding* (SD 2-801). New York: ATCO Records, 1972.

90. Helen Reddy, *Helen Reddy's Greatest Hits* (ST 511467). New York: Capitol Records, Inc., 1975.

91. Jimmy Reed, *The Greatest Hits of Jimmy Reed—Volume I* (KST 553). Los Angeles, California: Kent Records, n.d.

92. Jimmy Reed, *Jimmy Reed's Greatest Hits—Volume 2* (KST 562). Los Angeles, California: Kent Records, n.d.

93. Paul Revere and the Raiders Featuring Mark Lindsay, *All-Time Greatest Hits* (CG 31464). New York: Columbia Records/CBS, Inc., 1972.

94. The Righteous Brothers, *The History of The Righteous Brothers* (SE 4885). Hollywood, California: MGM Records, 1972.

95. Johnny Rivers, *Superpack* (UXS 93). Los Angeles, California: United Artists Records, Inc., 1972.

96. Marty Robbins, *Marty Robbins' All-time Greatest Hits* (CG 31361). New York: Columbia Records/BCS, Inc., 1972.

97. Smokey Robinson and the Miracles, *Smokey Robinson and the Miracles' Anthology* (793 R 3). Hollywood, California: Motown Record Corporation, 1973.

98. Kenny Rogers, *Ten Years of Gold* (VA-LA 835 H). Los Angeles, California: United Artists Records, Inc., 1977.

99. The Rolling Stones, *Hot Rocks 1964-1971* (London 2PS 606-7). New York: ABKCO Records, Inc. (London), 1972.

100. The Rolling Stones, *Made in the Shade* (COC 79102). New York: Rolling Stone Records, 1975.

101. Linda Ronstadt, *Greatest Hits* (Asylum 7E-1092). Los Angeles, California: Elektra/Asylum/Nonesuch Records, 1976.

102. Linda Ronstadt, *A Retrospective* (SKBB 511629). New York: Capitol Records, 1977.

103. Diana Ross and the Supremes, *Diana Ross and the Supremes Anthology* (M7-794Ac). Hollywood, California: Motown Record Corporation, 1974.

104. Leon Russell, *Best of Leon* (SRL 52004). Los Angeles, California Shelter Recording Company, Inc., 1976.

105. Neil Sedaka, *Neil Sedaka's Greatest Hits* (PIG 5297). Universal City, California: Rocket Record Company, 1977.

106. Pete Seeger, *Pete Seeger's Greatest Hits* (CS 9416). New York: Columbia Records/CBS, Inc., n.d.

107 The Shirelles, *The Very Best of the Shirelles* (UA-LA 340E). Los Angeles, California: United Artists Records, Inc., 1975.

108. Carly Simon, *The Best of Carly Simon* (7E 1048). Los Angeles, California: Elektra/Asylum/Nonesuch Records, 1975.

109. Paul Simon, *Greatest Hits, Etc.* (JC 35032). New York: Columbia Records/CBS, Inc., 1977.

110. The Spinners, *The Best of the Spinners* (SD 19179). New York: Atlantic Recording Corporation, 1978.

111. Steppenwolf, *Steppenwolf Gold: Their Greatest Hits* (DSX 50099). New York: ABC Records, Inc., n.d.

112. Cat Stevens, *Greatest Hits* (SP 4519). Beverly Hills, California: A & M Records, 1975.

113. Barbra Streisand, *Barbra Streisand's Greatest Hits—Volume 2* (FC 35679). New York: Columbia Records/CBS, Inc., 1978.
114. James Taylor, *Greatest Hits* (BS 2979). Burbank California: Warner Brothers Records, Inc., 1976.
115. The Temptations, *The Temptations—Anthology: A Tenth Anniversary Special* (M 782 A3). Hollywood, California: Motown Record Corporation, 1973.
116. Three Dog Night, *Golden Biscuits* (DSX 50098). New York: ABC Records, Inc., n.d.
117. Three Dog Night, *Joy To The World—Three Dog Night: Their Greatest Hits* (DSD 50178). New York: ABC Records, Inc., 1974.
118. Joe Turner, *Joe Turner: His Greatest Recordings* (SD 33-376). New York: ATCO Records, 1971.
119. The Turtles, *The Turtles' Greatest Hits* (WW 115). Los Angeles California: White Wale Records, n.d.
120. Billy Ward and the Dominoes, *The Dominoes* (King 5008X). Nashville, Tennessee: Gusto Records, 1977.
121. Dione Warwick, *Dione Warwick's Golden Hits—Part One* (SPS 565). New York: Scepter Records, Inc., n.d.
122. The Who, *Meaty Beaty Big and Bouncy* (DL 79184). Universal City, California: MCA Records, Inc., 1971.
123. Hank Williams, *24 of Hank Williams' Greatest Hits* (SE 4755-2). Hollywood, California: MGM Record Corporation, n.d.
124. Otis Williams and the Charms, *Otis Williams and His Charms* (King 5015X). Nashville, Tennessee: Gusto Records, Inc., 1978.
125. Chuck Willis, *Chuck Willis: His Greatest Recordings* (SD 33-372). New York: ATCO Records, 1971.
126 Jackie Wilson, *Jackie Wilson's Greatest Hits* (BL 754140). New York: Brunswick Record Corporation, 1968.
127. Wings, *Wings Greatest* (500 11905). New York: Capitol Records, 1978.
128. Stevie Wonder, *Looking Back* (M 804 LP 3). Hollywood, California: Motown Record Corporation, 1977.
129. Z Z Top, *The Best of ZZ Top* (PS 706). New York: London Records, Inc., 1977.

C. Recordings of "Live" Performances

1. Joan Baez, *From Every Stage* (SP 3704). New York: A & M Records, Inc., 1976.
2. The Beatles, *The Beatles At The Hollywood Bowl* (SMAS 11638). Hollywood, California: Capitol Records, 1977.
3. The Beatles, *The Beatles Live! At The Star-Club in Hamburg, Germany 1962* (LS 2-7001). London, England: Lingasong, Ltd. 1977.
4. Harry Belafonte, *Belafonte at Carnegie Hall: The Complete Concert (LSO 6006). New York: RCA Victor, n.d.*
5. *Glen Campbell, Glen Campbell Live at the Royal Festival Hall* (SWBC 11707). Hollywood, California: Capitol Records, 1977.
6. Johnny Cash, *Johnny Cash at Folsom Prison* (CS 9639). New York: Columbia Records/CBS, Inc., n.d.
7. Johnny Cash, *Johnny Cash at San Quentin* (KC 9827). New York: Columbia Records/CBS, Inc., n.d.
8. Harry Chapin, *Greatest Stories—Live* (E7-2009). Los Angeles, California: Elektra/Asylum/Nonesuch Records, 1976.
9. Ray Charles, *Ray Charles Live* (SD 2-503). New York: Atlantic Recording Corporation, 1973.

10. Joe Cocker, *Mad Dogs and Englishmen* (SP 6002). Hollywood, California: A & M Records, 1970.
11. Niel Diamond, *Hot August Night: Recorded In Concert at the Greek Theatre in Los Angeles* (MCA 2-8000). Universal City, California: MCA Records, Inc., 1972.
12. Neil Diamond, *Love At the Greek* (KC 2-34404). New York: Columbia Records/CBS, Inc., 1977.
13. Bob Dylan and The Band, *Before the Flood* (Asylum AB 201). New York: Elektra/Asylum/Nonesuch Records, 1974.
14. Peter Frampton, *Frampton Comes Alive!* (SP 3703). Beverly Hills, California: A & M Records, Inc., 1976.
15. Aretha Franklin, *Aretha—Live At Fillmore West* (SD 7205). New York: Atlantic Recording Corporation, 1971.
16. Tom Jones, *Live in Las Vegas—At The Flamingo* (PAS 71031). New York: Parrot Records, n.d.
17. Doug Kershaw, *Alive and Pickin'—Recorded Live in Atlanta* (BS 2851). Burbank, California: Warner Brothers Records, Inc., 1975.
18. Albert King, *Live Wire/Blues Power* (STS 2003). Memphis, Tennessee: Stax Records, n.d.
19. B.B. King, *Live in Cook County Jail* (ABCS 723). Los Angeles, California: ABC/Dunhill Records, Inc., 1971.
20. B.B. King and Bobby Bland, *Together For the First Time...Live* (DSY 50190/2). Los Angeles, California: ABC Records, Inc., 1974.
21. Jerry Lee Lewis, *The Greatest Live Show on Earth* (SRS 67056). Chicago: Smash (Mercury) Records, n.d.
22. Little Richard, *Little Richard's Greatest Hits* (OKS 14121). New York: Okeh Records, 1967.
23. Barry Manilow, *Barry Manilow Live* (Arista 8500). New York: Arista Records, Inc., 1977.
24. Curtis Mayfield, *Curtis/Live!* (CRS 8008). New York: Buddah Records (Curtom). n.d.
25. Les McCann and Eddie Harris, *Swiss Movement* (SD 1537). New York: Atlantic Recording Corporation, 1969.
26. Willie Nelson, *Willie and Family Live* (KC 2-35642). New York: Columbia Records/CBS, Inc., 1978.
27. Peter, Paul and Mary, *In Concert* (2 WS 1555). Burbank, California: Warner Brothers Records, n.d.
28. Elvis Presley, *Elvis: Aloha From Hawaii via Satellite* (CPD 2-2642). (New York: RCA Records, 1972.
29. Elvis Presley, *Elvis in Concert* (APL 2-2587) New York: RCA Records, 1977.
30. Otis Redding and the Jimi Hendrix Experience, *Otis Redding/The Jimi Hendrix Experience* (MS 2029). New York: Reprise Records, 1970.
31. Paul Simon, *Live Rhymin': Paul Simon in Concern* (PC 32855). New York: Columbia Records/CBS, Inc., 1974.
32. Wings, *Wings Over America* (SWCO 11593). New York: MPL Communications (Capitol Records), Inc., 1976.

D. Special Collections
1. Otis Blackwell, *These Are My Songs!* (I.C. 1032). New York: Inner City Records, 1977.
2. Otis Blackwell, Eddie Cooley, Lincoln Chase, Winfield Scott, Ollie Jones, and Billy Dawn Smith, *We Wrote 'Em and We sing 'Em* (MGM E 3912). Hollywood, California: MGM Record Corporation, n.d.

3. Ray Charles, *A 25th Anniversary Show Business Salute to Ray Charles: His All-Time Great Performances* (ABCH—731). New York: ABC Records, Inc., 1971.
4. Arthur "Big Boy" Crudup, *Arthur "Big Boy" Crudup—The Father of Rock and Roll* (LPV 573). New York: RCA Records, 1971.
5. Willie Dixon, *I Am The blues* (CS 9987). New York: Columbia Records/CBS, Inc., n.d.
6. Aretha Franklin, *The Gospel Soul of Aretha Franklin* (CH 10009). New York: Chess/Janus Records, 1972.
7. Jerry Lee Lewis, *The Session* (SRM 2-803). Chicago: Phonogram, Inc., (Mercury), 1973.

III. Standard Albums
  A. Individual Artists
    1. Robert Gordon, *Rock Billy Boogie* (AFL 1-3294). New York: RCA Records, 1979.
    2. Janis Ian, *Between the Lines* (PC 33394). New York: Columbia Records CBS, Inc., 1975.
    3. Billy Joel, *The Stranger* (JC 34987). New York: Columbia Records. CBS, Inc., 1977.
    4. Elton John, *Captain Fantastic and the Brown Dirt Cowboy* (MCA 2142). Universal City, California: MCA Records, Inc., 1975.
    5. B.B. King, *Indianola Mississippi Seeds* (ABCS 713). Los Angeles, California: ABC/Dunhill Records, Inc., 1970.
    6. Carole King, *Tapestry* (SP 77009). Hollywood, California: A & M Records, 1971.
    7. John Lennon, *Rock 'N' Roll* (SK 3419). New York: Apple Records, Inc., 1975.
    8. Barry Manilow, *Tryin' To Get The Feeling* (Arista 4060). New York: Arista Records, 1975.
    9. Lee Michael, *Barrell* (SP 4249). Hollywood, California: A & M Records, n.d.
    10. Johnny Rivers, *Blue Suede Shoes* (UA-LA 075F). Los Angeles, California: United Artists Records, Inc., 1972.
    11. Linda Ronstadt, *Living in the USA* (6E 155). Los Angeles, California: Elektra/Asylum Records, 1978.
    12. Neil Sedaka, *Sedaka's Back* (MCA 463). Universal City, California: MCA Records, Inc. (The Rocket Record Company, Ltd.), 1974.
    13. Paul Simon, *Still Crazy After All These Years* (PC 33540). New York: Columbia Records/CBS, Inc., 1975.
    14. Donna Summer, *Bad Girls* (NBLP 2-7150). Los Angeles, California: Casablanca Records, Inc., 1979.
    15. Taj Mahal, *The Natch'l Blues* (CS 9698). New York: Columbia Records, n.d.
    16. Stevie Wonder, *Songs in the Key of Life* (T13-340C2). Hollywood, California: Motown Record Corporation, 1976.
  B. Group Performances
    1. The Beatles, *Sgt. Pepper's Lonely Hearts Club Band* (SMAS 2653). Hollywood, California: Capitol Records (EMI), 1967.
    2. Crosby, Stills, Nash and Young (with Dallas Taylor and Greg Reeves) *Deja vu* (SD 7200). New York: Atlantic Recording Corporation, 1970.
    3. Derek and the Dominos (Eric Clapton), *Layla* (ATCO SD 2-704). New York: ATCO Records, 1970.
    4. The Eagles, *Hotel California* (Asylum 6E-103). Los Angeles, California: Elektra/Asylum/Nonesuch Records, 1976.

5. Fleetwood Mac, *Rumors* (BSK 3010). Burbank, California: Warner Brothers Records, Inc., 1977.
6. Buddy Holly and the Crickets, *The Buddy Holly Story* (SRL 57279). New York: Coral Records, Inc., n.d.
7. The Jefferson Airplane, *Volunteers* (LSP 4238). New York: RCA Records, 1969.
8. Loggins and Messina, *"So Fine"* (PC 33810). New York: Columbia Records, Inc., 1977.
9. Steve Miller Band, *Book of Dreams* (SO 11630). Los Angeles, California: Capitol Records, Inc., 1977.
10. The Persuasions, *The Chirpin' Persuasions* (7E 1099). Los Angeles, California: Elektra/Asylum Records, 1977.
11. The Rolling Stones, *Some Girls* (COC 39108). New York: Rolling Stones Records, 1978.
12. Bob Seger and the Silver Bullet Band, *Stranger in Town* (SW 11698). Hollywood, California: Capitol Records, 1978.
13. Simon and Garfunkel, *Bridge Over Troubled Water* (KCS 9914). New York: Columbia Records/CBS, Inc., n.d.
14. Simon and Garfunkel, *Sounds of Silence* (CS 9269) New York: Columbia Records, 1965.
15. Ike and Tina Turner, *Workin' Together* (LST 7650). Los Angeles, California: Liberty/U.A., Inc., n.d.
16. The Who, *Tommy* (MCA 2-10005). Universal City, California: MCA Records, Inc., 1973.
17. Jackie Wilson and Count Basie, *Manufacturers of Soul* (BL 754134). New York: Brunswick Record Corporation, 1968.

IV. Other Types of Albums
   A. Motion Picture Soundtracks
      1. *American Graffiti* (MCA 2-8001). Universal City, California: MCA Records, Inc., 1973.
      —Features the Crests, the Heartbeats, Frankie Lymon and the Teenagers, Buddy Knox, the Clovers, and others.
      2. *American Hot Wax* (SP 6500). Beverly Hills, California: A & M Records, Inc., 1978.
      —Features the Spaniels, Little Richard, the Moonglows, Buddy Holly, the Drifters, Jackie Wilson, and others.
      3. *Animal House* (MCA 3046). Universal City, California: MCA Records, Inc., 1978.
      —Features Sam Cooke, Chris Montez, Paul and Paula, Bobby Lewis, and others.
      4. The Band, *The Last Waltz* (3 WS 3146). Burbank, California: Warner Brothers Records, Inc., 1978.
      —Features Bob Dylan, Neil Diamond, Joni Mitchell, Ringo Starr, Neil Young, Eric Clapton, and others.
      5. *Banjoman* (SA 7527). Los Angeles, California: Sire Records, Inc., 1977.
      —Features the Earl Scruggs Revue, the Nitty Gritty Dirt Band, Joan Baez, the Byrds, Ramblin' Jack Elliott, and others.
      6. The Beatles, *Yellow Submarine* (SW 153). Hollywood, California: Capitol Records, Inc., 1968.
      7. Gary Busey, *The Buddy Holly Story* (SE 35412). New York: Epic Records, 1978.
      8. *Bye Bye Birdie* (LSO 1081). New York: RCA Records, 1963.
      9. *Car Wash* (MCA 2-600). Universal City, California: MCA Records, Inc., 1976.

10. *Cooley High* (M7 840 R2). Hollywood, California: Motown Record Corporation, 1975.
    —Features Diana Ross and the Supremes, Stevie Wonder, the Four Tops, Martha Reeves and the Vandellas, the Marvellettes, the Temptations, Mary Wells, and others.
11. *F.M.* (MCA 2-12000). Universal City, California: MCA Records, Inc., 1975.
    —Features Boston, Jimmy Buffett, the Doobie Brothers, the Eagles, Foreigner, Billy Joel, Steve Miller, Queen, Linda Ronstadt, Boz Scaggs, Bob Seeger, James Taylor, Joe Walsh, Steely Dan, and others.
12. *Godspell: A Musical Based Upon the Gospel According to St. Matthew* (Bell 1102). Scarborough 703, Ontaria, Canada: Quality Records, Ltd. (Bell Records), 1971.
13. *The Graduate* (OS 3180). New York: Columbia Records/CBS, Inc., n.d.
    —Features Simon and Garfunkel
14. *Grease* (RS 2-4002). Los Angeles, California: RS0 Records, Inc., 1978.
    —Features Sha-Na-Na, Frankie Valli, John Travolta, Oliva Newton-John, Frankie Avalon, and others.
15. *Hair: The American Tribal Love-Rock Musical* (LSO 1150). New York: RCA Records, Inc., 1973.
16. Marvin Hamlisch, *The Sting* (MCA 2040). Universal City, California: MCA Records, Inc., 1973.
17. *Jesus Christ Superstar* (MCA 2-11000). Universal City, California: MCA Records, Inc., 1973.
18. *Let the Good Times Roll* (Bell 9002). New York: Bell Records, 1973.
    —Features Chubby Checker, Bill Haley and the Comets, Danny and the Juniors, Fats Domino, the Shirelles, the Coasters, Bo Diddley, the Five Satins, and Little Richard
19. *Looking for Mr. Goodbar* (JS 35029). New York: Columbia Records/CBS, Inc., 1977.
    —Features Donna Summer, the Commodores, Thelma Houston, Diana Ross, the O'Jays, Boz Scaggs, Bill Withers, and others.
20. Curtis Mayfield, *Superfly* (CRS 8014-ST). New York: Curtom (Buddah) Records, 1972.
21. *Rocky* (UA-LA 693 G). Los Angeles, California: United Artists Records, Inc., 1976.
22. Diana Ross, *Lady Sings the Blues* (M 756 D). Detroit, Michigan: Motown Record Corporation, 1972.
23. *Saturday Night Fever* (RS 2-4001). Los Angeles, California: RSO Records, Inc., 1977.
    —Features the Bee Gees, Yvonne Elliman, Walter Murphy, the Tavares, K.C. and the sunshine Band, and the Trammps.
24. *Sgt. Pepper's Lonely Hearts Club Band* (RS 2-4100). New York: RSO Records, Inc., 1978.
    —Features Peter Frampton, the Bee Gees, Aerosmith, Alice Cooper, Billy Preston, Earth, Wind and Fire, and others.
25. *"Thank God It's Friday"*. Los Angeles, California: Casablanca Records, Inc., 1978.
    —Features Donna Summer, Diana Ross, the Commodores, Santa Esmeralda, Thelma Houston, Cameo, and others.
26. *Tommy* (PD 2-9502). New York: Polydor, Inc., 1975.
    —Features Elton John, Eric Clapton, Tina Turner, the Who, and others.
27. *Wattstax: The Living Word* (STS 2-3018). Memphis, Tennessee: Stax

Records, Inc., 1973.

—Features Kim Weston, Johnny Taylor, Isaac Hayes, and others.

28. *Wattstax 2: The Living Word* (STS 2-3018). Memphis, Tennessee: Stax
Records, Inc., 1973.

—Features Kim Weston, Johnny Taylor, Isaac Hayes, and others.

29. John Williams, *Close Encounters of the Third Kind* (AL 9500). New
York: Arista Records, Inc., 1977.

30. *Woodstock* (SD 3-500). New York: Cotillion Records, 1970.

—Features Jimi Hendrix, Jefferson Airplane, Richie Havens, Arlo
Guthrie, Country Joe McDonald and the Fish, Joan Baez, and others.

B. Comedy Albums

1. Buchanan and Goodman, *The Original Flying Saucers* (NCS 9000). New
York: IX Chains, Inc., n.d.

2. *25 Years of Recorded Comedy* (3 BX 3131). Burbank, California: Warner
Brothers Records, Inc., 1977.

—Features Lenny Bruce, Shelley Berman, Richard Pryor, Lily Tomlin,
Gabriel Kaplan, Stan Freberg, Cheech and Chong, David Frye, and
others.

C. Bootleg Albums*

D. Imported Recordings**

1. *The American Dream: The Cameo-Parkway Story, 1957-1962* (Dream
U 3/4). London: London Records, n.d.

—Features Chubby Checker, Dee Dee Sharp, the Orlons, the Dovells, Jo
Ann Campbell, Charlie Gracie, the Rays, and others.

2. *Charly's angels* (CR 30143). London: Charly (Pye) Records, n.d.

—Features the Shangri La's, the Jelly Beans, the Ad Libs, the Butterflies,
Evie Sands, and the Dixie Cups.

3. Fats Domino, *The Fats Domino Story—6 Volumes* (UAS 30067/68/69/
99/100/118). London: United Artists Records, 1977.

4. *Don't You Step On My Blue Suede Shoes* (CR 30119). London: Charly
(Pye) Records, n.d.

—Features Charlie Rich, Johnny Cash, Carl Mann, Roy Orbison, Warren
Smith, Jerry Lee Lewis, and others.

5. *Flashbacks: 20 Rock and Roll Favourites—Volume 1* (SNTF 780).
London: Sonet Productions, Ltd., 1978.

—Features Don and Dewey, Lloyd Price, Little Richard, Sam Cooke, and
others.

6. Buddy Holly, *Legend* (CDMSP 802). Middlesex, England: MCA Coral,
n.d.

7. Elvis Presley, Elvis: The '56 Sessions—Volume 1 (PL 42101). London:
RCA LTD., 1978.

8. *The Red Bird Era: The Hit Factory—Volume 1* (CR 30108). London:
Charly (Pye) Records, n.d.

—Features the Dixie Cups, the Shangri La's, the Ad Libs, the Jelly
Beans, the Tradewinds, Sid Barnes, Sam Hawkins, and the Robbins.

9. *The Red Bird Era: The New York Sound and the New Orleans
Connection—Volume 2* (CR 30109). London: Charly (Pye) Records, n.d.

—Features Alvin Robinson, the Dixie Cups, the Ad Libs, Evie Sands,
the Robbins, "Shadow" Morton, Jeff and Ellie, and the Butterflies.

10. *Sun—The Roots of Rock: The History of the Legendary Sun Record
Company of Memphis, Tennessee—13 Volumes* (CR 30101-06/14-17/
26-28). London: Charly Records, n.d.

11. *Walking the Back Streets and Crying: The Stax Blues Masters*

(STM 7004). Middlesex, England: Stax (EMI Records, Ltd.), 1978.
—Features Little Milton, Little Sonny, Albert King, Johnnie Taylor, Freddie Robinson, and Isreal "Popper Stopper" Tolbert.

E. Special Collections and Documentary Recordings

1. *The Beatles' Story: A Narrative and Musical Biography of Beatlemania* (STBO 2222). Hollywood, California: Capitol Records, n.d.

2. *50 Years of Film: Original Motion Picture Soundtrack Recordings of the Great Scenes and Stars From the Warner Brothers Classics, 1923 to 1973.* Burbank, California: Warner Brothers Records, Inc., 1973.

3. Buddy Holly, *Buddy Holly "Live": The Only Unreleased "Live" Recordings of Buddy Holly and His Crickets—Volume 1* (C 001000). N.P.: Cricket Records, n.d.

4. Buddy Holly, *Buddy Holly "In Person"—Volume 2* (C 0020000). N.P.: Cricket Records, n.d.

5. *The Motown Story* (MS 5-726). Detroit, Michigan: Motown Record Corporation, 1970.

6. Elvis Presley, *Elvis—The King Speaks: February 1961 in Memphis, Tennessee* (GNW 4006). Seattle, Washington: Great Northwest Music Company, 1977.

7. Elvis Presley, *"The Elvis Tapes"* (GNW 4005). Seattle, Washington: Great Northwest Music Company, 1977.

8. *Elvis Presley: Interviews and Memories of the Sun Years* (Sun 1001). Memphis, Tennessee: Sun International Corporation, 1977.

9. Elvis Presley, *Elvis: A Legendary Performer—Volume 1* (CPL 1-0341). New York: RCA Records, 1973.

10. Elvis Presley, *Elvis: A Legendary Performer*—Volume 2 (CPL 1-1349). New York: RCA Records, 1976.

11. Elvis Presley, *Elvis: A Legendary Performer—Volume 2* (CPL 1-3082). New York: RCA Records, 1978.

12. Twenty-Five Years of Recorded Sound From the Vaults of M-G-M Records. New York: DRG Archive, 1979.

*A Librarian seeking to fulfill a patron's request for a bootleg album should contact Mr. William L. Schurk, Director of the Audio Center at the Bowling Green State University Library. The exorbitant prices of bootleg discs and the lack of quality control in these recordings should discourage all but the most specialized collectors from attempting to add bootleg items to standard audio holdings.

**It may seem peculiar that Japan, England, Holland, and Germany are producing some of the best re-issue recordings of American Rock Music. The albums listed in this section are currently available in most large record stores at prices which are competitive with American records.

IV. Concluding Comments

Potential criticism of the preceding discography will be legion. Why aren't the albums identified according to traditional musical genre—"Rock," "Jazz," "Folk," "Soul," "Country" and so on? Shouldn't *all* of Bob Dylan's releases be listed? Isn't there an anti-British bias in the discography, particularly since so few albums by the Beatles and the Rolling Stones are recommended? Conversely, why is so much emphasis placed on recordings by black artists? Is there sufficient representation for country music? Should there be additional "Motown Sound" entries? Why is Linda Ronstadt included when Jessi Colter is not? Where are the albums by Led Zeppelin? All of these questions merit consideration, but not here or now. The primary issue remains—: "Are librarians prepared to accept the challenge of developing collections of popular record resources which are academically functional and systematically organized for educational access?" The author hopes that the response of the library community will be affirmative.

Notes

*The author wishes to thank Dr. Wayne A. Wiegand of the University of Kentucky for his constructive comments on this text and Dr. John B. Romeiser of Clemson University for providing English translations of several German discographic articles from *Buch und Bibliographie*.

¹Exceptions to this generalization are:
Gordon Stevenson, "Race Records: Victims of Benign Neglect in Libraries," *Wilson Library Bulletin*, L (November 1975), pp. 223-232; Gordon Stevenson, "Sound Recordings" in *Advances in Librarianship*, Volum3 5 (New York: Academic Press, Inc., 1975), pp.279-320; Gordon Stevenson, "The Wayward Scholar: Resources and Research in Popular Culture," *Library Trends*, XXV (April 1977), pp. 779-818; and Gordon Stevenson, "Popular Culture and the Public Library," in *Advances in Librarianship*, Volume 7 (New York: Academic Press, Inc., 1977), pp. 177-229.

²B. Lee Cooper, "Teaching Contemporary History From an Audio Perspective— 'The Image of American Society in Popular Music'," *Library-College Experimenter*, (II (November 1976), pp. 22-34.

³Frank Hoffmann, "Popular Music Collections and Public Libraries," *Southeastern Librarian*, (XXIII (Winter 1974), pp. 26-31; Christopher May, "A Basic List of Rock Records, *BRIO*, XIII (Autumn 1976), pp. 34-38; Jim O'Connor, "A Rock and Roll Discography," *School Library Journal*, XXII (September 1975), pp. 21-24; Michael Olds, "From Sergeant Pepper to Captain Fantastic: A Basic Rock Collection," *Hoosier School Libraries*, XVI (December 1976), pp. 17-19; and Ulrich Raschke, "One Hundred Times Pop Music: Concrete Advice for the Construction of a Basic Collection," *Buch und Bibliographie*, XXVII (July-August 1975), pp. 661-682.

⁴Bob Sarlin, *Turn It Up (I Can't Hear the Words): The Best of the New Singer/Song Writers* (New York: Simon and Schuster, 1973); B. Lee Cooper, "Review of *Chuck Berry's Golden Decade*," *History Teacher*, VIII (February 1975), pp. 300-301; Harold F. Mosher, Jr., "The Lyrics of American Pop Music: A New Poetry," *Popular Music and Society*, I (Spring 1972), pp. 167-176; David E. Morse, "Avant-Rock in the Classroom," *English Journal*, LVIII (February 1969), pp. 196-200 ff.; and Barry Wallenstein, "Leonard Cohen and The Poets of Rock," *The Chronicle of Higher Education*, XIII (January 17, 1977), p. 18.

⁵Critical commentaries by Joan Peyser (musical), Spiro Agnew (political/social), Marion Meade (Social), and Gary Allen (political) can be found in two popular culture anthologies: Jonathan Eisen (ed.), *The Age of Rock: Sounds of the American Cultural Revolution* (New York: Vintage Books, 1969), pp. 126-137 and R. Serge Denisoff and Richard A. Peterson (eds.), *The Sounds of Social Change: Studies in Popular Culture* (Chicago: Rand McNally and Company, 1972), pp. 79-91, 151-166, 173-177, and 307-310. For sources of theological criticism, see B. Lee Cooper, "Rock Music and Religious Education: A Proposed Synthesis," *Religious Education*, LXX (May-June 1975), pp.289-299.

⁶B. Lee Cooper, "Social Change, Popular Music, and the Teacher," *Social Education* XXXVII (December 1973), p. 776-781, 793; B. Lee Cooper, "Images of the Future in Popular Music: Lyrical Comments on Tomorrow," *Social Education*, XXXIX (May 1975), pp. 276-285; and Richard A. Rosenstone, " 'The Times They Are A-Changing': The Music of Protest," *The Annals of the*

American Academy of Political and Social Science, CCCLXXXI (March 1969), pp. 131-144.

[7]Undated letter from Mr. Charles Briefer, Manager of Columbia Records' Library Subscription Services located at 51 West 52nd Street in New York City 10019, addressed to the "College Librarian" at Newberry College in Newberry, South Carolina.

[8]Friedrich Summan and Manfred Jagnow, "A Basic Collection of Rock 'N' Roll Records and Tape Cassettes," *Buch und Bibliographie,* XXVII (July-August 1975), p. 683.

[9]Ulrich Raschke, "One Hundred Times Pop Music...," p. 662.

[10]Irwin Stambler, "Twenty Years of Rock 'N' Roll Soul: A Casual Summary." In *Encyclopedia of Pop, Rock, and Soul,* compiled by Irwin Stambler (New York: St. Martin's Press, 1974), p.13.

[11]R. Serge Denisoff, *Solid Gold: The Popular Record Industry* (New Brunswick, New Jersey: Transaction Books, 1975), p. 39.

[12]Carl Belz, *The Story of Rock,* 2nd ed. (New York: Harper and Row, 1972), p. vii.

"Popular culture may be trivialized, often tasteless, and largely ephemeral, but it is not meaningless. Obviously, its manifestations strike responsive chords in the populace; that's what makes it popular. The unbending library, heedless of the popular chant, ignores it at its own risk."

Bruce A. Shuman, "Marshall McLuhan Burns His Library Card: Reflections on the Public Library in the Global Village"

XVI

What if Marshall McLuhan is even a *little bit* right in his pronouncements—what might that mean to *your* library? From the catchy title of this article to its end, this question is the challenge; and, like McLuhan, Bruce Shuman leaves the answer to the reader. Shuman ends with a quotation from McLuhan, "There is no inevitability as long as people are willing to think." So let's think: throughout the library articles in this book, "print" appears to be an enemy. It is not really so—the enemy is exclusive print—*orientation*, just as in the museum essays it was the exclusiveness of *first, best, greatest* and *only* that stands between everyday human experience and history. Thus, Shuman is nowhere asking us to buy, accept or even *analyze* McLuhan. Rather he is asking us to consider what is the culture of the people, what are the indications of direction for the future—and what does this mean for the public library? As with Kenneth Hopkins' essay on the regional museum, Shuman's article insists that the real test of 20th-century popular culture in libraries will be the 21st century, and thus makes a fitting end to this collection.

Bruce A. Shuman, who is an Associate Professor in the Graduate School of Library and Information Studies at Queens College, Flushing, New York, has taught in the schools of library science at the University of Oklahoma, Indiana University, the University of Texas and the University of Washington. He has had professional library experience in North Carolina, Florida, Illinois and Indiana. His many articles, speeches and seminars have been particularly concerned with intellectual freedom, with library futures and with the professional training of librarians.

Bruce A. Shuman

Marshall McLuhan Burns His Library Card—
Reflections on the Public Library
in the Global Village

A MORE-OR-LESS TYPICAL ISSUE of the *Journal of Popular Culture* lists articles dealing with such diverse topics as *Star Wars, Roots,* Southern Cultural Stereotypes, Juvenile Literature, British Royalty, Flirtation Walks in South America, Bestsellers, Witches, Race Relations, Right Wing Politics in Fiction, and Contemporary Urban Problems.[1] If there is any unifying theme in such a potpourri, it is that popular culture embraces just about everything people talk about, are interested in, view with alarm or point to with pride.

By a not-so-curious coincidence, not lost on those responsible for the production of this book, the public library has, as part of its charter and mission statement, a range of interests and a scope equally wide. The public library which seeks to ignore popular culture, in favor of "serious" or "classical" works is likely to find itself underfunded, underused, and, worst of all, undernoticed. The Demand Principle rules the public library today, and, for better or worse, determines what it will contain. Everything it contains, everything it circulates is a product of popular culture, and, in its own way, contributes to that culture.

Other types of libraries can afford to be selective or exclusive, defining their areas of interest as those which support a specific curriculum or enrich the cultural heritage of users. The public library, however, is funded for the purpose of being RELEVANT to the lives of those who pay for it, and, in pursuit of that relevance, it embraces and reflects the culture of those who support it. A diversity of tastes dictates a diversity of materials and services, and the library seeks to please all people with its normally inadequate resources, failing in the attempt as it must, given the circumstances. Something is happening here, and we are having a difficult time identifying it, coming to terms with it, and understanding it. It is therefore natural that we seek the word of one who can make it clear to us, to render intelligible the seeming chaos of the library's labors. There was one who spoke to us of media struggles, of technological warfare, of popular culture, but his star has waned now. And besides, he didn't really address himself specifically to libraries and their problems. His scope was cosmic, his theories were abstruse, his attention was wide-ranging, and his personality was as infuriating as it was ubiquitous. His name was Marshall McLuhan, and we librarians have much we may learn from him. For McLuhan addressed himself to issues which surround us all, and we, dealing in the media as we do, ignore his injunctions at our peril.

"Marshall McLuhan, What're Ya Doin'?" This catchy couplet amused the audience of a popular television show[2] in 1969, but not nearly so many of us would understand its reference, or find it amusing today. Herbert Marshall McLuhan was born about seventy years ago, in Canada. This fact has great meaning to him, for he feels that, in coming from a 19th century nation, he is better equipped to understand the 20th century problems of our country, which he says we are too numb to perceive, because of our immersion in America. "Your chances of understanding anything going on in your own time are remote," he intones,[3] assuring us that his Canadian perspective endows him with sight superior to our own.

Patriotism and ego combine to anger us at this remark. Can this be true? Can he be right? McLuhan then unloads further weaponry, telling us that it doesn't matter a damn whether he is right or wrong! So long as he can make us think, he is content. "I'm the probe, not the package,"[4] meaning that he is freed from the cumbersome burden of proving anything, and that he wishes only to provoke, to tease, to sting one's intellect.

Naturally this philosophical stance has earned McLuhan a generous measure of scorn from academic communities, and he has been labeled everything from the grudging "The High Priest of Popular Culture," to "That Crackpot Professor from Canada." Of late, he has been almost totally ignored, which is perhaps worse than being savaged in print. Two years ago, *Newsweek* felt it necessary to perform an "update" on the man, clearly a retrospective, which might have begun with the words, "whatever happened to...?"[5] Has McLuhan's muse deserted him? Not likely. A book-length biography of his writings[6] (and writings about him) indicates that his formidable output persisted unabated throughout the 1970s, and that, if there is a gap between thinker and receptor, it lies in a pervasive dismissal from his audience rather than a stagnating intellect.

Let us examine some of McLuhan's more pithy and telling statements, most of which were made in his heyday, the 1960s. You remember. He's the man who gave the world "Global Village," and "We look at our world through a rear-view mirror," and "The Medium is the Message (massage)," and, to the confusion of most of us, "Media are Hot or they are Cool." These theories, ten to fifteen years ago, were hotly discussed in our universities, on our talk-show programs, at chic cocktail parties, and down at the corner bar. Libraries viewed them askance. If McLuhan were right, they reasoned, we librarians are doing all the wrong things. Such an admission called for immediate retrenchment, retrofitting, and wholesale change in our mission and our services programs. Such rapid change, without proper preparation, could lead to Future Shock, and Future Schock was an illness with little in the way of cure. So we rejected him, the man, and his far-out theories. Dissenting voices were raised, McLuhan's articles were assailed, challenged and dismissed. Yet his unconquerable nonchalance prevails. Through a writing career spanning over forty years, and from today until he enters the ultimate medium, McLuhan will preach to us, contradicting himself without worrying about it overmuch, and will beckon us to follow. Let's see what we librarians (and archivists, and media specialists) can glean from his "wisdom." And remember, along the way, it doesn't really signify anything to be "right." Such a distinction is trivial and dysfunctional. Just stop and open your mind to what he says (as interpreted in a library context by the present author) and see if any of it registers meaningfully. If not, don't worry about it. Go home and relax. But if anything hereinafter causes you the slightest worry about what you're doing all day in your library, maybe you'd do well to check out your own well-thumbed copy of *Understanding Media*[7] and browse. Here goes....

Global Village. McLuhan feels that tribal society, with its concomitant interinvolvement of group members, persisted as long as individuality was infeasible or impossible. With the invention of the print technology (Gutenberg, or whomever you credit with it) in the mid-15th century, it became possible for individuals to exist. Prior to that time, reading meant necessarily reading aloud, and individual learning, at one's own pace, was rarely possible.

Then came books. Thousands of titles on almost as many subjects. Suddenly, as time is considered, one could educate oneself. One could purchase and possess knowledge not shared with his fellows. One could take knowledge to a mountaintop or across the sea. Individuality was born. The tribal dance was ended, and each was now free to go his way. McLuhan now envisions, beginning with the midpoint of this century, a new era; an electronic age. The telephone, the telegraph, network television, and computerization have conspired to re-enact tribal village, on a global scale. "We are now doing the tribal dance on the village green once again," says McLuhan, "only this time we are doing it with our eyes wide open."[8] Through television, it is possible to see oneself as interconnected, as involved with people in foreign lands who heretofore could not affect your environment at all. Events taking place around the globe, far out at sea, or inside the atmosphere of Venus are brought into the living room nightly, and they change and affect us all. Pollution in Leningrad, a nuclear test in China, political unrest in Iran, all impinge on your life, your family, your welfare. Global village is upon us, mirroring tribal village in its reliance on interdependence. Are we wiser than those primitive tribesmen who danced away the evil spirits? We can't be sure. More sophisticated, certainly. Better?

You decide.

Libraries must cope with global village. The day is long past when a library might say that it stocks no titles in foreign languages because no one in the community reads foreign languages. No longer can a librarian refuse to buy books on the black experience in America, arguing that since the community has no black members, such books would be unused and superfluous. Buckminster Fuller's concept of Spaceship Earth, with all that the idea entails, affords us no chance to be insular. We're all in this thing together, and it matters a great deal what goes on in Africa or Asia. Therefore, a McLuhanesque library would spend liberally to bring the world outside into the community. A variety of media formats must be employed to keep us current and aware. John Donne said, "Any man's death diminishes me"[9] almost four hundred years ago, and it was never more true.

McLuhan's next theory for consideration is twofold. Interrelated ideas, so to speak. "The Book is Dead" was a pronouncement widely greeted with catcalls and other derision, while "The Medium is the Message" was more often met with uncomprehending murmurs. See, Marshall McLuhan chooses to present his theories in the context of "illustrative examples," and just doesn't have time to stop for questions. Too much analysis won't do in confronting the theories of McLuhan, and besides, one misses the point, that way. A theory should tantalize, provoke, cause one to consider, and then be rejected or accepted on its "rightness," when subjected to one's own inner voices. As with a poem, too much stress on what-the-hell-it-means is counterproductive. Therefore, when McLuhan tells us that "The Book is Dead," he refers not to the date by which the last communication in book form rolls off the presses, but rather to the superfluous and far-too-slow nature of the old, print technology, which renders the book obsolete as a viable form of dissemination of ideas.

By way of example, McLuhan points to our children. Most of them are thoroughly screen-oriented, quite accustomed, from birth, to receiving information, entertainment and diversion through a common household appurtenance, television. Through television, we receive knowledge, a picture of the world (one's own cognitive map of the world varies with how much television he watches) and recreation. Some, such as Mander,[10] deplore this phenomenon, saying that television's very power to influence behavior makes it as terrifying as any dictator. "It is possible to speak through media directly into people's heads and then, like some otherworldly magician, leave images inside that can cause people to do what they might otherwise never have thought to do."[11] Most of us would agree with Mander's gloomy admission, and even McLuhan speaks of television-watching as being entertainment in exchange for manipulation. The difference is that Mander and others see television as embodying the potential for unparalleled evil, while

McLuhan is generally pleased by its effects on the human psyche and consciousness.

In explaining why "The Medium is the Message," McLuhan asserts that it is of no real consequence that one watches one program or another. It is the act and process of *watching* television which has significance, he says. In his film *The Medium is the Massage* [*sic*], McLuhan employs the analogy of a baker kneading and working dough to indicate the effect of television watching on one's mind. Saying that it matters little what is in it or on it, McLuhan compares watching television to being kneaded, massaged, bumped around, twisted, compressed, expanded, and, eventually, improved. While it may be acknowledged that *some* television is edifying, and *some* programs are educational, most of us would stop short of testifying that watching *Masterpiece Theatre* compares to watching *Gomer Pyle, USMC,* for the fourth time. Still, McLuhan persists in his vision that you are better for it, and that is the way it is.

About this time, you may be saying that you don't believe any of this, and that his theories make no sense to you. Fine, says McLuhan, if you reject my theories, let's hear yours. Now how can you reason with a person like that? He never backs down or renounces his theories, and certainly never concedes error, but he is blandly willing to permit you the right to hold opinions different from his and bears you no malice whatsoever for your open skepticism.

What the significance of "The Book is Dead" is for libraries is found in his insistence that television has changed the way in which one thinks. The media now tell us not only what to think, but what to think about! Television has erected an atmosphere of "allatonceness" which renders the print technology of letters forming words, words forming lines, lines in sequence, pages in a linear arrangement, front to back, just too slow and too regimented to have any real relevance to the lives of those children who have been reared to perceive the world in several dimensions, augmented by sound effects. After you have been massaged by television, and after events occurring in Munich, Jonestown, Guyana (where's that old atlas, Maw?), and Peking have been sent, live, into your consciousness, books just don't make it anymore. And what of our generation, still steeped in the old culture, the book and print technology? We shall resist, with some success, the incursions of the new media into our lives. We shall cling to books and magazines, as they are familiar and meaningful to us. Eventually, we shall die, and new generations will arise which know not the love of books. Literacy will become a lost art, practiced by a few. The era of "allatonceness" will suffuse our collective lives until some new development, for better or worse, alters its influence.

But for now, libraries may take heart to know that books will be a part of the American scene for our lifespans, and beyond. McLuhan consoles us when we lament the fact that Johnny (and

Janey) can't read. They are ahead of us, he tells us. They have learned what we will have great difficulty mastering, and they have done so effortlessly. They perceive the world in several dimensions, they are tuned into the media voices which seem to us discordant and jangling. They are much better at survival in the technological world of the future than we are, and so there is cause for rejoicing if our children seem illiterate to us. They don't have to be literate: they need fluency in media, not marinating in the words of the past. History is irrelevant, and books are relics of our collective past. Librarians take note.

Next we find McLuhan rhapsodizing on a favorite theme of his: The Medium is the Message. Many librarians and communications people have had much to say concerning the importance of getting information across to people, without much concern on either the part of purveyor or recipient with the packaging of that information. As Guy Garrison predicts, "the future of libraries depends on less attention to the information itself."[12] McLuhan, naturally, disagrees, re-emphasizing that the format is not irrelevant, but is all-important in the nature and shape of the message being transmitted. If he is wrong, we may think little about his statement's impact on the library community. But should he be right, we would do well to consider the ramifications of maintaining our present course and speed on the intellectual climate of the world in which we live.

One statement of McLuhan's for which there is ample evidence is that contemporary society prefers to view the world through a rear-view mirror. McLuhan claims that the preponderance of Americans, when confronted with the bewildering and often dangerous (it is the business of the future to be dangerous) choices of the future, prefer to comfort themselves with visions of the recent past. For evidence, he cites television programming which has proven itself to be most popular. *Gunsmoke* ran for eighteen years. Recent top shows (in terms of popularity, anyway) include *Happy Days* and *Laverne and Shirley* (set in the late 1950s), *Little House on the Prairie* (the 1870s) and *The Waltons* (at this writing, entering World War II). Somehow, we feel safer in a world evocative of the past. Traditional values, primitive technology or lack of technological change are comforting to us, as we worry about the hazards of computerization, biological warfare and recombinant DNA. Here, the message for libraries is clear. Libraries which reflect the homey and traditional values of the past, even though they present them in modern, electric formats, are those with the best prognosis for success in the troubled times awaiting us, while those which try too hard to inundate us in the new ways may be seen as discordant and frightening. If the foregoing seems, on inspection, a contradiction in terms, let it be. The library of today, and of tomorrow, is a contradiction in terms.

Finally, McLuhan offers us his much-discussed and, frankly, confusing, theory of Hot and Cool. Media, he says, are either hot (extending one sense in one direction) or cool (multi-sensory). Radio is hot. Print is hot. Television is cool. The electronic communications industry is cool. Any questions? What he seems to mean is that any medium which involves only one sense in its transmission is hot, and therefore bad, in the sense that it is not involving. Television is cool, in that it is multisensory and involving. The mind must work to apprehend it, and that work brings the individual into the medium, rather than keeping him or her at arm's length. Such involvement is beneficial in its ability to convey the sense of purposeful participation, and therefore cool media should supplant hot ones wherever and whenever possible.

This theory has caused much head-scratching in a considerable cross-section of America. McLuhan claims, for example, that film is hot, and television is cool. True to form, he offers nothing by way of "proof," but only a handful of discrete examples to make his points. He offers nothing in answer to the very real question of what happens when a film is shown on television. To suggest that taking a feature-length film and chopping it to suit the requirements of both standards and commercial messages renders the product more involving is pure rubbish. Finkelstein[13] terms this unintelligible dichotomy "obscurantist gobbledygook," and recommends that we pay no heed to it. But just pretend for a few moments that McLuhan is right. Or not "right," exactly, for the terms right and wrong have little relevance to what he's trying to tell us. Imagine, as a librarian, now, that his distinction of hot and cool media means something. The implication is clear: libraries must move ahead full-throttle in their transformation to telecenters. The cool medium of television (and why cool; why not cold?) is replacing the hot media of print and film and radio, and we must modify ourselves radically to suit a radically-changed environment. We librarians must harness the growing energy of television and make it work for us. We must become "cool" or we run the risk of being dropped like the hot potato of the simile. Just in case the terminology pertains to our situation, we want to be on the right side, the winning side, in this war, don't we? The alternative is death, for the library, for the print technology, for traditional culture.

Summation and Interpretations

It is highly likely that Marshall McLuhan is rightly dismissed as an original thinker who just happened to be wrong. And if he is wrong, librarians need worry about him no further. His theories will continue to be read and discussed, perhaps, but will generally end up atop (or underneath) the scrapheap of other discredited ideas, not because they are evil or stupid, but because they failed the empirical tests which we, as pragmatists, apply to them. One is not sure what to make of his ideas. Some of them strike responsive chords in the subconscious; others just couldn't be important enough to bear further consideration.

But if the reader will permit just one further willing suspension of disbelief, here is what his collected pronouncements may mean to libraries as they confront the future:

1) The death of the book is possible, even likely, but not necessarily to be feared. The book's decline will not leave the human race in stone-age illiteracy, but will rather usher in an age of the realm of sensory involvement, in which all participate freely in learning, pleasure and exchange of ideas.
2) Global Village is already upon us, and will continue to bring other people, other places and other worlds into our home-town environments. Growing awareness of our interconnectedness, and our interdependence, will cause libraries to expand their horizons, break down their walls, and reach out into the universe. The go-it-alone spirit of the past will be economically, socially and politically impossible, and the sooner we realize it, the better.
3) Since it is the process that matters, and not the content of a medium, any medium which extends our senses in more than a single direction is to be encouraged, and to be adopted, in libraries. The future of libraries depends upon people being able to perceive them as integral and vital to the daily conduct of our lives. Already, many find television to be necessary to their well-being. But a significant percentage of those people will be unable to tell you where the library is located, or how it is funded, or what they do there besides check out books.

All the foregoing seems to show that we don't have to bring in Marshall McLuhan to act as a consultant to know that we librarians have an image problem. *American Libraries* reports that an estimated 70% of Americans cannot or do not pronounce the two "r"s in "library." *If* the medium is the message, we must become masters at the art of communication, understanding media and their capabilities and limitations better than those who are to form our audiences. And even if McLuhan is wrong (remember: probe, not package), libraries would do well to consider the wisdom of retooling their services to meet and anticipate the expanded communication of the next twenty-five years. Such radical change may evade the entropy which we fear, and provide continuing relevance, in any of a number of future situations.

It is possible that turning the library, the repository of what is known, into an "experience parlor" (a combination TV studio, disco, amusement gallery and recreation center) would be a suicidal act, the contemporary equivalent of Romans assisting in the sack of Rome. The dangers of status-quo are, however, very real. Ask any public library in California what the mood of the people is. They'll tell you that people will pay only for that which they perceive to be beneficial, necessary, and pleasurable. Popular culture may be trivialized, often tasteless, and largely ephemeral, but it is not meaningless. Obviously, its manifestations strike responsive chords in the populace; that's what makes it popular. The unbending library, heedless of the popular change, ignores it as its own risk. To Marshall McLuhan an institution bending to the popular will is preferable to its dying a solitary death in its ivory tower. Voices may be heard saying that, unless it is seen as necessary to change, it is necessary *not* to change. This author contends that the necessity lies in recognition that change will occur with or without the participation of the library, and we're running out of chances to change with society. For we can affect and guide that change, if we're a part of it. If we miss this plane, we are powerless to influence any future society which may come about.

Marshall McLuhan tells us that "there is no inevitability as long as people are willing to think."[14] What if he is right?

Notes

[1]*Journal of Popular Culture*, Summer, 1977 issue.
[2]Uttered by Henry Gibson on Rowan & Martin's *Laugh-In*, 1969.
[3]Film: *This is Marshall McLuhan, The Medium is the Message*, 1968.
[4]*Ibid.*
[5]*Newsweek*, September 22, 1975.
[6]*The Writings of Marshall McLuhan Listed in Chronological Order, from 1934 to 1975.* Wake-Brook House, 1975 (bibliography)
[7]McLuhan, Marshall, *Understanding Media: The Extensions of Man*, Signet Books, 1964.
[8]Film in Note 3.
[9]Donne, John (1573-1631), "No Man Is an Island...."
[10]Mander, Jerry, *Four Arguments For the Elimination of Television*, Morrow, 1977.
[11]*Ibid.*, p. 3.
[12]Garrison, Guy, "The Metropolitan Matrix of Libraries and Users," *Library Trends* (October, 1974), p. 194.
[13]Finkelstein, Sidney H. *Sense and Nonsense of McLuhan*, International Press, 1968, p. 23.
[14]Film in note 3.

Appendix A

Audio Center Materials Selection Policy

The Audio Center is an archival and research center and service unit to the University, the surrounding community, and serious scholars throughout the nation and world. The areas of concern in the Center include all fields of endeavor surrounding the Audio recording medium and the material contained within.

Materials included in the collection are of both a primary and secondary source nature. They are intended for studies up to and including those for doctoral research.

Types of material included in the Audio Center are as follows:

A. Audio recordings
  1. Phonograph records (all sizes, speeds, and groove cuts, and of all ages, from their inception up to the present; both disc and cylinder)
  2. Tape recordings (open reels concurrent with the speed capabilities of the Center's playback equipment, and cassettes)
  3. Piano rolls (Center retains a large collection, but does not have a player piano in its collection as of yet)
  4. Wire recordings (None are presently in the collection, however, this does not preclude the possibility of the Center acquiring a machine and wire in the future)
B. Audio recording and playback equipment
  1. The console includes a complement of equipment to handle most of the tape and record configurations used on a daily basis
  2. A secondary collection of working historical machines for record playback are included both for historical study and for reproducing non-standard record configurationss (i.e. cylinders and "Hill and Dale" discs manufactured by Edison and also Pathe Bros.)
C. Printed support materials
  1. Reference books (i.e. discographies, bibliographies, biographical directories, heavily illustrated monographs, books issued with accompanying recordings, and historical studies of recordings and related subjects
  2. Periodicals (i.e. trade, critical, and scholarly journals, newstand magazines, fanzies, and collector-oriented publications)
  3. Sheet music and song folios
  4. Dealer, manufacturer, and auction catalogs
  5. Record promotional material (i.e. posters, flyers, handbills, and retail establishment paraphernalia)
  6. Biographical and record promotional materails issued for media publication
  7. Record company release notices

Subjects included on the recordings and in the printed materails are as follows:

A. Popular music (personality, country, rhythm & blues and soul, rock and roll, regae, etc.)
B. Jazz, big band, and the blues
C. Folk music and folk-lore
D. Musical revues and motion-picture music
E. Gospel and sacred
F. Comedy, and humorous songs
G. Poetry, prose, drama, and related readings
H. Documentary and histories
I. Old-time radio programs and television music
J. Conferences, seminars, presentations, panel discussions, etc., relating to all academic areas
K. Classical (an archive is being maintained through gifts and inexpensive purchases. A working collection for current music students can be found in the College of Musical Arts (Audio Lab)
L. Juvenile stories and music
M. International music
N. Miscellaneous

The Audio Center does not maintain a collection of language instruction recordings.

William L. Schurk
Audio Center Director

—Features Roy Milton, Don and Dewey, Larry Williams, Lloyd Price, Little Richard, and others.

B. Random Song Order:

1. And The Rock Lives On.... A Voyage SWVL 1021-2/122, Sunnyvale, California: Sunnyvale Records, 1978.

—Includes Gene and Johnny, The Capris, Billy Bland, The Ikenas, The Heartbeats, Lee Allen, B.B. King, The Fathoms, and others.

2. At The Hop/AA III-1312, Los Angeles, California: ABC Records, Inc., 1978.

—Includes Danny and The Juniors, Three Dog Night, Del Shannon, The Impressions, Lloyd Price, Sonny James, The Royal Teens, Pat Boone, George Hamilton IV, and others.

3. The Blues—2 volumes (LPS-4026/2/27), 45-311, Chicago: Cadet (Chess) Records, n.d.

—Includes Little Walter, Chuck Berry, Howlin' Wolf, Muddy Waters, Willie Mabon, and others.

4. Boo Boom and All I/19371, New York: Chocolate City Records, 1978.

—Includes Muddy Waters, ... Bo Diddley, Chuck Berry, and others.

5. Sweet Relief ... SWVL 1021, ... Sunnyvale, California: Sunnyvale Records, 1978.

—Features ... Junior Parker, Larry Davis, The Clovers, The Radio Shakes, Otis Redding, Johnny Thunders, and Bobby Blue ...

6. Classic Blues—4 volumes (RRL 7653/654), New York: ABC Records, Inc., 1978.

—Features Ray Charles, T-Bone Walker, ... and others.

...

8. Rock 'n' Roll—2 volumes, Hollywood, California: Motown Record Corporation, 1973.

—Includes Stevie Wonder, Martha Reeves and The Vandellas, The Temptations, Junior Walker and The Allstars, Marvin Gaye, and others.

9. Legends of a Rock Era—4 Volumes UPF-115, ... New York: Roulette Records, Inc., 1971.

—Features Sonny Til and The Orioles, the Penguins, the Moonglows, Maurice Williams and the Zodiacs, Mary Wells, the Shirelles, and others.

10. The 50's Greatest Hits (3 discs), New York: Columbia Records (CBS), Inc., 1972.

—Features Johnny Mathis, Doris Day, Johnny Ray, the Four Lads, and others.

11. 14 Golden Recordings From the Historic Vaults of Duke/Peacock Records—2 Volumes (ABCX 784/785), New York: ABC Records, Inc., 1973.

—Features Johnny Ace, Bobby Bland, Roy Head, Earl K. Dee, Junior